The Glorious Life

OF

Śrīla Narottama Dāsa Ṭhākura

Śītalā dāsī

Printed in the United States of America
ISBN: 978-1-880404-27-0 Paperback edition
ISBN: 978-880404-28-7 Ebook

Paperback and Ebook editions published by
Bookwrights Press
a publishing devision of The Bhaktivedanta Center, Inc.
www.bookwrightspress.com
www.bhaktivedantacenter.com
publisher@bookwrightspress.com

The prayers of Narottama dāsa Ṭhākura... this sound is above the material platform. It is directly from the spiritual platform. And there is no need of understanding the language. It is just like a thunder-burst. Everyone can hear the sound of thunder, there is no misunderstanding. Similarly, these songs [of Narottama dāsa Ṭhākura] are above the material platform, and they crack like thunder within your heart.

– Śrīla A. C. Bhaktivedanta Swami Prabhupāda

Acknowledgments

I offer my sincere obeisances and gratitude to everyone who contributed to the production of this book. I want to thank Kaiśori dāsī, who is a wizard with words, for kindly editing the text, and Jāhnavī Harrison who also helped give it shape. Raivata dāsa patiently assisted with layout and design. Thanks to the scholarly Haripriyā dāsa from Gopīnātha Gauḍīya Math for his helpful review. And much appreciation to Advaita Chandra dāsa for his professional support, as well as his daughter, Kiśori Rādhā, for her artistic input.

I especially want to thank my dear friend Prāṇadā dāsī who stepped in to save the day with her expert assistance on pretty much everything – layout, design, proofreading, and putting it all together to get the hard-cover edition of the book to the printer.

My deepest indebtedness is to Indradyumna Swami and Chaturātma dāsa for their enthusiasm and dedication to teaching the glories of Śrīla Narottama dāsa Ṭhākura and for urging me to print this book. Finally, thank you to all the devotees who have a special affinity for hearing about Śrīla Narottama dāsa Ṭhākura – the

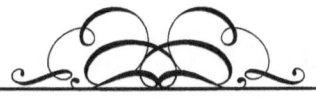

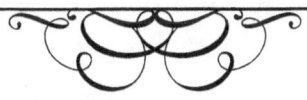

"Narottama bhaktas" – who inspired me to write and speak about his glories.

I am greatly indebted to the generous devotees whose donations made it possible to print this book. Although they wish to remain anonymous, I pray that the blessings of Śrīla Narottama dāsa Ṭhākura flood their hearts.

And of course, my gratitude always goes to my good husband, Hari Śauri Prabhu, and my dear daughter, Rasarānī Priyā, for their support, tolerance, and love.

I would also like to express my heartfelt gratitude to Kiśorī dāsī (Australia) and Kṛṣṇa Mādhurī dāsī (Mayapur) who contributed generously towards the second printing of the hardcover edition. I pray they, and their families, receive the merciful blessings of Śrīla Narottama dāsa Ṭhākura.

This paperback edition was executed by Bookwrights Press, the publishing arm of the Bhaktivedanta Center, Inc., and thanks go to them for making it happen!

Contents

Acknowledgments v
Foreword ix
Introduction xi

CHAPTER ONE: LORD CAITANYA'S PREDICTION 1

CHAPTER TWO: BIRTH & YOUTH 7
A Prince Is Born 7
Childhood 14
Youth 27
Escape 38

CHAPTER THREE: VRAJA 47
Mathurā 47
Entering Vṛndāvana 52
Initiation 62
Meeting at Govardhana Hill 72
Boiling the Milk 77

CHAPTER FOUR: THE MISSION 81
Śrī Jīva's Request 81
The Journey 91
Return to Kheturi 97

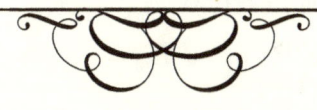

Chapter Five, Pilgrimage 117
Navadvīpa 117
Jagannātha Purī 134
Ekacakrā 149

Chapter Six: The Festival 155
Preparations 155
Guests Arrive 168
Deity Installation 171
Mahā-saṇkīrtana 174

Chapter Seven: Preaching 187
Harirāma & Rāmakṛṣṇa 187
Gaṅgā-nārāyaṇa Cakravartī 199
The Challenge 208
Chand Rāya 231

Chapter Eight: Final Pastimes 253
Seclusion 253
Trip to Gambhila 258
Disappearance 268

Endnotes 275

Foreword

Śrīla Narottama dāsa Ṭhākura was born at an important juncture in Gauḍīya Vaiṣṇava history, appearing soon after the *yuga-avatāra*, Lord Caitanya Mahāprabhu, returned to the spiritual world. Along with two of his closest friends, Śrīnivāsa Ācārya and Śyāmānanda Paṇḍita, Narottama dāsa Ṭhākura rallied an entire generation of devotees who were experiencing intense separation from Lord Caitanya. The three of them also initiated a movement of systematic preaching of Mahāprabhu's doctrine.

Narottama dāsa Ṭhākura was not only a fearless preacher but also a deep, *rasika* devotee, as evinced in his many songs. As such, he has always been highly esteemed by generations of devotees, who have followed in his footsteps by spreading the teachings of Lord Caitanya.

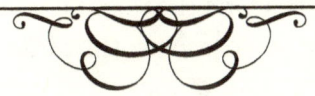

This is true even today. Our spiritual master, His Divine Grace A. C. Bhaktivedanta Swami Prabhupada, often quoted the great saint Śrīla Narottama dāsa Ṭhākura in his books and lectures. He was also fond of singing the *bhajanas* composed by Narottama dāsa Ṭhākura. In his purport to *Śrīmad-Bhāgavatam* 1.10.20, Śrīla Prabhupāda writes: "There are songs of Ṭhākura Narottama dāsa, one of the *ācāryas* in the Gauḍīya-*sampradāya*, composed in simple Bengali language. But Ṭhākura Viśvanātha Cakravartī, another very learned *ācārya* in the same *sampradāya*, has approved the songs by Ṭhākura Narottama dāsa to be as good as Vedic mantras."

Following in Śrīla Prabhupāda footsteps, members of the Hare Kṛṣṇa movement strive to emulate Narottama dāsa Ṭhākura's example as a stalwart preacher, and they see him as a hero in every sense of the word.

It is for these reasons that I am convinced this book, *The Glorious Life of Śrīla Narottama dāsa Ṭhākura,* will be widely read and much appreciated by devotees. Like Narottama dāsa Ṭhākura's own writings, it is simple and easy to read, yet reveals profound meaning about the life and teachings of this great *ācārya*. Śītala Devī Dāsī spent a great deal of time poring over various scriptures and historical materials to present Śrīla Narottama dāsa Ṭhākura in an authorized way. Her own love for him shines forth in her writing, helping us to not only appreciate him as a great devotee but also to imbibe his teachings. By doing so we can easily attain the perfection of life, which Śrīla Prabhupāda defines, in connection with Narottama dāsa Ṭhākura, in his purport to *Śrīmad-Bhāgavatam* 4.29.68: "Narottama dāsa Ṭhākura advises everyone to stick to the principle of carrying out the orders of the spiritual master. One should not desire anything else. If the regulative principles ordered by the spiritual master are followed rigidly, the mind will gradually be trained to desire nothing but the service of Kṛṣṇa. Such training is the perfection of life."

We give our heartfelt thanks to Śītala Devī Dāsī for enriching our lives with the pastimes of Śrīla Narottama dāsa Ṭhākura, whose association even Lord Caitanya hankered for when He famously called out "Narottama! Narottama! Narottama!" on the banks of the Padma River.

Indradyumna Swami

Introduction

To explain the origins of this book I have to go back to the early 1980s, when I had the good fortune of serving part-time at the Institute for Vaiṣṇava Studies in New Delhi. My dear friends Dayānanda and Nandarāṇī were heading up the Institute's work, focusing primarily on acquiring and translating old Vaiṣṇava texts, and gathering biographies of Vaiṣṇava saints. Intrigued by the project, I volunteered to help–in my spare time typing, editing, and doing whatever I could. Through this service I developed a keen interest in the lives of the saintly personalities who have shaped Gauḍīya Vaiṣṇava history. Unfortunately, the Institute eventually dissolved.

But my interest was piqued, so I considered how I could continue to immerse myself in these histories. I thought I could write a series of books for young adults about the lives of the *ācāryas*, using the materials I had acquired in my service with the Institute. This would serve my purpose to remain absorbed, and provide inspirational literature for devotee youth.

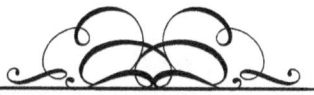

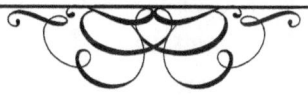

Inspired by the prospect, I started with the life of Śrīla Narottama dāsa Ṭhākura. I had recently edited newly translated versions of *Narottama-vilāsa* and *Prema-vilāsa* for the Institute, and become captivated by his story. I felt that his remarkable life, filled with challenges, adventure, and divine encounters, would likely catch the interest of young readers.

I studied various accounts of Narottama's life, gathering information in the hope of weaving a story that would convey the nature and qualities of this great personality who is one of the most significant *ācāryas* in our Gauḍīya Vaiṣṇava line. The more I read, the more questions arose, and the more I felt the need to explore further. Fitting together the pieces of the puzzle of the Ṭhākura's life became a kind of spiritual hobby. Gradually, the book I was writing changed into something no longer exclusively for young people. This was a story anyone might relish.

While researching Narottama's life, I quickly found that ascertaining historical facts was difficult. *Līlās* were recorded in various ways, time lines conflicted, and there were large gaps in the storyline. It became clear that history, in our Western, linear sense of it, was not as important to those who had recorded Narottama's story. Historians of Vedic thought have also noted that the Vedic literature–and Indian thought in general–places less emphasis on chronologies and more on the emotional and philosophical content of the histories they tell. So, rather than strive for precise historical data, I tried to extract details from a variety of sources that would bring out the personality, mood and mission of Narottama dāsa Ṭhākura. In doing so I often paraphrased the *līlās* in my own words, or added background information to make something more informative and understandable for my readers.[1]

I finished writing this book about twenty-five years ago. It was an enlivening exploration for me, but when it came time to acquire artwork and then get the layout done, I began to drag my feet. Other services came to the foreground, and I slowly lost interest in publishing. In the meantime, new books on the life of Narottama dāsa Ṭhākura were published in English, making it seem unnecessary to publish my own. Consequently, the manuscript sank into the shadowy depths of my computer, only to be brought out for special occasions, and my dream of a series of books faded away.

So why publish now? One reason is that a number of devotees who have read or heard me speak from the manuscript have urged me to print it. I am printing now simply to honour their requests.

But the primary reason I am finally printing this text is that over time, I have come to deeply appreciate just how beneficial for our spiritual development it is to learn about the history of our *sampradāya* and to form attachments to our spiritual predecessors. This awareness dawned on me gradually as I explored the life of Śrīla Narottama dāsa Ṭhākura. Through that meditation, he no longer seemed a distant historical figure, but a real, relevant and palpable presence; a shelter; an inspiration.

These feelings were amplified whenever I had the opportunity to speak about his life. Seeing the devotees captivated and enlivened by his story helped to increase my appreciation for both Narottama dāsa Ṭhākura and the devotees who were inspired by him. Thus, the purifying power of such immersion became more evident, and gave me a taste of the satisfaction that arises from the awareness that we are all connected, sheltered and surrounded by the blessings of some of the greatest personalities who have ever walked the earth.

By the grace of Śrīla Prabhupāda, we do have an intimate connection with the previous *ācāryas* in our line, and cultivating that nourishing connection by reflecting on the life and teachings of saints like Narottama dāsa Ṭhākura, attachment for them grows and our lives are truly enriched and inspired. According to Śrīla Bhaktivinoda Ṭhākura, forming such attachment is the "very root of the tender creeper of divine love." If we root our devotional creepers in such attachments, all things are attained.

The songs of Śrīla Narottama dāsa Ṭhākura brim with such conviction: *chāḍiyā vaiṣṇava sevā* . . . Even Kṛṣṇa Himself says, "Only a person who claims to be the devotee of My devotee is actually My devotee." To quote His Holiness Rādhānāth Swami: "In *bhakti* it's not what you know but who you know."

To get to know Śrīla Narottama dāsa Ṭhākura is to meet a true spiritual hero. His life is an epic tale of one of the greatest pioneers of Śrī Caitanya Mahāprabhu's mission. He was a trailblazer in spreading Kṛṣṇa consciousness. His compassion was so great that despite opposition, prejudice, and even hatred, he persevered. Through the power of his devotion he broke the bonds of stifling social traditions to bring the message of Lord Caitanya to the broadest audience possible – from dacoits to *brāhmaṇas*. By encapsulating the deepest and highest truths in simple Bengali song, he opened the door of *bhakti* to the common man.

Śrīla Narottama dāsa Ṭhākura is the "person *bhāgavata*." He demonstrated the highest levels of attainable love along with the humility and determination required to reach such heights. Example is better than precept. We all need heroes, but what good are the type of heroes we encounter in myth and fiction? Who needs Superman or Wonder Woman? Rather, we need heroes who inspire us to give up our materially conditioned nature and to break free from the modes of material nature. We need heroes that teach us to seek out our highest potential as servants of the Supreme Lord. Śrīla Narottama dāsa Ṭhākura is just such a hero.

Where would we be today if he had not made such monumental efforts? His songs resound in thousands of temples and homes around the world, and people from all walks of life are given entrance into the highest spiritual understanding. His dedication paved the way for *bhakti* to spread through the ages, and daily we receive his mercy as we associate with him through his profound songs of devotion. We certainly owe him a great debt of gratitude. To develop awareness of this and to feel that gratitude deeply is to create fertile ground for love to sprout in our hearts.

These are the reasons I've finally decided to print this book. The glories of Śrīla Narottama dāsa Ṭhākura are so vast and sublime that there can never be too much said about him. We can go on hearing about him again and again from different angles of vision and always be benefited. My words here are only a modest attempt at praising him. As a bird can only fly as high as its capacity can take it, my spiritual realization and writing capacity are very limited and this book therefore has many imperfections. Still, if even one person feels closer to Narottama dāsa Ṭhākura after reading it, I will consider my endeavour worthwhile.

Śītala Dāsī

śrī-kṛṣṇa-nāmāmṛta-varṣi-vaktra-
candra-prabhā-dhvasta-tamo-bharāya
gaurāṅga-devānucarāya tasmai
namo namaḥ śrīla-narottamāya

I repeatedly offer my respectful obeisances to Śrīla Narottama Dāsa Ṭhākura, a pure-hearted servant of Lord Gaurāṅga. From his splendorous moonlike lips pours a radiant shower of nectar in the form of Śrī Kṛṣṇa's holy name that dissipates the darkness of ignorance.

Narottama-prabhor-āṣṭaka, Verse 1

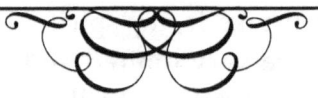

Chapter One

Lord Caitanya's Prediction

Chattering monkeys scampered through the trees, gawking curiously at the group of bright-faced devotees jubilantly singing the Lord's holy names. The *kīrtana* party slowly wound its way through the lush green countryside, their sweet, melodious chanting echoing through the thick canopy of palm and coconut trees: "Hare Kṛṣṇa, Hare Kṛṣṇa, Kṛṣṇa Kṛṣṇa, Hare Hare . . ." Losing themselves in the joy of the *kīrtana*, the devotees chanted with full absorption, their voices brimming with devotion. Śrī Caitanya Mahāprabhu danced in the center of the devotees, His radiant, golden body swaying gracefully to the beat of the pulsating drums.

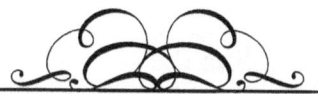

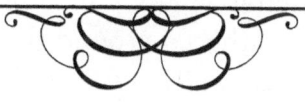

As they walked, the *mṛdaṅga* players quickened the beat. The brass *karatālas* chimed in time, flashing in the morning sunlight. Powerful waves of ecstasy surged through the *kīrtana* party as Śrī Caitanya Mahāprabhu raised His long graceful arms and leapt into the air. The devotees surrounded Him, dancing with wild abandon, their bare feet pounding the soft ground, raising clouds of dust.

Suddenly, Śrī Caitanya Mahāprabhu stopped dancing. Standing motionless, He stared intently into the distance and fervently called, "Narottama! Narottama!" His body trembled and tears poured from His eyes with uncontrollable force. Overwhelmed with ecstatic love, He grabbed on to Nityānanda Prabhu for support, but then collapsed to the ground and rolled in the dust, crying again and again, "Narottama! Narottama!"

Bewildered by the Lord's sudden outburst, the devotees stopped singing. Glancing at each other with uncertainty, they gathered around the Lord and softly sang the holy names, waiting for His ecstatic trance to abate.

Kneeling, Śrī Nityānanda Prabhu whispered sweet, pacifying words in the Lord's ear. Caitanya Mahāprabhu, however, simply threw His arms around Nityānanda Prabhu's neck and continued to cry.

Worried, Śrī Nityānanda Prabhu turned to Vakreśvara and Haridāsa. "I've never seen Him shed such profuse tears."

Hoping to revive the Lord, Vakreśvara led the devotees in loudly chanting the name of Lord Jagannātha.

Hearing this, the Lord regained His composure. Sitting up, He wiped the tears from His eyes and motioned to Nityānanda Prabhu to come closer. "Nitāi," He whispered, "You know that *saṅkīrtana* is everything to Me. It is My very life. I want everyone in this world to taste the nectar of the holy name. But soon You and I will leave this world. Who will spread this chanting after we are gone? Who will keep the flame of love I have brought into the world burning? Before I leave, I must empower someone to carry on this wonderful *saṅkīrtana* movement. I have such a wealth of love of God, and I must leave it with someone. But who is qualified to inherit such riches?"

"My Lord," said Nityānanda softly, "You know everything. Only You can answer that question. Is there anyone capable of carrying on Your mission? Who is worthy of inheriting Your love?"

"Yes, Nitāi, there is someone. His name is Narottama."

"Narottama?" Nityānanda Prabhu asked. "Who is Narottama? Just a few minutes ago You were calling his name and crying so hard I feared for Your life. But I don't know of anyone named Narottama among Your associates."

"Narottama has not yet appeared in this world," the Lord replied. "But soon he will take birth, nearby, on the other side of the Padmavatī River, in the town of Kheturi. Narottama will be such a wonderful devotee that every word coming from his mouth will be filled with love of God. And anyone who sings his praises will certainly attain love of God. If I leave My love with him, it is certain that the nectarean ocean of *saṅkīrtana* will continue to flood the universe."

Puzzled, Nityānanda inquired, "But if Narottama has not yet been born, how will You give him Your love?"

Śrī Caitanya Mahāprabhu smiled. "Tomorrow I will enter the Padmavatī River and deposit My love for Narottama to receive in the future. At the appropriate time You must guide Narottama to the riverbank to collect the divine treasure that awaits him." The Lord then stood and resumed His chanting.

That evening the devotees spoke among themselves in hushed voices. "Who is this Narottama the Lord called for?" No one except Nityānanda Prabhu could answer, but He remained silent.[2]

The following morning, the *kīrtana* party moved slowly along the sandy footpath, chanting and dancing as they sang the holy names. As they reached a clearing in the trees, the deep blue of the Padmavatī River came into view. At the riverbank, Nityānanda Prabhu turned to the devotees and stopped the *kīrtana*. "Watch carefully," He said. "Something extraordinary is about to take place. Śrī Caitanya Mahāprabhu is going to place His divine love into the Padmavatī River. Sometime in the future this love will be given to a devotee named Narottama.

The devotees watched curiously as Śrī Caitanya stepped with His lotus feet into the water and slowly waded toward the river's center. To their amazement, the placid river swelled with joy. Transformed by the Lord's touch, the water appeared to dance in glee, swirling and gurgling as it rose higher and higher. Within moments the river overflowed with ecstasy, spilling over its banks and gushing onto the land.

All at once, an extraordinarily beautiful woman rose from the waves. She stood before Śrī Caitanya Mahāprabhu with folded palms. Her silken garments shimmered in the breeze, and her jeweled crown sparkled in the morning sunlight. She asked, humbly, "My Lord, how can I serve You?"

"Oh goddess of this river, Padmavatī Devī," Mahāprabhu said. "I want to leave My transcendental property in your care. Please take My love and keep it with you until a devotee named Narottama bathes here. At that time, deliver this love to him."

"Yes, my Lord," she replied submissively. "But how will I recognize Narottama?"

"When a young, dark-complexioned boy, who is filled with love for God, enters your waters, causing them to surge and flood the land as they did today, you will know that is Narottama."

"But, My Lord," she asked, "if this boy has so much devotion that his touch will cause me to overflow with ecstasy even before he has received Your divine treasure, what will his condition be after receiving Your love?"

"Don't worry," the Lord interrupted. "Narottama will sustain My love. When he comes, simply give My love to him."

Quivering with joy, Padmavatī Devī received Mahāprabhu's love, offered her obeisances, and disappeared into the receding waters.

The devotees who observed this exchange stood transfixed, mouths agape and eyes wide with astonishment. Śrī Caitanya Mahāprabhu turned to them and said, calmly, "Begin *kīrtana*."

News of this miraculous incident quickly spread throughout the land. Devotees everywhere waited eagerly for Narottama's appearance, each of them hoping for the opportunity to meet such a special devotee.

saṅkīrtanānandaja-mānda-hāsya-
danta-dyuti-dyotita-diṅ-mukhāya
svedāśru-dhārā-snapitāya tasmai
namo namaḥ śrīla-narottamāya

I repeatedly offer my respectful obeisances to Śrīla Narottama Dāsa Ṭhākura, whose face is bathed in perspiration and torrents of tears due to the bliss of chanting the holy names. His gladdening smile and shining teeth illuminate all directions.

Narottama-prabhor-āṣṭaka, Verse 2

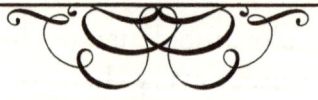

Chapter Two

Birth and Youth

A Prince Is Born

The sun rose over the palm trees, illuminating the village of Kheturi. As the warm rays streamed through the window of his palace, King Kṛṣṇānanda Datta sat silently, worshiping his family Deity. Picking up a handful of *tulasī* leaves, he gently placed them at the Lord's feet, thus completing his *pūjā*. Staring intently at the Deity, bowing his head and folding his hands he humbly pleaded, "My dear Lord, if You so desire, please bless our family by sending us a son."

The king offered his obeisances and walked out onto the veranda. Surveying the capital of his small kingdom, his heart swelled with pride to see the well-kept village homes surrounded by gardens that overflowed with fruits, vegetables, and grains. "What a paradise!" he thought. "The soil in Kheturi is so fertile that practically anything grows here." Kṛṣṇānanda's gaze swept the horizon. For as far as he could see, the countryside was lush with banana, jackfruit, mango, and coconut palm trees, which spread their deep green foliage beneath a clear blue sky. Inhaling deeply, he savored the exquisite fragrances of the many varieties of flowers carried on the morning breeze. "It's truly a blessing to rule over such opulence," he reflected. "I have everything a man could want: land, wealth, and a devoted wife. The Supreme Lord has certainly been kind to me. Yet," and the king's brow furrowed slightly, "all these blessings cannot fill the void in my heart. Without a son, my home appears empty and lifeless. To whom shall I turn over my kingly responsibilities when I am old? And how can I pacify my good wife Nārāyaṇī, who suffers without a child to nurture?" Kṛṣṇānanda shook his head sadly. "I know I am becoming too old to entertain such thoughts, but I just cannot give up my desire for a son." Then sighing, he turned from the window. "Well, I mustn't waste the day dreaming. The Supreme Lord knows that my wife and I are anxious to have a child. But we must wait to see what He desires."

Kṛṣṇānanda sat alone in his chamber, reflecting on the affairs of the village. His thoughts were interrupted by a loud voice that echoed in the room. "Soon you will be the father of a son named Narottama. This boy will shower the earth with love of God."

Stunned, Kṛṣṇānanda looked around himself to see who had spoken, but he found no one to match the extraordinary voice. Spellbound, he waited expectantly for the voice to continue. But nothing more was said.

"What? Am I in my right senses?" he whispered to himself, doubting the reality of what he had heard. "Did

I really hear that voice, or was I merely dreaming? Am I a victim of delusion, imagining good news?" Kṛṣṇānanda shook himself. "No, no," he assured himself emphatically. "I definitely heard a voice. It was no dream. My eyes are open, and I am fully conscious. What I heard could be nothing other than a divine prophecy." His heart leapt to think that his desire for a son might be fulfilled. He hurried to share the good news with his wife.

A few days later, in the early morning, Nārāyaṇī rushed into her husband's chamber, her face flushed with excitement. "Prabhu, last night I dreamed that an extraordinary person came from your body and entered mine. This must be another omen that we will have a son!"

Kṛṣṇānanda looked unsure. "Your dream confirms the oracle I heard the other day. But don't raise your expectations too high. Whatever the Supreme Lord ordains, that we must accept."

"Yes, Prabhu," she said, and silently left the room. Despite her husband's advice, hope blossomed within her heart.

Neither of them mentioned the omens again, but they couldn't stop their minds from dwelling on the prospect of having a child.

Shortly after this incident, Kṛṣṇānanda was relaxing in his chamber when an astrologer paid him an unexpected visit. Always a gracious host, Kṛṣṇānanda welcomed him. "Come in, friend. Make yourself comfortable. I'll have the servant bring you a cool drink. Then please let my wife and I hear something about our future."

The learned *brāhmaṇa* accepted the gracious hospitality, sipping his drink as he settled down, cross-legged on a cushion. Spreading some charts out before him, he silently made several complicated calculations.

The King and Queen waited anxiously. Suddenly the astrologer gasped, and smiled brightly. "Oh, this is wonderful!" he exclaimed. "You will certainly have a son who will be a remarkable devotee of the Supreme Lord. He will have the power to destroy the world's miseries, and he will bring great happiness and fortune to your family."

Delighted by his words, Kṛṣṇānanda showered the astrologer with gifts and bid him farewell. Now he and his wife felt certain that their long-cherished dream would come true.

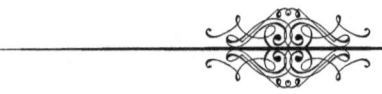

Nārāyaṇī was soon pregnant. The elated couple waited impatiently for the months to pass, hardly able to think of anything other than their unborn child. Finally, at six o'clock in the morning, on the full moon day of Magha (January–February), Nārāyaṇī gave birth to a healthy male child.[3] When the child appeared, an unearthly effulgence illuminated the delivery room and profound happiness swelled in the hearts of everyone present.

Nārāyaṇī gazed lovingly at the charming face of her son. "Just see how beautiful he is!" she exclaimed to the midwives. "His features are exquisitely fine, and his eyes are like lotus petals." Embracing her child tightly, she wept with joy.

One of the midwives rushed out of the room and announced the good news. Kṛṣṇānanda beamed with delight and hurried to see his son. The musicians waiting in the palace courtyard for the birth announcement played celebratory music, and the village *brāhmaṇas* loudly chanted auspicious Vedic hymns.

News of the child's birth spread quickly. The residents of Kheturi, having great affection for their Rāja and Rāṇī, rushed to the palace with gifts for the newborn child. Everyone wanted a glimpse of the little prince. Though Kṛṣṇānanda could barely take his eyes off his child's face, the proud father managed to welcome each visitor warmly.

Amid this excitement, Nārāyaṇī suddenly saw the most beautifully resplendent figures enter her room. One of them was glowing like molten gold, and another had a creamy white complexion and wore brilliant blue garments. Amazed, Nārāyaṇī sat upright, staring with wide eyes as the extraordinary personalities danced ecstatically in her home. Bewildered, she looked around, but no one else in the room seemed to notice the remarkable scene. When she turned again to look at the dancers, they had vanished. Nārāyaṇī sank back onto her pillow. Overcome with confusion, excitement, and fatigue, she thought, "I must be imagining things." Unable to comprehend that the Supreme Lord

Himself, Śrī Caitanya Mahāprabhu, and His associates had blessed her home with their presence, she simply turned back to look at her son's face. In moments, she had forgotten everything else. Feeling herself the most fortunate woman in the universe, her heart overflowed with happiness and contentment.

When all the visitors had left, Kṛṣṇānanda made arrangements for an eight-day celebration. Calling his servants, he declared, "I want huge quantities of clothing, blankets, utensils, and *prasāda* to be given to all the people of Kheturi, especially the *sādhus* and *brāhmaṇas*. Spare no expense. Everyone should feel satisfied and happy. The child will thus receive everyone's blessings."

Soon after, Kṛṣṇānanda called a few local *paṇḍitas* to calculate the child's astrological chart and to recommend a suitable name. After carefully studying the chart, the astrologers agreed it was extraordinarily auspicious.

"This is definitely not the chart of an ordinary person," one of them announced. "We can also understand this simply by looking at the auspicious signs on the child's body."

"Yes," another astrologer agreed. "This child will have all good qualities and be extremely religious. He will bring great fortune to everyone in this region."

Glowing with both pride and happiness, Kṛṣṇānanda asked, "What shall we name him?"

The *paṇḍitas* discussed at length and eventually concluded, "We all agree the boy's name should contain one or more of the syllables *na*, *ra*, and *ta*. We think Narottama would be a most suitable name, because *nara* means "man" and *uttama* means "topmost." It is clear from this boy's chart that he will indeed be the greatest of men."

"Splendid," Kṛṣṇānanda exclaimed. "How amazing it is," he said softly to his wife, "that these astrologers have chosen the same name the oracle predicted before the child's conception." Turning to the astrologers the King asked, "Now tell me what else you see in his chart."

Each astrologer then gave an enthusiastic interpretation of the chart, describing in detail various aspects of the boy's character and destiny. One of the *paṇḍitas*, however, warned, "Majumadāra, I must caution you that there is one thing to watch out for. Be careful when you take your son to the river. It could be dangerous for him there."

Rāja Kṛṣṇānanda shivered at the thought of *any* possible danger to his son, and firmly resolved that although he lived a short distance from the Padmavatī River, he would keep Narottama away from the water.

Six months passed swiftly as Kṛṣṇānanda and Nārāyaṇī doted on their growing child, who was the joy of their lives. Kṛṣṇānanda sent out invitations inscribed on golden plates to all his friends and relatives, inviting them to attend the baby's *anna-prāśana* ceremony, at which Narottama would be offered his first grains.

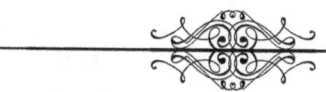

At the ceremony, guests and family members gathered around the infant, eager to watch him taste his first rice, but to everyone's dismay, the child refused to open his mouth. They coaxed him again and again, but Narottama repeatedly turned his head away in disgust. The guests looked at each other nervously, and the festive mood was replaced with confusion. No one knew what to do.

Then, one thoughtful *brāhmaṇa* stepped forward and reassured everyone, "Don't worry. This baby won't eat the sweet rice because it hasn't first been offered to Lord Kṛṣṇa."

Realizing they had somehow forgotten to offer the food, Kṛṣṇānanda quickly placed it on the altar. Then, once again, his mother offered Narottama a spoonful. To everyone's relief, the child happily devoured the rice.

Kṛṣṇānanda mused, "For generations, worship of the Supreme Lord has been customary in our family. This child, although still so young, is already teaching us to be more mindful of our religious duties." Then Kṛṣṇānanda announced, "My son should be given only the Lord's *mahā-prasāda* from now on."

Childhood

Rāja Kṛṣṇānanda sat next to his brother Puruṣottama Datta in the main room of the palace, surrounded by many servants. "There are less than two months left until the Ratha-yātrā in Jagannātha Purī," he announced. "Soon hundreds of pilgrims will pass through Kheturi on their way to the festival. It's our duty to receive them properly and make their stay in Kheturi as comfortable as possible. We must start preparing the accommodations and set up a kitchen to feed them all. Everything should be organized perfectly – no one should feel any inconvenience while they are here in Kheturi."

After assigning different responsibilities to the servants, Kṛṣṇānanda said, "There is no time to lose. Work must begin immediately. Already some Vaiṣṇava pilgrims have arrived. Tonight, one of them will give a discourse in the courtyard of the palace temple." Saying this, the king dismissed everyone and entered his private chambers.

Looking out his window, Kṛṣṇānanda noticed little Narottama playing in front of the palace with some village children. "Naru! Oh Naru!" he called affectionately, "Where are you going?"

Narottama waved happily, "I'm going, Pitā. I'm going to see the big river with my friends."

"What? You come back into the palace right now," Kṛṣṇānanda ordered. Rushing outside, he swept Narottama up in his arms and hugged him tightly to his chest. "Naru, you know you don't have to leave the palace for anything. Whatever you want we will bring to you here."

"But Pitā, I want to go to the river."

"No! I've told you many times that rivers are dangerous for you." Seeing the hurt in his son's eyes, Kṛṣṇānanda spoke more gently, "Don't worry, Naru. I will have a pond dug next to the palace and fill it with water from the Padma. Then you can learn to swim with the guards watching you. Now run along inside and take your bath. Tonight we will listen to the *sādhus* speak."

Narottama ran obediently into the house, and Kṛṣṇānanda turned to the village children. "Don't ever mention the river to Narottama again," he fumed. The children ran away, and Kṛṣṇānanda turned to the guards near the palace door. "What is this nonsense? Why didn't you bring my son back inside? You know that he is absolutely forbidden to go to the river. Never, ever let this happen again."

That evening, many of Kheturi's residents gathered in the palace courtyard and waited for the lecture to begin. When Kṛṣṇānanda and Nārāyaṇī came out with Narottama by their side, the villagers greeted their Rāja and Rāṇī respectfully, then turned their attention to the town's favorite son. Someone called out affectionately, "Oh! Here is our Rāja Kumāra Narottama! Come over here and talk to your uncle." Many of the ladies hurried toward Narottama to play with him and pinch his cheeks. Everyone was captivated by Narottama's bright, handsome face. Accustomed to such pampering and coddling, Narottama simply smiled good-naturedly.

As the lecture was about to begin, Kṛṣṇānanda grabbed Narottama's hand, walked to the front of the courtyard, and took his seat directly in front of the speaker. Narottama sat beside him. "Sit quietly, Narottama, and listen respectfully to the instructions of the *sādhus*," he whispered. "Even if we don't understand much of what they say, we should still listen respectfully and try to receive their mercy."

The speaker uttered auspicious prayers of invocation and began his lecture, explaining the importance of detachment from material pleasure. "As a boy, Śrī Caitanya Mahāprabhu's follower, Śrī Raghunātha Dāsa, lived like a prince. His father was a big land owner and earned over 200,000 gold coins a month. But Raghunātha Dāsa was so attracted to Śrī Caitanya Mahāprabhu's lotus feet that he had no interest whatsoever in his father's wealth. Eventually, he managed to run away from home and went to Purī. There he fell at the feet of Śrī Caitanya Mahāprabhu and surrendered his life to Him. From that day on, Raghunātha Dāsa was totally absorbed in loving service to Mahāprabhu and never worried about how he himself would be maintained. He ate only the few morsels of food he managed to beg from pilgrims passing the Siṁha-dvāra gate. After some time, he even stopped begging and instead went to the drain where the refuse from the kitchen was thrown. Taking a handful of discarded, rotting rice, he washed it off and made it his meal."

Narottama listened, enthralled, his eyes wide open. He loved to hear about these wonderful devotees the *sādhus* described. His heart was filled with both awe and respect. "I would like to be a great devotee like Raghunātha Dāsa," he thought.

After the lecture, Kṛṣṇānanda and his family went into their private rooms. "Narottama, come sit next to me and have some sweet rice," Kṛṣṇānanda said.

"But, Pitā, what is Raghunātha Dāsa eating? Do you think we should eat such opulent food? Raghunātha simply begged his food at the Siṁha-dvāra gate."

Nārāyaṇī laughed. "Naru, do you think you have become a *sādhu* like Raghunātha Dāsa?"

"Clever child," Kṛṣṇānanda chuckled. "He listens nicely." Patting Narottama on the head, he said, "You're a good boy, Narottama. If you learn to take guidance from *sādhus* and serve the Vaiṣṇavas nicely, you will be a very good king when you grow up."

Nārāyaṇī filled silver bowls with sweet rice, and Narottama and Kṛṣṇānanda began to eat.

After a few minutes Narottama said, "Pitā, why don't we leave home?"

"Ha! Leave home? Why should we leave home? Everything is so nice here."

"No, Pitā," Narottama said seriously. "We should run away like Raghunātha Dāsa did. We can stay in a *dharmaśālā*. But make sure your servant doesn't bring gold coins with him. Remember the story we heard about Sanātana Gosvāmī? His servant almost got them killed because he secretly brought gold coins."

Amused by Narottama's childish talks, Kṛṣṇānanda laughed again. "Naru, stop fantasizing. We cannot imitate devotees like Raghunātha Dāsa. These are great souls. They are worshipable people. We can worship them, but we can never become like them. We have to perform our own duties to care for our citizens."

"Yes, Pitā," Narottama said submissively. But he thought, "Yes, *you* cannot become like them, but *I* can and I *will*."

"Hurry, Naru," Nārāyaṇī called. "Everyone is waiting. You mustn't be late for your first day of school." Grabbing her son's hand, Nārāyaṇī hurried with Narottama down the steps and into the room in the palace that had been set up as a classroom.

Kṛṣṇānanda and many *paṇḍitas* and friends were waiting there, and they greeted Narottama happily when he arrived. "Come over here, Narottama," Kṛṣṇānanda said. Kneeling, he wrapped his arm around his son's waist. "Just see what elaborate arrangements I have made for you, Naru," he said proudly. "I have brought the greatest teachers from far and wide to ensure that you receive the best education possible. Now, just sit here, and one of your teachers will show you how to write the letters of the Sanskrit alphabet. Then the *paṇḍitas* will offer some prayers and perform a *yajña* to create an auspicious beginning for your education."

Bright-eyed and innocent, Narottama dutifully sat down to begin his education. Turning to the *paṇḍitas* Kṛṣṇānanda instructed, "I don't want my son to feel any anxiety or misery. He should simply study and become well educated. That will make him fully qualified to care for all the property here and to serve the people of Kheturi when I no longer can."

Over the next few years, Narottama listened dutifully as his teachers taught. He quickly mastered Sanskrit, logic and rhetoric. They marveled at his brilliance, especially his sharp memory and peaceful, submissive attitude toward his teachers. Yet Narottama's heart was not in his studies. He wanted to learn more about spiritual topics.

Closing his grammar book one day, he offered obeisances to his teacher and hurried up the steps to his room. Peering out an open window, he looked out over the village. His eyes fell on a group of pilgrims walking toward the large pavilion his father had erected to accommodate *sādhus* passing through Kheturi. "Those Vaiṣṇavas must be returning from Jagannātha Purī," he thought. Intrigued, he watched them carefully.

Hundreds of pilgrims filed into the pavilion, each searching for a place to lay his or her belongings and the *kuśa* mat each pilgrim travelled with. The place bustled with activity, and the pilgrims were talking excitedly among themselves as scores of servants scurried around, tending to their needs. In the kitchen area, Narottama saw fires ablaze and dozens of cooks stirring the contents of gigantic pots. Returning his gaze to the pilgrims Narottama began to study their faces. They were glowing with happiness. "I want to understand their joy," Narottama thought. "What did they see in Jagannātha Purī that made them so wonderfully effulgent?"

Turning away from the window, Narottama ran to one of the servants at the palace door and tugged at his sleeve. "Please take me outside. I want to get a closer look at the pilgrims."

"I'm not sure if your father . . . "

"*Please*," Narottama pleaded sweetly.

"Well, I guess it can't do you any harm," the servant said. He took Narottama by the hand and the two of them wandered through the village observing the pilgrims.

From that day onward, whenever Narottama had spare time, he would ask a servant to accompany him so he could go out and mingle with the pilgrims and listen to their discussions. One day he noticed a very old man addressing the crowd. The man's eyes were bright and clear and his speech so sweet that Narottama was immediately drawn to him. Narottama remembered seeing the same *sādhu* talking to his father at the palace.

Narottama whispered to his servant escort, "Who is that man?"

"Oh," the servant said with surprise, "don't you know? That's Kṛṣṇadāsa Bābājī. He was a personal associate of Śrī Caitanya Mahāprabhu. He is living in Kheturi now."

Narottama moved into the crowd and sat down to listen. When Kṛṣṇadāsa finished, Narottama walked up to him and asked shyly, "Please tell me about Śrī Caitanya Mahāprabhu."

A broad grin spread across the old *brāhmaṇa's* face. "Oh, Rāja-kumāra Narottama, you have asked a very nice question. But my dear boy, even if I spoke for a thousand years with a thousand tongues I could never properly describe the glories of Mahāprabhu. Still, I will happily tell you what I know about Him."

Kṛṣṇadāsa caught hold of Narottama's hand and pulled him down next to him. His eyes sparkled as he began to speak.

"Śrī Caitanya Mahāprabhu appeared in Nadia as the son of Śacī-mātā and Jagannātha Miśra. Though acting like an ordinary child, He is actually the Supreme Personality of Godhead, who came to earth to teach us how to develop love for God."

Narottama's eyes widened. "The Supreme Lord?" he interrupted excitedly. "He is here in this world? Is He in Nadia or Jagannātha Purī?"

Kṛṣṇadāsa heaved a deep sigh. "No, my boy, I'm sorry to say that He is not in Nadia or Purī."

"Well, where is He then? Can I see Him?"

Kṛṣṇadāsa fell silent and tears welled in his eyes. "Son," he said gravely, "You can see Śrī Caitanya Mahāprabhu only with the eyes of devotion now, because unfortunately, He no longer walks among us in this mortal world."

Narottama could hardly believe his ears. "What? He's gone? But I've heard pilgrims passing through Kheturi speak of a golden *avatāra* named Śrī Caitanya Mahāprabhu."

Kṛṣṇadāsa said sadly. "For years Mahāprabhu's devotees visited Him in Purī around the Ratha-yātrā festival, but those days of ecstatic dancing with the Lord are gone. Śrī Caitanya is no longer there. He has returned to His supreme abode."

Narottama's face paled as he tried to grapple with this tragic news. "You mean the Lord was here just a little while ago and now I'll never be able to see Him?" Young Narottama was devastated. "Oh, why wasn't I born a few years earlier?" he cried. "How could I be so unfortunate?"

Placing a hand on Narottama's shoulder, Kṛṣṇadāsa said softly, "Don't worry, Narottama, Śrī Caitanya Mahāprabhu lives in the hearts of His devotees. He can appear to them as He likes, and simply by hearing about His pastimes and associates one can feel His presence."

Tears welled up in Narottama's eyes as he sat lost in thought. He was deeply disappointed, yet the calming words of Kṛṣṇadāsa soothed his burning heart. After some time, he resolved to shake off his despondency. Wiping his eyes, he looked hopefully at Kṛṣṇadāsa and with a quivering voice asked, "Well, then, could you tell me more? I want to know everything there is to know about Śrī Caitanya Mahāprabhu and His devotees." Narottama's eager inquiries tumbled out one after another: "Where did He live? What did He look like? What did He teach His devotees?"

A smile lit Kṛṣṇadāsa's face, and he began to answer Narottama's questions. He spoke at length of Mahāprabhu's *līlās*, but the boy's thirst appeared unquenchable. Finally, late into the afternoon, Kṛṣṇadāsa said, "Hold on, my son. The glories of Śrī

Caitanya Mahāprabhu are fathomless and unlimited. You cannot learn everything in a day. Don't worry, I'll come to see you at the palace tomorrow, and we can continue our discussion. I have much more to tell you."

Kṛṣṇadāsa was intrigued and enchanted by Narottama's sincere desire to hear about Caitanya Mahāprabhu and His associates. Thus, he began to visit the palace every afternoon to share his spiritual wisdom with Narottama and anyone else who was interested to listen.

Each day after finishing his studies, Narottama waited impatiently for Kṛṣṇadāsa to come. Whenever he finally did arrive, Narottama would rush to sit at his feet, ready to hear the exciting narrations about the great saints. Sometimes relatives or palace staff would sit to listen for a while, but Narottama was always riveted and would not move. However long Kṛṣṇadāsa would speak, Narottama could listen without becoming tired or distracted.

Enthused by the boy's eagerness, Kṛṣṇadāsa said much, describing not only the life of Śrī Caitanya but the lives of His greatest devotees – Nityānanda Prabhu, Śrī Gadādhara, Śrīvasa Paṇḍita, Svarūpa Dāmodara, Rūpa Gosvāmī, Sanātana Gosvāmī, and Haridāsa Ṭhākura.

"Today," Kṛṣṇadāsa said, "I will tell you about a very special devotee, one who is the embodiment of humility and renunciation. His name is Lokanātha Gosvāmī."

Narottama's attention was riveted on the nectar flowing from Kṛṣṇadāsa's mouth.

"When he was a young man," Kṛṣṇadāsa began, "Lokanātha decided to renounce worldly life, so he set out for Navadvīpa with the hope of living in the sweet company of Śrī Caitanya Mahāprabhu. On reaching Mahāprabhu's home, He saw the Lord sitting outside surrounded by Murāri, Gadādhara, Śrīvasa, and other devotees. Overcome with love, Lokanātha fell prostrate at the Lord's feet. The Lord too was filled with delight at the sight of Lokanātha. 'Lokanātha, you have come!' he said, his voice choked with emotion. Mahāprabhu then lifted Lokanātha from the ground and embraced him tightly to His chest.

"After they had spent the afternoon together, Mahāprabhu told Lokanātha, 'You must be tired after your long walk here. Go and rest. Come again tomorrow morning, and I will open My heart to you. Kṛṣṇa has kindly sent you to Me to fulfill a great task.'

"Lokanātha *was* tired, but that night he was unable to sleep. The Lord's words continued to ring in his ears: 'Kṛṣṇa has kindly sent you to me to fulfill a great task.' He could hardly bear the suspense. What could that task be?

"The next morning, he went to see Śrī Caitanya Mahāprabhu. The Lord embraced him lovingly and said, 'Lokanātha! You are very fortunate. Kṛṣṇa has chosen you for a task which is dear to Him. The sacred land of Lord Kṛṣṇa's loving pastimes, Śrī Vṛndāvana, is now a deserted forest. I want you to go to that holy *dhāma* and reclaim the holy places associated with Kṛṣṇa's *līlā*. You should devote yourself to this great service. There is no need for you to stay here in Navadvīpa.'

"Lokanātha was stunned. Hot tears sprang from his eyes, and he felt faint. Desperately he begged with folded hands, 'Prabhu, I renounced the world and came here to drink the nectar of Your association. I planned to spend the rest of my life with You. Now You are sending me away. Why are You being so cruel to me? What offense have I committed to receive such punishment? How can I live without You? You are the life of my life.'

" 'No, Lokanātha, this is not punishment,' the Lord said. 'I am giving you the rare privilege of serving the transcendental land of Vṛndāvana. Don't you know how dear Vṛndāvana is to Kṛṣṇa? He is not pleased so much by His own service as by service to His *dhāma*. Vṛndāvana is My heart and soul. By sending you there I am keeping you close to My heart.'

"Lokanātha's voice shook, 'Please, Prabhu, don't trick me like this. Haven't You the slightest place in Your heart for me? If so, why are You pushing me away as soon as I have come?'

" 'Lokanātha,' the Lord said softly, 'I'm not kicking you away. I am sending you to Vṛndāvana, where staying even one day enables a person to attain the highest goal of life – *kṛṣṇa-prema*.'

"Falling at Mahāprabhu's feet Lokanātha cried, 'Prabhu, I have no desire to attain anything except Your lotus feet.'

"Placing His hand gently on Lokanātha's head, Śrī Caitanya Mahāprabhu lovingly replied, 'Just try to understand the importance of the work I want you to do. Kṛṣṇa manifested Śrī Vṛndāvana, His spiritual abode, on earth for the benefit of all souls, but Vṛndāvana's beauty and grandeur have become covered. I want you to rediscover and revive Vṛndāvana so it will be accessible to everyone. If you want to make Me happy, start this work immediately. Remember, Lord Kṛṣṇa said that all devotees are dear to Him, but those who try to help others attain Him are the most dear.'

"Lokanātha contemplated the Lord's words. Nothing Mahāprabhu had said about Vṛndāvana and its importance had persuaded him to leave the Lord's company, but His last point had struck a chord: there was only one thing that could encourage Lokanātha to leave Śrī Caitanya Mahāprabhu, and that was the happiness of Mahāprabhu Himself. With the realization that his actions could make the Lord happy, Lokanātha surrendered to the Lord's wishes. He understood that pleasing Śrī Caitanya by serving His preaching mission was more important than having the Lord's personal association."

Narottama gasped and interrupted Kṛṣṇadāsa's narration. "But how could he leave Caitanya Mahāprabhu's personal association? It must have been so difficult. Did he ever see the Lord again?"

"Well," Kṛṣṇadāsa said, "yes and no. When Lokanātha left Nadia, Caitanya Mahāprabhu promised he would meet him in Vṛndāvana. But after Lokanātha and Bhūgarbha . . . "

Rāja Kṛṣṇānanda stood quietly in one corner of the room observing the aged *sādhu* and his beloved son, deep in conversation. The king's brow knitted with concern. "Narottama is spending too much time listening to these stories," he thought. "I must put a stop to it, but I don't want to offend the great soul, Śrī

Kṛṣṇadāsa." Kṛṣṇānanda called out gently, "All right, Narottama, it is getting late. Your mother has *prasāda* ready for you."

His reverie broken, Narottama looked up. "Oh, Pitā, is it late already? But Bābājī Mahārāja was telling me the most wonderful story."

"That's nice, Naru, but it *is* late. Go find your mother."

Kṛṣṇadāsa chuckled. "Run along, Narottama. I will tell you more stories tomorrow."

With regret, Narottama offered his humble obeisances to Kṛṣṇadāsa and then hurried from the room, his mind racing as he remembered all that he had just heard.

Youth

Nārāyaṇī sat down next to her husband, her face tense with worry. "Prabhu, I'm concerned about Narottama. He's become indifferent to everything. His mind isn't on his studies anymore, and he shows no interest in village affairs. He doesn't even enjoy playing with other children. He seems interested only in hearing Kṛṣṇadāsa's stories and doing *pūjā*." Nārāyaṇī wrung her hands in despair and looked at her husband for his advice. She added, "It's fortunate he has such strong spiritual inclinations, but too much detachment is unnatural and unhealthy for a boy that age and especially for the son of a king. What will become of him?"

Kṛṣṇānanda furrowed his brow. "What you say is true. I don't know what to do with him either," he said shaking his head. "He is no longer a child. He has to start thinking of his future responsibilities. But he seems overly detached from everything worldly. I'm getting old. It won't be long before he'll have to relieve me of my duties."

He sighed. "It's good he's a religious boy, but he seems too carried away by it all. We are *kāyasthas* and must manage the affairs of our village and collect taxes. Narottama too will have this responsibility. He's our only son. He's getting too old to behave as if he were a *sādhu*."

Kṛṣṇānanda sat silently, lost in thought. Finally, he turned to Nārāyaṇī and announced, "I think I know what we can do. Let's arrange Narottama's marriage. That will ground him and wake him up to his responsibilities."

Nārāyaṇī agreed. Confident they had found a solution, she and Kṛṣṇānanda began to search for a suitable bride.

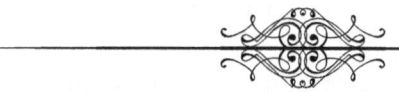

Narottama lay on his bed staring into the darkness of night, his mind spinning. "I can't bear to hear another word about property management or collecting taxes. I have absolutely no interest in those things. I just want to dedicate my life fully to the service of Śrī Caitanya Mahāprabhu." He sighed deeply. "I want so much to be in Vṛndāvana. I desperately want to meet the personal associates of Mahāprabhu still living there – Śrī Rūpa, Sanātana, Raghunātha Dāsa. . . . Many of them are very old. How much longer can they remain in this world? I have to get there before it's too late."

Narottama lay awake with these thoughts for a long time. Finally, he decided, "I see no other alternative. I have to leave home."

Late into the night, as sleep overtook him, Narottama had a startling vision. Śrī Nityānanda Prabhu appeared before him. The Lord's face was more beautiful than millions upon millions of moons. He had a tall, strong, heroic stature. His hands, arms, and legs were beautifully formed, and His eyes resembled lotus flowers. He wore golden earrings, armlets, and bangles. Smiling, He told Narottama, "Go at once to the Padmavatī River to bathe. Padmavatī Devī has been keeping a gift for you, and she will deliver it when you come. She has been waiting for you." Then the Lord disappeared.

Narottama woke with a start. Astonished and overcome with transcendental ecstasy, he jumped out of bed. He had to get out of the palace and down to the Padmavatī immediately. Afraid he might be seen by one of the ever-protective household servants, Narottama decided to climb out through his window. He stacked the furniture under a small window high up on the wall. Scaling it, he then squeezed through and pulled himself out onto the roof. As silently as possible, he slid down to the eaves and dropped quietly to the ground.

By the arrangement of Providence, the sun had not yet risen and there were no guards in sight. Narottama rushed toward the Padmavatī River, softly chanting the holy name all the way. When he reached the bank, he bowed down in the moist earth and then stepped into the shallows, calling out the name of Gaurāṅga. The cool, dark water swirled around his legs and immediately began to rise higher and higher. Within moments, the river's waves surged over the banks and onto the land.

Narottama suddenly saw the goddess Padmavatī Devī standing before him. Shocked, he stared at her with wide eyes.

Padmavatī Devī smiled warmly at him. "Before you were born," she said, "Śrī Caitanya Mahāprabhu left His divine love in my care and instructed me to give it to a boy named Narottama, whose touch would make my waters rise in the same way they did when Śrī Caitanya Mahāprabhu Himself came here. Clearly you are the rightful recipient of this most extraordinary gift. I have been waiting for a very long time for your visit. Now, please take this topmost treasure." Saying this, Padmavatī Devī moved towards Narottama with outstretched hands, holding what appeared to be a radiant golden lotus flower.

Without warning, the goddess Padmavatī disappeared, and Narottama was astonished to see the golden lotus transform into a luminous golden-colored boy. This exquisite form, which was none other than Śrī Caitanya Mahāprabhu Himself, danced toward him and entered his body. Narottama felt Mahāprabhu's essence engulf him. Powerless in the grip of the Lord's ecstasy, he shouted, "Gaurāṅga! Gaurāṅga!" As the Lord's love infused his every limb, Narottama's swarthy complexion lightened, transforming his skin into a beautiful golden color. His skin also slackened, and he shivered and trembled uncontrollably. The current of divine love that coursed through his body was so intense that Narottama couldn't contain his emotions. Staggering out of the water, he laughed, cried, sang, and danced furiously on the banks of the Padmavatī, lost in the ecstasy of love and oblivious to everything around him.

Narottama was abruptly brought back to external consciousness when he heard his father's frantic shouts. "Naru! Naru! Where are you? Look! – there's someone over there. . . . It doesn't look like Narottama. Oh, my dear Lord, what has happened to my son?"

Squinting in the predawn darkness, Narottama saw a large crowd of people rushing toward him with torches. To his surprise, he heard his mother's hysterical voice, "It *is* Naru! Can't you recognize your own son? Look! He's wearing Naru's ornaments!"

Nārāyaṇī ran to where Narottama stood and kissed his face again and again. "Naru, Naru," she cried. "Why did you sneak off like this? Why didn't you tell us where you were going? We were so frightened when we found your room empty! We searched everywhere for you. I was frantic!"

Taking Narottama's face in her hands she looked at him in bewilderment. "What has happened to you? Why do you look so strange? What happened to your skin?" Her voice shook. "Are you all right?"

"I'm . . . I'm fine," Narottama managed to stutter as he tried to compose himself. But thoughts of Lord Caitanya again surged in his heart, and he pulled away from his mother, yelling, "Gaurāṅga! Gaurāṅga!" Tears of ecstasy streamed from his eyes, as he danced around the crowd of confused relatives and friends.

Kṛṣṇānanda gaped at his son in disbelief. "What is this bizarre behavior?" he cried. "It's like he's possessed by a ghost. I've heard a terrible *brahma-rākṣasa* lives in that tamarind tree over there. Perhaps he has entered Naru's body. This is horrible! Quick, let's get him home."

Bewildered and frightened, Kṛṣṇānanda grabbed hold of Narottama. Nārāyaṇī pleaded with her son, "Stop this, Narottama. Please come home with us now."

With great difficulty they managed to get their son home and into his bed.

Realizing the anxiety he was causing, Narottama tried to calm himself, but the golden Lord he had seen at the Padmavatī appeared within his mind, and he again became wild. Thrashing about on the bed and with tears shooting from his eyes, he called, "Gaurāṅga! Gaurāṅga!" Suddenly his mood changed and he began to laugh loudly. Several times he tried to jump from the bed, but Kṛṣṇānanda forcibly held him down. All the while Nārāyaṇī was frantically fanning him to cool him down.

Concerned relatives and friends stood around Narottama's bed, all of them helpless and perplexed as the boy repeated over and over, "That boy . . . golden . . . my body . . . entered . . . "

Not knowing what else to do, Kṛṣṇānanda ordered one of the servants, "Bring a tantric to help cure my boy."

An exorcist soon arrived and began chanting *mantras* and waving peacock feathers in front of the boy's face. Narottama, however, continued to flail his arms and legs and mumble incoherently about a golden boy. Finally, the exorcist turned to Kṛṣṇānanda and said, "Don't worry, it's not a ghost in your son's body."

"What do you mean?" Kṛṣṇānanda demanded. "Just look at him! He must be possessed."

"No," the exorcist said, "he is simply suffering from an imbalance of air. I suggest you rub jackal oil on his stomach to cure him." Saying this, the tantric left.

Eventually, Narottama stopped thrashing and, exhausted, fell asleep. Kṛṣṇānanda and Nārāyaṇī sat next to his bed, utterly confused. Nārāyaṇī sobbed miserably. "My child, my dear son, please, please, be your sweet, normal self."

Kṛṣṇānanda's face was pale and drawn. "I tried," he said, tears welling up in his eyes. "I tried my best to give him everything – to make him happy – to keep him away from the river. Now just see his pathetic condition. I cannot bear to see my son like this." He heaved a deep sigh and looked at his wife. "We can only pray he will be all right."

Narottama continued to cry incessantly all the next day, and his worried parents continued to watch over him helplessly. Kṛṣṇānanda tried to tell Narottama what the exorcist had said. Narottama, however, only laughed. "Do you think you can cure me by killing an animal to make medicine? Please do not commit this sinful act out of blind affection for me. Oh, Pitā, can't you understand? I am not haunted by a ghost, and I have no disease. I'm feeling intense love for the Supreme Lord. This is what makes me cry."

Kṛṣṇānanda and Nārāyaṇī looked at each other blankly. They had never seen anyone behave like this before. They were simple, pious people, but they knew nothing about the exalted states of extreme devotion to God.

His parents stepped out of Narottama's room to talk. "I believe Narottama is telling us the truth," Kṛṣṇānanda said. "Perhaps he is not haunted by a ghost. Perhaps he had some sort of extraordinary mystical experience when he went to the Padmavatī the other night. That would account for why he can't think of anything else. I think the golden boy he speaks of is Śrī Caitanya Mahāprabhu."

"But . . . but, he's just a child," Nārāyaṇī sobbed. "What kind of religious experience could a young boy have?"[4] She wrung the folds of her sari in desperation, crying, "What are we going to do? Oh, what are we going to do?"

Kṛṣṇānanda shook his head. "I don't know, but I think he will be all right in time. Go now and rest. I will stay with him."

Despite these reassuring words to his wife, Rāja Kṛṣṇānanda sat silently, tormented by remembrance of the ominous words of the astrologers spoken so many years ago. . . . "Rivers are dangerous for your boy."

Nārāyaṇī was beside herself. For days she watched Narottama cry incessantly. Nothing she said or did made any difference. She begged him, "Narottama, please, tell us how we can *help* you. We cannot understand what has happened to you. Why are you crying in such a pathetic way?"

Narottama was sad to see his parents' distress. He loved them, and didn't want to hurt them, but he knew he was no longer their little Naru – he had been touched by the love of Śrī Caitanya Mahāprabhu and would never be the same. He couldn't stop the tears of love of God that constantly welled up in his eyes. He tried to reveal his heart to his distraught mother. "Mātā, if you really want to help me, then let me to go to Vṛndāvana and dedicate my life to the Supreme Lord's service. That's the only medicine for my disease. Let me go to Vṛndāvana and become healthy."

Nārāyaṇī was shocked. She grabbed hold of her son and cried, "Don't even think of such a thing! You can love God here in your own home. We would rather drink poison than live without you. Do not speak about this anymore. Do not even think of such a thing!"

Seeing his mother's state, Narottama said no more about it. He simply asked for something to eat and fell silent.

By the time Narottama had finished eating, Kṛṣṇānanda had returned home for the day. Narottama thought his father might be more understanding. "What can I do, Pitā? Śrī Caitanya Mahāprabhu has entered my body and transformed my mind. I can no longer stay here. I *must* go to Vṛndāvana." And then Narottama was again overcome with ecstatic emotions. Crying and shivering, he called out, "Gaurāṅga," then fell to the ground unconscious.

Kṛṣṇānanda cradled his son's limp body in his arms until Narottama's eyes fluttered open. Tears rolled down his cheeks, as he spoke softly to Narottama. "My son, why do you keep talking about going to Vṛndāvana? It's not necessary for you to go anywhere to lead a spiritual life. Everything you can do in Vṛndāvana you can do here. We eat only *prasāda* in this house. We listen to *śāstric* discourses. The Supreme Lord is here in our home as the Śālagrāma-śilā. Why don't you dedicate your life to His service right here? What's the problem?"

Narottama sat up and looked lovingly at his father. "Yes, Pitā, what you say may be true, but I'm not content simply following the family traditions and rituals. I don't want to live a comfortable, pious life of sense enjoyment. That is only the skeleton of our religion – there's no soul in it. Without elevation to Kṛṣṇa consciousness through the mercy of Lord Caitanya and Lord Nityānanda, life is simply spoiled in the animal propensities of sense gratification. I want to dedicate my entire life to the mission of Śrī Caitanya Mahāprabhu. I want to give myself completely to Him – mind, body, and words. To me, only that is real life. Everything else is death."

"Don't think it is so easy to live like a *sādhu* Naru," Kṛṣṇānanda said. "It is a very, very austere life. You are a prince. You could never live like a *sādhu*. It is not in your nature. Of course, it is a nice idea to leave everything to become a follower of Mahāprabhu. I would also like to join His mission. But Naru, we must also be responsible. We have our own duties to perform. We are the patrons of so many Vaiṣṇavas here in Kheturi, and they look to us to feed, clothe, and protect them. Don't you think Caitanya Mahāprabhu would be pleased if you cared for His devotees?"

Narottama fell silent. His parents would never understand. He wondered whether Vṛndāvana would forever remain an unattainable dream. As he wondered, his throat tightened and tears welled up in his eyes, spilling over into the torrential crying that his love for God evoked in him.

Kṛṣṇānanda now knew his son's intense determination to leave home was greater than ever. He gave the guards a firm order: "Watch my son twenty-four hours a day. Do not let him out of your sight for even a minute." Entering the adjoining room, he sank onto a cushion next to Nārāyaṇī. "Well, I've done it," he said, his voice tired and worn. "I've hired strong men to keep a constant watch on Narottama." He let out an anguished sigh. "I hate to do this to our own son, but I'm afraid if we don't do something drastic, he'll run away and become a renunciate. We must protect him. He's naïve – he doesn't know how difficult it is to live like a *sādhu*. He also doesn't realize we can't live without him."

Nārāyaṇī chewed her lip nervously. "Guards or no guards," she thought, "I will have no peace of mind."

Narottama could indeed see how desperate his parents were to keep him in Kheturi, and he couldn't see a solution to this problem. He could not be cured of the love God had placed in his heart. All he could do to ease the situation was to try to behave like an obedient son, and to trust Kṛṣṇa to make some arrangement for him to somehow get to Vṛndāvana.

Seeing Narottama's changed behavior – how he didn't cry nearly so much, and especially how he no longer spoke of becoming a *sādhu* – his parents were relieved. But they didn't realize their home had become like a prison for him, and that he still constantly longed to be free. He said nothing more to them of Vṛndāvana, yet he awaited his opportunity to leave. He knew it would come somehow.

Nights were especially difficult for Narottama. Unable to control his distress, he was not able to sleep. Sometimes he paced impatiently in his room, or pleaded for the Lord's help. Raising his arms, he begged, "My dear Lord, please be merciful to me. Who can be more merciful than Your Lordship within these three worlds?

You came just to reclaim the fallen conditioned souls. You will not find a more fallen soul than me. Therefore, please place my claim first. Oh Lord Gaurāṅga! Nitāi! Advaita! Please let me serve You."

Escape

One night, Narottama lay on his bed thinking. "How much longer can I go on secretly worshiping the Lord in my room at night? When will Śrī Caitanya Mahāprabhu give me His mercy? When will I be able to live with His devotees in Vṛndāvana?" Eventually, Narottama fell into a fitful, dream-filled sleep.

In his dream he saw the gorgeous golden form of Śrī Caitanya Mahāprabhu. Narottama stared in astonishment at His exquisite, moonlike face. Beautiful curling black hair adorned His shoulders, vividly colorful garlands draped around His neck, and His petal-soft hands rested gracefully near His knees.

When Narottama's eyes met Śrī Caitanya Mahāprabhu's infinitely deep, loving gaze he thought his heart would explode. Overcome with emotion, he fell at the Lord's feet.

Śrī Caitanya Mahāprabhu gently placed His foot on Narottama's head and said, "Don't worry about anything. I have many plans for you to carry out. Go straight to Vṛndāvana. There you will be initiated by My dear devotee, Lokanātha. He will pour the nectar of the holy name into your ears."

Then, without warning, the Lord disappeared.

Narottama woke up gripped by the intense feelings of separation from his Beloved. Full of anguish, he beat his fists into his pillow and cried, "Where *are* You my

Lord?" He felt that without his Lord, he was enveloped in darkness within and without. He tossed and turned on his bed, his heart burning with grief.

Over many hours he calmed and eventually fell back asleep. Once more the Lord appeared to him in his dream, but this time He stood on the bank of the Ganges in Navadvīpa surrounded by Nityānanda Prabhu, Advaita Ācārya, Gadādhara Paṇḍita, and Śrīvasa Ṭhākura. There were many other devotees there too, but Narottama didn't recognize them. All of them were dancing and chanting ecstatically. It seemed to Narottama that the entire population of Navadvīpa had swarmed onto the riverbank, eager to get a glimpse of this divine pastime. Narottama could even see Lord Brahmā, Lord Śiva, and other demigods and goddesses in disguised forms walking among the people and straining to catch a glimpse of the extraordinary *saṅkīrtana*. Even animals and birds looked on with wide eyes, captivated by the beautiful scene.

To his astonishment, Narottama was not merely to be a spectator of this extraordinary scene. Rather, he was allowed entrance into it, and he found himself again at the Lord's lotus feet. Narottama fell to the ground, weeping in disbelief and joy.

Lord Caitanya gently lifted him and embraced him. Narottama felt his heart melting with such exchanges of love. The Lord's embrace seemed timeless, and Narottama wished it would never end. As Lord Caitanya finally withdrew His arms from Narottama's shoulders, Narottama began to fall again. Other devotees, however, caught him in their arms, also warmly embracing him. Many encouraged him to go to Vṛndāvana without delay.

For a second time that evening, Narottama awoke. He lay on his bed, crying with joy. He now had full confirmation of what to do next; he would go to Vṛndāvana soon. He just had to wait for the right moment.

A few days later, a horseman arrived at the palace with a message for the king. Kṛṣṇānanda frowned as he read its contents.

"What is it, Prabhu?" Nārāyaṇī asked with concern.

"It's from the Nawab. He's heard about Narottama."

Nārāyaṇī raised her eyebrows. "What does that mean?"

Kṛṣṇānanda put down the letter and took a deep breath. "Well, it seems Narottama's unusual behavior has drawn attention." He looked at Nārāyaṇī with concern. "He says he wants to meet Narottama."

Nārāyaṇa nearly fainted at the thought. "No!" she cried.

Kṛṣṇānanda sat back in his chair, his face solemn and pale. The very idea of Narottama leaving them disturbed him. "What can we do?" he whispered. "Although I'm considered the king here, I'm only allowed to govern at the pleasure of the Muslim rulers. I am their servant. If I don't do as they ask, there may be trouble."

He leaned forward and touched Nārāyaṇī's hand to reassure her. "Don't worry, I will send a convoy of armed guards to protect Narottama."

Nārāyaṇī looked mildly relieved. She closed her eyes and sighed a reluctant agreement.

When Kṛṣṇānanda told his son about the trip, Narottama knew this was the chance he had been waiting for.

The next day, numerous guards assembled in front of the palace with a palanquin ready for the journey. Narottama lightly stepped into his palanquin, apprehending that his freedom was finally at hand.

Nārāyaṇī was on the verge of tears. She pulled her son tightly to her chest. "Hurry home, Naru," she said, her voice choked. Then she kissed him on the cheek. "When you return we shall begin preparations for your marriage."

Narottama smiled sweetly at his mother, "Don't worry, I'll be back soon."

The procession headed north, passing through one village after another. Narottama watched intently from his palanquin, waiting for the right moment to escape.

When the convoy stopped the first evening, Narottama couldn't sleep. He was anxiously waiting for midnight. At the appointed hour he slipped silently from his bed. Creeping slowly through the camp, he saw that even the watchmen were asleep. This was his chance. His heart was pounding so loudly he felt sure it would wake the guards. Sweat streamed from his forehead. He hardly dared even to breathe. Once he had cleared the camp, he crept through dense underbrush and then stood up in a forest. Narottama then ran like lightning through the jungle maze. Nothing now would stop him from finding his way to the holy land of Vṛndāvana.[5]

As the sun slowly arced through the sky, Narottama ran without a pause, oblivious to the intense heat. Sweat soaked his clothes and his throat was parched, but he forced himself to continue, his mind focused on one thought only: "Vṛndāvana."

Despite the intense physical strain, Narottama's heart overflowed with joyful, ecstatic love. Days passed, and still Narottama ran, never daring to rest for more than an hour or two at a time.

One late afternoon, he flopped down, utterly exhausted, under a tree. He turned his head sharply at the snapping of a twig in the nearby bushes. Someone was coming. He stood to run, but it was too late – he was surrounded by his father's hired guards.

"Ah! Rāja-kumāra!" one of them called out. "We have found you at last."

Another scolded, "Do you realize that hundreds of men have been scouring the countryside for days looking for you? You must return to Kheturi at once. Your parents are sick with anxiety."

Another said, "When your poor mother heard you had run away, she fainted."

All the men nodded in disapproval at the distress Narottama had caused his parents. Narottama was genuinely sorry he had hurt them, but he knew he could not go back. He said, gently, "I cannot return to Kheturi with you. I am firmly resolved to go to Vṛndāvana. I am dedicating my life fully to the Supreme Lord."

"Forget this madness!" the senior man among them protested. "It's not fitting for a prince to behave like vagabond."

Narottama replied, "On the contrary. It would not be fitting for me to return to Kheturi. A faithful widow may decide to join her husband on his funeral pyre. I have decided to climb the pyre of pure Kṛṣṇa consciousness and leave my material life behind. It's not right for you to try to dissuade me."

"Rāja-kumāra, we cannot return without you. What will your father say to us?" another man pleaded. "Please forget all this and come home with us. Give life back to your suffering parents."

Narottama was not daunted. He smiled sweetly and said, "When a woman wants to show her devotion to her dead husband in this extreme way it's natural for her well-wishers to try to stop her. I understand you don't want me to enter the fire of God consciousness. But please understand that I would be less than a faithful servant of my Lord if I didn't attempt to enter that fire."

Moved by Narottama's poetic analogy, the men on the search party stared at his charming golden face. What could they say to this determined young boy? He was obviously not an ordinary person, and his resolution was clearly unshakable.

Without even bidding the men good-bye, Narottama turned and resumed his journey. He was confident the men would be afraid to stop him since he had made it clear his path was the one of the saints. And he was right – no one even called out a farewell.

Narottama walked on and on, not knowing how much further he had to go to reach Vṛndāvana. He was exhausted and hungry, and his palace-soft feet were blistered. His entire body ached with his exertion. But his attraction to Vṛndāvana pulled him forward. Though alone, he realized he wasn't lonely. Being fully immersed in thoughts of Śrī Caitanya Mahāprabhu, he felt the Lord Himself was his travel companion.

After many days of traveling, he was finally overtaken completely by fatigue. Dropping to his knees, he crawled for a short distance and then collapsed beneath a tree and fell asleep.

Narottama awoke a short while later. Despondent, he beat the ground with his fists and lamented, "Oh Gauracandra, Rūpa, Sanātana! Will I ever reach Vṛndāvana?"

Seemingly from nowhere a golden-skinned *brāhmaṇa* boy suddenly appeared before him and offered him a pot of milk. "Drink this," the boy said. "It will take away your aches and pains." Narottama lifted his weary head to look at the boy, but he was much too tired to drink the milk. Again, sleep overcame him. This time he had a vivid dream.

Both Rūpa Gosvāmī and Sanātana Gosvāmī appeared. Glowing with a natural effulgence the two brothers stood before him wearing sacred threads, *tulasī mala*, and beautiful *tilaka*. Their lips were curved into gracious smiles, and they chanted the holy names, counting the *mantras* on their fingers. Narottama could smell the sweet aroma of their bodies when they leaned over and placed their hands on his chest.

Śrī Rūpa Gosvāmī said, "Narottama, you are still a child, and you are also the son of a wealthy man. You have never experienced this kind of suffering. But we know Mahāprabhu has empowered you to flood the world with love of God and deliver the fallen, conditioned souls. If you distribute this love, even the most sinful of men will be delivered. In the future, thousands and thousands of people will embrace Śrī Caitanya Mahāprabhu's teachings and thus attain love of God. So don't worry. Your suffering will soon end. Seeing you so tired from your journey, Śrī Caitanya Mahāprabhu personally brought that milk for you. Drink it and then go on to Vṛndāvana." With these words, Rūpa and Sanātana vanished.

Narottama awoke. He rubbed his eyes, staring at the earthen pot left on the ground before him. "Śrī Caitanya Mahāprabhu personally brought me this gift?" Hardly able to believe this fortune, he carefully lifted the pot to his lips, afraid to spill even one drop. As he gulped down the sweet, rich liquid, all his pain and fatigue disappeared. From head to toe, he felt fully rejuvenated.

With Śrī Rūpa's encouraging words still resonating in his heart, he stood stronger than before. Feeling confident of his success, he resumed his journey.

Narottama traveled undauntedly now along the main roads, deeply immersed in intense feelings of separation from Lord Caitanya and convinced of the Lord's protection. Sometimes he sang loudly, and sometimes he softly spoke about Lord Caitanya's glories to himself. At other times he simply called out, "Gaurāṅga! Gaurāṅga!" while tears coursed down his cheeks.

Narottama caused a stir in every village he passed through. The villagers were spontaneously drawn to him, and they would come out to stare as he passed. "Who is this dust-covered, lotus-eyed boy? He looks half mad, but he must be a *sādhu*. Who are his fortunate parents?"

The village women worried about him. "Such a young *sādhu*! Look at his beautiful face and large eyes. He's obviously from a good family. Why is he wandering alone in the forest? I wonder how his parents are living without him! I cannot bear to see his beautiful body covered in dust!"

Some villagers eagerly served him, bringing him things to eat or offering him a bed for the night. But Narottama was so absorbed in the ecstasy of love that he barely ate, and he spent most of his nights chanting the holy name, oblivious to his body's needs.

Curious villagers often tried to stop him from leaving them in the morning, but each morning, Narottama begged their leave and continued. He walked like this for weeks, through village after village, until he reached Vārāṇasī, and then Prāyaga, coming ever closer to Vṛndāvana.

mṛdaṅga-nāda-śruti-mātra-caṣcat-
padāmbujāmanda-manoharāya
sadyaḥ samudyat-pulakāya tasmai
namo namaḥ śrīla-narottamāya

I repeatedly offer my respectful obeisances to Śrīla Narottama Dāsa Ṭhākura. Just by hearing the sound of the *mṛdaṅga*, his lotus feet would begin to dance in a way that fully enchants the mind, and the hairs of his body would stand on end in ecstasy.

Narottama-prabhor-āṣṭaka, Verse 3

Chapter Three

Vraja

Mathurā

By the end of two months of walking, Narottama was emaciated and his feet were severely cracked and blistered. Yet his excitement continued to increase with every step. He was nearly mad with anticipation.

One day, as he stepped into a clearing, he tried to get his bearings and gauge how much farther it was to Vṛndāvana. He thought he saw a city on the horizon. Nearby, he could see a farmer plowing his field. He called out a greeting, ran up to him and asked, "Is that a city up ahead?"

The farmer eyed Narottama curiously. "That's Mathurā, of course. Have you lost your way, son?"

Hearing the name Mathurā, Narottama fainted. When he opened his eyes the bewildered farmer was peering down at him. "Are you all right?"

Narottama was so excited he could hardly speak. He blurted out his thanks, leaped to his feet and ran toward the city.

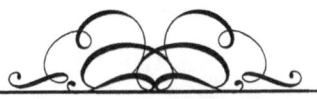

Entering the busy metropolis, he found himself before a huge ornate gateway. "Where am I?" he asked a local resident.

"Why this is Raṅga Bhūmi," he said, "the place where the colossal elephant Kuvalayāpīḍa blocked Kṛṣṇa's entry into the wrestling arena!" The man pointed to another site down the road. "And over there is where Kṛṣṇa and Balarāma wrestled the giants Cāṇūra and Muṣṭika!"

Delirious with joy at having at last found the places of Kṛṣṇa's pastimes, Narottama rushed to the site of Kṛṣṇa's birth. When he arrived, he fell flat on the ground and offered prayers. Then, in ecstasy, he hurried on to Vishram Ghat to see where Kṛṣṇa had bathed and rested after killing Kaṁsa. Refreshing his own tired body in the same cooling waters, Narottama couldn't believe his good fortune. Was it true that his body was touching the same sacred Yamunā? Was he finally so close to Śrī Vṛndāvana-dhāma?

He sat on the Yamunā's sandy bank and watched breathlessly as a coral sun set over the dusky horizon. Overwhelmed with joy, Narottama sang prayers in glorification of Kṛṣṇa.

An elderly *brāhmaṇa* passing by heard Narottama's sweet voice and noticed that although the boy's body was emaciated, and his scant clothing tattered and worn, he was glowing with happiness and appeared rapt in meditation. Fascinated by this charming youth, the *brāhmaṇa* quickly went home and made Narottama a large plate of *prasāda*. Rushing back to the bank of the river, he called sweetly, "Oh, child! Please come and eat!"

Narottama looked up from his singing and smiled brightly, touched by the *brāhmaṇa's* generosity.

He and the *brāhmaṇa* then shared the sumptuous *prasāda* together, relaxing on the bank of the Yamunā. Innocently, Narottama asked, "How is everything in Vṛndāvana? Are Śrī Rūpa Gosvāmī and Sanātana still busy writing books?"

The *brāhmaṇa's* face darkened.

Narottama tensed. "What's wrong?"

The *brāhmaṇa* turned to stare at the river, unable to look into Narottama's eager eyes. Sighing heavily, he gazed into the flowing current, tracing a finger awkwardly through the damp sand. Narottama took hold of the *brāhmaṇa's* feet. "Please tell me what's wrong."

The *brāhmaṇa* remained silent. Then letting out a heavy sigh, he turned and looked deeply into Narottama's eyes, his own filling with tears.

"My heart aches to tell you," he faltered, "Rūpa . . . and Sanātana . . . " He broke off and wiped tears from his eyes. " . . . they . . . they have both left this mortal world."

Narottama didn't respond immediately. Stunned, he stared at the *brāhmaṇa* in disbelief. Then, his heart pounding, he searched the brāhmaṇa's face – could this really be true?

The *brāhmaṇa* continued, "Not only them, but Śrī Raghunātha Bhaṭṭa and Kāśīśvara Paṇḍita – they have also returned to the Lord's abode."

Narottama could bear the pain no more. Jolting as if struck by lightning, he collapsed into the soft sand of the bank. Nearly senseless with despair, he struck his head on the ground again and again. "Oh Rūpa! Oh Sanātana! Where are you? Raghunātha Bhaṭṭa! Kāśīśvara! Why have you left me here alone? Is my heart made of stone that I still live after receiving such news?" Narottama's tears flowed, hot and fast. "How is this possible? I have been waiting my whole life to meet these great personalities! I plotted, I planned, I hoped, I dreamed–I endured so many hardships and walked for so many miles!" He gasped for air, a fresh wave of tears welling.

"Now in one ghastly moment, my hopes have been shattered." Sick with grief, he sobbed uncontrollably. "I am so unfortunate. I was born too late to take part in Śrī Caitanya Mahāprabhu's pastimes. Now again I am cursed and have lost the chance to associate with His devotees."

Narottama sat stunned and silent, like a lifeless doll.

The *brāhmaṇa* was distraught to see Narottama's state and tried to comfort him by embracing him. "Please don't cry, my son. I understand your disappointment, but there are still many great devotees in Vṛndāvana, and you can still meet them."

Narottama blinked back his tears and nodded weakly.

"Why, Śrī Raghunātha dāsa Gosvāmī, Śrī Jīva Gosvāmī, and many other wonderful Vaiṣṇavas are still with us."

Narottama did not dispute that there were other devotees. But Rūpa and Sanātana were his childhood heroes. He had been waiting for years to meet these great souls, who were direct associates of Caitanya Mahāprabhu. They were irreplaceable. What was the point of even going to Vṛndāvana now? What was the point of even going on living?

Sensing the depth of Narottama's despair, the *brāhmaṇa* didn't dare to leave him alone that evening. He stayed with Narottama, and they talked late into the night. Finally, fatigue overtook them and they fell silent.

Although Narottama was tired, he couldn't fall asleep. He stared up at the multitude of brilliant stars in the clear night sky. Suddenly, all the great souls he had longed to meet were before him. Śrī Rūpa, Sanātana, Bhaṭṭa Raghunātha, and Kāśīśvara Paṇḍita came forward and embraced Narottama, showering him with their blessings. Each of them spoke to him lovingly, pacifying him and encouraging him to go on to Vṛndāvana. They reminded him of Śrī Caitanya Mahāprabhu's instruction that he was to be initiated by Śrī Lokanātha Gosvāmī. Narottama felt boundless happiness in their company.

Then, as suddenly as they had appeared, they vanished. Narottama sat up and looked around in all directions. Those great devotees had appeared so vivid just a moment before. Where were they? His eyes searched the darkness but could only see the faint outline of trees and buildings. He desperately wanted to see them again.

The elderly *brāhmaṇa* had been fortunate enough to witness the vision and hear the transcendental discussion. He now looked at Narottama with amazement, for he had never seen such profound devotion. The *brāhmaṇa* tearfully embraced Narottama. "Thank you for giving me your purifying association. Since it is now morning, please come to my house and rest for a while."

Narottama bowed respectfully to the *brāhmaṇa*. "You have been kind to me, but I cannot wait another moment. I must go to Vṛndāvana and see the Gosvāmīs living there. Who knows how much longer Lokanātha Gosvāmī will remain in this world? I don't want to waste another minute! Please give me your blessings so I may leave immediately."

The *brāhmaṇa* nodded his reluctant consent. As Narottama left Mathurā, the *brāhmaṇa* walked along with him, unable to give up his saintly company. He walked as far as his frail legs would carry him, then waved good-bye when he could go no further.

Entering Vṛndāvana

Narottama walked swiftly, heading north along the dusty pathway. As eager as he was to reach Vṛndāvana, the closer he came to it, the more uneasy he became. "How could Lord Caitanya have sent such a low and unqualified person as me to this sacred land? I know so little about spiritual life. Will a great soul like Śrī Lokanātha Gosvāmī accept me as his servant? Will Śrī Gopāla Bhaṭṭa allow me to touch his lotus feet? Will Śrī Jīva Gosvāmī love a fallen soul like me?"

As he neared the transcendental land of Vṛndāvana, Narottama's heart raced and his body trembled. He was becoming overwhelmed by the intensity of the spiritual atmosphere that permeated everything around him. Everything seemed to be shimmering. Narottama picked up a handful of sand. It sparkled like diamonds in the sun. "This is *cintāmaṇi*," he marveled. "Everything here is made entirely of divine touchstones. This land is identical to Kṛṣṇa's transcendental abode in the spiritual sky, Goloka Vṛndāvana." He let the sand slip through his fingers and momentarily closed his eyes. "But one must have transcendental eyes to see it," he thought.

Stopping to gaze at a few cows sheltering from the sun under a small kadamba tree, Narottama felt his heart fill with reverence. "This is the actual place where Kṛṣṇa herded His cows! This is where He danced with the *gopīs* and played with the other cowherd boys! He killed demons here and protected the Vrājavāsīs! Please, my Lord," he begged, "help me cleanse my mind of all material anxieties and desires so I will be able to understand Your Vṛndāvana. Then my spiritual life will be successful."

Entering a forest thick with *tulasī* plants, Narottama gazed up at a magnificent banyan, then at other trees – neem, mango, and *kadamba* – all spreading their bright green leaves under the clear blue sky. He watched monkeys scamper through the trees and flocks of bright green parrots chirping and swooping in and out of the leaves. Spellbound, he thought, "Every living being in Vṛndāvana is special. When Kṛṣṇa was present here, all the residents of Vṛndāvana – even the birds, trees and cows – were absorbed in trying to please Him. That was their spirit. They loved Kṛṣṇa so much that they had no care for their own happiness. They simply wanted to make Kṛṣṇa happy. How wonderful it would be, to be so unselfish and loving."

A peacock's loud mournful wail filled the air, sending shivers up Narottama's spine. His thoughts turned to Lord Caitanya. During the Lord's first journey to Vṛndāvana He had become mad with ecstatic love for Kṛṣṇa upon hearing a peacock's call or a cowherd boy playing a flute. In His ecstasy, Lord Caitanya would ask the birds and plants if they had seen Kṛṣṇa. "Now here I am in that same transcendental land of Vṛndāvana," Narottama thought, "hearing the same sounds and seeing the same sights as Śrī Caitanya Mahāprabhu." Narottama's ecstasy increased with every step he took.

Tears flowed from his eyes so profusely that he could barely see the path in front of him.

The pathway widened, and several *sādhus* joined Narottama on the road. They passed clusters of small mud huts, and Narottama asked his companions, "Have I reached Vṛndāvana?"

The *sādhus* nodded and chanted, "Rādhe! Rādhe!" Intense love swelled again in Narottama's heart – he was actually in the topmost holy *dhāma*! He knelt down and touched his forehead to the ground, then smeared the dust on his head. To think that not only did Lord Kṛṣṇa walk on this ground, but so did Mahāprabhu!

The faint chime of *karatālas* in the distance reminded Narottama of his mission. He stood up and squinted into the distance. *Karatālas* means *kīrtana*, and *kīrtana* means devotees. Maybe Lokanātha Gosvāmī, Gopāla Bhaṭṭa Gosvāmī or Śrī Jīva Gosvāmī were there. He could just make out the outline of a temple.

A group of barefoot village women, balancing clay pots filled with water on their heads, came down the path talking and laughing. Narottama interrupted their chatter, "Excuse me, dear ladies. What temple is that, please?"

Peering at him curiously through their veils, one of the women answered, "Govindajī Mandira."

Narottama thanked her and then broke into a run toward the temple. Breathless, he entered the courtyard and then fainted in ecstasy.

It seemed that news of his arrival had spread quickly, for when Narottama opened his eyes, he found himself surrounded by a large group of curious devotees. He was surprised to hear one of them announce to the rest, "This is indeed Narottama." This effulgent devotee leaned over him. His face radiated strength, warmth, and love. "Narottama," he said softly, "welcome to Vṛndāvana. I am Jīva Gosvāmī."

Narottama's eyes widened. "Ji . . . Jīva?" and again he fainted.

Śrī Jīva sprinkled a few drops of water on Narottama to revive him, and Narottama came to for a second time and saw Śrī Jīva's smiling face. Narottama slowly sat up, and the devotees gathered around closer, lovingly welcoming him. The head priest of the temple brought garlands worn by the Deity and placed them gently around Narottama's neck.

Narottama was floating on a cloud of ecstasy. His long-cherished dream had finally come true.

"How do you know who I am?" Narottama asked Śrī Jīva Gosvāmī.

Śrī Jīva smiled enigmatically, and then said, "Śrī Caitanya Mahāprabhu told us of your birth and mission years ago. All the Vṛndāvana devotees have been waiting eagerly to meet the special devotee destined to carry out the Lord's order. We are elated to finally see you face to face.

"Come, Narottama," Śrī Jīva said, "and take *darśana* of Śrī Govindadeva."

Narottama's entire body trembled with ecstasy as he followed Śrī Jīva into the temple room. Falling flat before Śrī Govindadeva, he cried out heartfelt prayers of gratitude. As he rose, the *pūjārī,* Śrī Kṛṣṇa Paṇḍita, brought the Lord's garland and placed it around Narottama's neck. Again, Narottama fell to the ground in thankful obeisances.

After *darśana* Śrī Jīva introduced Narottama to the other devotees and brought him some *prasāda.* Then Narottama bathed and rested. After, Śrī Jīva asked,

"There is someone I want you to meet. Are you strong enough to walk a little distance with me?"

"Oh, yes," Narottama affirmed, jumping up enthusiastically.

He followed Jīva Gosvāmī through the forested walkways of Vṛndāvana to a quiet, secluded hermitage. Peering through the bushes, Narottama saw a very old, emaciated *sādhu* sitting on the bare ground, quietly uttering the names of the Lord. The *sādhu* was oblivious to all else. He was clearly a great saint.

"That is Lokanātha Gosvāmī," Śrī Jīva whispered.

Narottama was enthralled. This was the culmination of everything he had been looking for. His heart pounded as the full realization dawned on him: "I have found my shelter, my spiritual master. This person can actually guide me to receive the mercy of Kṛṣṇa and Lord Caitanya."

"He has been in Vṛndāvana for many, many years – long before anyone else came," Śrī Jīva said softly. "Nowadays Vṛndāvana is filled with temples and devotees, but when Lokanātha and Bhūgarbha came here, Vṛndāvana was a dense forest full of wild animals. Only a few tribal people lived here. Vṛndāvana had been ravaged again and again by foreign invaders."

"Were there no temples then?" Narottama asked.

Śrī Jīva shook his head. "All the temples were demolished and the Deities stolen or hidden in groves and ponds. There was no sign of the holy places connected with Śrī Kṛṣṇa's pastimes. The beauty and grandeur of Vṛndāvana was covered, and this highest place of pilgrimage was reduced to a mere hunting ground for Mohammedan rulers.

"What did Lokanātha and Bhūgarbha do in such a dangerous place?" Narottama asked.

"Not knowing what else to do, when they first arrived in Vṛndāvana they wandered throughout Vrāja, paying obeisances again and again, sometimes crying, and sometimes shouting, 'Kṛṣṇa! Rādhe! Lalite! Viśākhe! Where are you? Please help us to find the sites of your transcendental pastimes!' They carried out their search undaunted, sometimes even risking their lives. If they came across the ruins of an ancient temple or the sign of a divine pond, their hearts would leap with joy. If they didn't find anything, they begged Vṛndā Devī, 'How long will you keep the pastime sites hidden from our view? When will you manifest Nandagrāma and Varsana? When will we see Śṛṅgāra-vata, Vaṁśī-vaṭa, Keśī-ghāṭa, and Kālīya-daha?"

Narottama listened intently as Śrī Jīva continued. "The forest dwellers, who were busy making arrangements to secure their own safety, found it miraculous that these two young *brahmacārīs* made absolutely no endeavor to find a place to stay or something to eat or to protect themselves at night. Though the Vrājavāsīs were completely bereft of devotion for Kṛṣṇa, as they watched Lokanātha and Bhūgarbha praying day and night, crying and calling out to the Lord, their devotional inclinations began to surface and they began to come forward to help. Gradually, many of the Lord's pastime sites were found."

The story was incredible. And to think that here he was now, watching this elevated soul chanting in the groves of Vṛndāvana! Narottama's heart was drawn to him like a magnet. He turned to Śrī Jīva and asked, "Where does Śrī Lokanātha live?"

Śrī Jīva whispered, "He spends most of his time here in this beautiful *kuñja* with his dear friend, Bhūgarbha

Gosvāmī, chanting and doing *bhajan*. He is the embodiment of humility and kindness and such a *vairāgī* that he doesn't even go out to beg. If food comes to him, he eats. Otherwise, he fasts. Ever since Lokanātha missed Mahāprabhu's visit to Vṛndāvana, he has been deeply absorbed in an intense mood of separation from the Lord."

"Missed Mahāprabhu's visit?" Narottama asked. "I thought Śrī Caitanya had promised to meet him here in Vṛndāvana?"

"Yes, that was His promise." Śrī Jīva said solemnly. "But, after many, many months alone in Vṛndāvana, Lokanātha and Bhūgarbha heard that Mahāprabhu had taken *sannyāsa* and gone on pilgrimage to South India. Their hearts yearned to see Him, so they left Vṛndāvana to search for Him. After weeks of travel, they then heard that Śrī Caitanya was actually in Vṛndāvana. They realized their mistake in leaving Vṛndāvana. In the madness of love, they had forgotten Mahāprabhu's order to dedicate themselves exclusively to the revival of Vṛndāvana."

Narottama gasped. He could imagine how heartbroken those two devotees must have been.

Śrī Jīva continued, "In great anxiety they rushed back to Vrāja, only to find that Mahāprabhu had just left."

Tears welled in Narottama's eyes. "They must have been utterly devastated," he said.

"Yes," Śrī Jīva said, "but Lokanātha was persistent. Desperate to see the Lord, he decided to try to catch up with Him. But in a dream, Caitanya Mahāprabhu told him to stay in Vṛndāvana and take solace in the memory of their inner relationship. He told Lokanātha he should meditate on Him as he had known Him in Navadvīpa before becoming a *sannyāsī*."

Narottama asked Śrī Jīva, "Śrī Lokanātha has entered my heart and made me his servant. I am completely sold out to him. Do you think he will accept me as his disciple?"

Śrī Jīva shook his head sadly, "I'm afraid not. He has taken a vow not to accept disciples. In fact, he rarely even talks with anyone."

Narottama's heart sank. "But," he stuttered, "I have already accepted him as my spiritual master." He looked pleadingly at Śrī Jīva. "Please, could I meet him?"

"Yes, of course," Śrī Jīva said. He stepped into the clearing and bowed at Lokanātha's feet. Softly he announced, "The son of the king of Kheturi, Narottama, has just arrived from Bengal."

Śrī Lokanātha looked up from his meditation and glanced at Narottama, who was still standing in the bushes.

Narottama hesitantly stepped forward and fell at Lokanātha's feet.

Śrī Jīva said, "This young boy's acute renunciation and devotion are inconceivable. He reminds me of Mahāprabhu, with his golden complexion and trembling body."

Lokanātha Gosvāmī smiled brightly at Narottama, tears welling in his eyes. "I knew you would come. It was revealed to me in a dream last night."

Narottama's hair stood on end . . . to be in the presence of Śrī Lokanātha Gosvāmī was overwhelming. Narottama knelt before the saint, trembling and speechless.

Śrī Jīva invited Lokanātha to take *prasāda* with them at the Govindajī Mandira, and to Narottama's delight Śrī Lokanātha agreed. Walking behind the two stalwart devotees, Narottama marveled, "Can this truly be happening? Will I wake up in a moment and find myself back in my father's palace in Kheturi? For so many years I listened to stories about these great saints, Caitanya Mahāprabhu's associates. I spent hours imagining how they looked, how they walked, what they talked about. I used to cry, wondering when I would get the chance to see these devotees. Now I am here, walking behind the exalted *ācārya* Śrī Jīva Gosvāmī, nephew of Śrī Rūpa and Sanātana and powerful leader of Śrī Caitanya's movement. He must surely be one of the greatest philosophers of all time. He actually went on a *parikrāma* of Navadvīpa with Lord Nityānanda Himself. He personally talked to and walked next to Nityānanda Prabhu!"

Narottama bent down to scoop up some of the dust from the footprints of these two great souls. He shivered in ecstasy as he sprinkled it on his head, thinking, "Śrī Caitanya Mahāprabhu actually embraced Śrī Lokanātha Gosvāmī with His own arms. These devotees are players in the great epic of Śrī Caitanya's transcendental *līlā*. And here I am, the most fallen insignificant soul, stumbling along behind them."

When they arrived back at Govindajī Mandira, three seats were arranged for them to take *prasāda* together. Narottama didn't feel qualified to eat with these two great personalities, so he hesitated to sit down, but Śrī Jīva motioned to him, insisting that Narottama join them.

During the meal, Śrī Jīva asked Narottama to tell Śrī Lokanātha Gosvāmī how he came to Vṛndāvana. Shyly, Narottama related how he had received the mercy of Śrī

Caitanya Mahāprabhu from Padmavatī Devī. Concluding his story, he said, "Actually, I have no right to sit with you and eat *prasāda* – I do not even have a *guru*."

To Narottama's surprise, Lokanātha Gosvāmī laughed heartily at this. "Śrī Caitanya Mahāprabhu, the *guru* of the universe, has given you divine love, the same love most devotees pray to attain their entire lives. What more do you want? What is the value of having another *guru*?"

"Prabhu," Narottama said humbly, "if you permit me, I would like to explain why I want to be initiated, and why it is you that I want as my spiritual master."

Lokanātha nodded, encouraging him to speak.

"It is true that Mahāprabhu is the only real *guru*. But it is His order that I take initiation from you. The Lord personally told me this in a dream."

Seeing that Lokanātha was unmoved by this, Narottama continued, "Śrī Caitanya Mahāprabhu is the spiritual master of the whole world. Still, the Lord Himself set the example of accepting a spiritual master, and all the Lord's associates and followers also accepted spiritual masters. The spiritual master's orders are the life and soul of the disciple. Simply by following the spiritual master's order, a disciple attains all perfection. A *guru* guides his disciple in practical spiritual life. I have no *guru*, so who will guide me on the path of devotion? Unless one serves a pure devotee, he cannot attain liberation by directly serving Kṛṣṇa. He must serve the servant of Kṛṣṇa. Who has ever been elevated without rendering service to a pure Vaiṣṇava?"

"Yes," Lokanātha replied, "certainly a *guru* is required. But one must find a qualified *guru*. I cannot even become a devotee myself, so how can I help you?"

"Please, Prabhu," Narottama begged. "People call me a prince, but actually I am a beggar. I have renounced the world and have come here in the hope of finding Kṛṣṇa. But I am like a ship without a rudder. I am not able to find the path along which I should travel. It's not possible to find Kṛṣṇa without the mercy of the *guru*."

Lokanātha waved his hand dismissively and said, "The scriptures recommend that an aspiring disciple chant the holy names of Kṛṣṇa for at least one year before he is eligible for initiation."

Narottama nodded, saying no more. He accepted this within his heart as the first order of his spiritual master.

Initiation

Narottama sat on the sandy floor of the cave, meditatively gazing at the Yamunā River, which was sparkling only a few feet away. He was startled when Śrī Jīva Gosvāmī appeared at the cave's mouth. Śrī Jīva ducked his head as he stepped inside and sat down. "How are you Narottama? You seem to be recovering nicely. You were nearly dead with exhaustion when we found you in Govindajī's courtyard."

It was true – a few days of rest in Śrī Jīva's secluded cave, along with the Gosvāmī's wonderful association, nice *prasāda*, Yamunā water, and *caraṇāmṛta* had worked wonders on Narottama's tired body. "By your mercy, I feel much stronger," Narottama said. "The blisters on my feet are almost gone."

"But you look sad," Śrī Jīva said. "What is it Narottama? What's bothering you?"

Narottama looked into the Gosvāmī's kind eyes. "My body has healed, but my heart is aching," he said. "I cannot stop thinking of Śrī Lokanātha Gosvāmī. Somehow, I must get his shelter. Can you help me?"

Śrī Jīva thought for a few minutes. "It will not be easy to persuade Gosvāmī to break his vow. He is so humble, and he feels unqualified to be a *guru*."

"How could such an exalted saint feel unqualified?" Narottama whispered.

"*Bhakti* and humility go together, Narottama. One cannot exist without the other. Genuine *bhakti* makes one so humble that even if he is the greatest of devotees, he regards himself as the smallest of the small and the lowliest of the lowly; even if he is completely pure and worshipable, he feels himself as impure and untouchable."

Narottama nodded in appreciation.

"Lokanātha Gosvāmī doesn't want to accept disciples," Śrī Jīva Gosvāmī continued, "because he knows that taking disciples means he will be glorified. Glorification means fame, and he is totally averse to fame. When Kṛṣṇadāsa Kavirāja asked Lokanātha for his blessings to write about Śrī Caitanya Mahāprabhu's pastimes, Gosvāmī gave his approval but forbade Kṛṣṇadāsa to mention his name in the book. So this is Lokanātha's mood. What can I say, Narottama? He is *niṣkiñcana*. His only interest is in *bhajan*."

Seeing the disappointment on Narottama's face, Śrī Jīva added, "I can only suggest that you pray to the Lord and chant sincerely for that one year Lokanātha indicated the other day. In the meantime, I have many students, and if you like you can sit with us and study the *bhakti-śāstras*."

"Yes, I'd like that." Narottama said. "I must be patient, and I'll do as you say."

"But first, I want to take you to a few places in Vrāja," Śrī Jīva said. "I know you're eager to meet the associates of Caitanya Mahāprabhu who are still living, and they are just as eager to meet you."

"For years I've waited for this opportunity," Narottama replied eagerly.

"My student Śrīnivāsa can come along with us," Śrī Jīva said. "We should leave immediately. There are so many extraordinary devotees to meet – Śrī Gopāla Bhaṭṭa Gosvāmī, Śrī Raghunātha dāsa Gosvāmī, Bhūgarbha Gosvāmī, and Śrī Kṛṣṇadāsa Kavirāja. I will also take you to the *samādhis* of Rūpa Gosvāmī and Sanātana Gosvāmī. When we have finished our *parikrāma,* we will return to my *āśrama* and you can begin your studies."

Narottama, Śrīnivāsa, and Duḥkhī Kṛṣṇadāsa sat next to each other at the front of Śrī Jīva Gosvāmī's class, their legs folded and backs straight, listening attentively to the Gosvāmī's every word. The three effulgent young Vaiṣṇavas had become close, and already their fame had spread throughout Vrāja as Jīva Gosvāmī's foremost students. In so many ways Narottama's life at Śrī Jīva's *āśrama* was perfect.

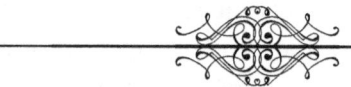

"And so," Śrī Jīva explained, "on the far shore of the Virajā River is the eternal, deathless, imperishable, unlimited, nectarean spiritual sky. It constitutes three fourths of the entire creation. That imperishable spiritual realm is the abode of the Supreme Personality of Godhead. It is made of the transcendental mode of pure goodness and is more splendid than millions of blazing suns."

Śrī Jīva's words, filled with authority, conviction, and love, carried the spirit of *bhakti* into the hearts of his students, illuminating and purifying them. With razor-sharp intelligence he explained the intricacies of the spiritual and material realms. He revealed the shallowness of materialistic life and exposed the hypocrisy of the impersonalists. As Ācārya, head of all the Vaiṣṇavas in Vṛndāvana, he spoke with tremendous potency, empowering his students to comprehend the highest spiritual truths.

"It's getting late," Śrī Jīva said, "so we'll stop here."

As the students got up to leave, Śrīnivāsa turned to his dear friend. "Come, Narottama, let's go to *ārati*."

"I'll be with you in a minute," Narottama replied. "I want to speak to Gosvāmī."

Kneeling down next to Śrī Jīva, Narottama watched him carefully wrap the palm-leaf manuscript in a cloth. When he finished, Śrī Jīva asked, "What is it, Narottama?"

"Prabhu, more than one year has passed since I first met Śrī Lokanātha Gosvāmī. Still he shows no signs of accepting me as his disciple. What should I do?"

"Many devotees, including me, have spoken to Gosvāmī on your behalf," Śrī Jīva said. "Yet for now he seems determined to keep his vow."

A stab of pain pierced through Narottama's heart. Tears began to well in his eyes.

Seeing the youth's distress, Śrī Jīva spoke gently, "I feel certain that you will get his mercy, Narottama. You are both sincere and determined. Why don't you render him personal service?"

"He doesn't want anyone to serve him," Narottama sobbed. "What can I do?"

"That's true," Śrī Jīva said. "Still, somehow you must serve him. *Tad viddhi praṇipātena* – you should both serve him and humbly inquire from him. Then, if he is pleased, he will accept you."

Narottama blinked back his tears and thanked his teacher. He hurried to the temple to join Śrīnivāsa at *ārati*.

The next morning Narottama rose early and went to the woods that bordered Lokanātha's hermitage. He peered through the thick foliage, watching Lokanātha Gosvāmī intently, trying to think of something he could do to serve the great *sādhu*. But he was perplexed. What service could he offer a person who simply sat in a grove chanting all day? "Lokanātha barely eats," Narottama thought, "He drinks only Yamunā water, and even then, scoops it in his own hands. He hardly sleeps, and when he does, he simply lies on a bed of dry leaves. He has only one cloth, which he rinses out when he bathes." What service could he render such a person who has no requirements at all? Lokanātha Gosvāmī's existence was simply spent performing *sādhana*. Filled with admiration, Narottama watched him chant.

Then, by Kṛṣṇa's mercy, an idea came to him. Inspired, he rushed back to Śrī Jīva's *āśrama* to join his friends for class.

The next morning, long before the sun rose, Narottama took a broom and walked to the bank of the Yamunā. Collecting sand and mud from the riverbank, he made his way to Lokanātha's *kuñja*, guided by the light of the moon. He was careful not to be seen or heard creeping through the bushes.

When he found the place where Lokanātha Gosvāmī went to evacuate, he thought, "Ah, this is the spot. Now I can serve my spiritual master."

With great enthusiasm he swept the area clean. He then spread dry sand all around, and placed a pile of Yamunā mud on the ground – perhaps Lokanātha would like to use the mud to clean his hands.

With a radiant smile Narottama quietly hurried out of the *kuñja* and back to the *āśrama*.

Early in the morning, Narottama picked up his broom and went to perform his usual service near Lokanātha's *kuñja*. As he began to sweep, a voice called out from the darkness: "Who's there?"

Clutching his broom tightly to his chest, Narottama froze, like a thief caught stealing. Squinting into the darkness he saw the faint outline of Lokanātha Gosvāmī visible through the trees. A shudder of fear ran through Narottama's body. "What if he's angry with me? I've been doing this service to get his blessings, but if he becomes upset, I will receive his curse instead."

Narottama took a deep breath and finally dared to say, "It is Narottama, your servant."

"Narottama? You?" Lokanātha was clearly upset. Stepping out from the undergrowth, Lokanātha Gosvāmī shook his head. "I knew someone had been secretly cleaning up after me for many months! It's not proper to allow someone to serve me in this way. I cannot tolerate it any longer! Come here."

Narottama stood before his master, frightened and speechless.

"How could you do this?" Lokanātha exclaimed. "I'm ashamed to accept such service. You, the son of a king, doing such menial service – I cannot allow it. I'm living in this *kuñja* and practicing detachment. Now here you are, a prince, cleaning up after me! Why are you trying to spoil my renunciation?"

His head still lowered, Narottama spoke in a subdued voice, "Gurudeva, please do not deny me the chance to serve you. After many lifetimes I finally have the opportunity to serve a great soul like you. Becoming your humble sweeper is a far more exalted position than ruling over any mundane kingdom. You are the lord of my life. I simply want to perform some *guru-sevā*."

"*Guru-sevā*?" Lokanātha said with surprise. "Who is the *guru*? I haven't made any disciples and have taken a vow never to accept disciples. If you are looking for a *guru*, you must find someone else."

Narottama humbly insisted, "Prabhu, I have already surrendered my mind and body to you. How can I offer to someone else what no longer belongs to me? If you will not give me your mercy, I will die. That is all I know. Please see my lowly condition and be merciful to me."

Clearly exasperated, Lokanātha said, "Narottama, Lord Caitanya is inside you! You have already developed pure love of God! What do you expect to achieve through initiation? You have already attained the ultimate purpose of practicing devotional service. What do you want *me* to give you? You ask me to deliver you, but what is it you want me to deliver you from? I do not see any bondage in you."

Narottama fell at Lokanātha's feet, crying. "Gurudeva, I am like a young woman who has already chosen her husband. My heart is clear and without doubt. A young woman who makes up her mind in this way prays that her father will agree with her choice. So I pray that our father, Śrī Kṛṣṇa, agrees with my choice."

Lokanātha's eyes softened and his tone became gentle. "Narottama, don't speak like this. I know you are an extremely qualified devotee. I am very attracted by your devotion. However, because of my vow I cannot accept you. Please, don't say anything more about it."

"But Gurudeva – " Narottama begged.

Lokanātha would hear no more. Shaking his head, he turned to walk back to his *kuñja*. Calling over his shoulder he repeated, "There is no point in serving me. I don't want your service, nor do I want to be anyone's master."

Narottama was devastated. He sat in silence for some time, trying to make sense of it all. Tears rolled down his cheeks as he contemplated life without the mercy of the Lord's pure devotee.

As the morning sun arced toward its midday position, Narottama moved closer to accepting the fact that Lokanātha Gosvāmī might never accept him as his disciple. Eventually, with a heavy heart, he started back to the *āśrama*.

The next morning, as he approached Lokanātha Gosvāmī's *kuñja*, Narottama was surprised to see his *guru* sitting near the entrance of the bower. He was even more surprised when that saintly person called him over in a mild voice.

Narottama's heart beat rapidly as he sat at his master's feet. Keeping his eyes on Lokanātha's feet, he dared not speak. After a few moments of silence, he shyly peered up at Lokanātha Gosvāmī's thin, radiant face. What magnetism! What wisdom! The sage's face seemed to embody all the attractive qualities of devotion: purity, truth, gentleness, and forgiveness.

Lokanātha Gosvāmī was gazing back at Narottama with warm, clear eyes that penetrated deep into Narottama's heart, touching the core of his being. "Narottama," he said gently. "Your fierce determination has conquered me. I didn't want to accept service from anyone, but you have melted my heart, forcing me to break my vow. I will accept you as my disciple."

Narottama's heart soared. He fell at his spiritual master's feet and cried with joy.

On the full-moon day of Śravana, Śrī Jīva Gosvāmī and his disciples walked to Lokanātha's *kuñja*. They carried *kuśa* grass, fruits, grains, ghee, wood, and other items necessary for Narottama's initiation ceremony.[6]

Narottama and a few other devotees were already at the *kuñja*, waiting expectantly for the auspicious ceremony to begin. Śrī Jīva told Narottama, "Go bathe in the Yamunā while we prepare everything."

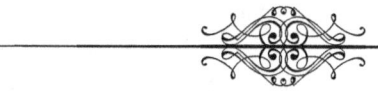

Narottama rushed to the river, washed his body, and put on new cloth. He then hurried back to the *kuñja*

where Śrī Jīva Gosvāmī and his disciples had built a *yajña-śāla* with mud and cow dung in the middle of the *kuñja*, and had decorated it with colorful rice flour designs. Pots filled with mango leaves and coconuts had been placed in each of the four corners of the space, and a pile of kindling and a bowl of ghee sat next to the pit where the fire would be lit.

The preparations complete, Śrī Jīva stood before the crowd of devotees and announced, "This ceremony will be the first of its kind. We will follow the initiation procedure outlined by Śrī Sanātana Gosvāmī in his *Hari-bhakti-vilāsa*." Then he sat down to conduct the elaborate ceremony.

Narottama's heart pounded as he watched Śrī Jīva Gosvāmī perform *ācamana*. He glanced nervously at Lokanātha Gosvāmī as Śrī Jīva chanted *mantras* to invoke auspiciousness.

When the rituals were complete, Lokanātha Gosvāmī walked over to the *yajña-śāla*. Slowly, he knelt down, then lay prostrate on the ground. Narottama heard his soft prayer, "My dear Lord Śrī Caitanya, please accept this boy. Give him Your mercy so he will have the strength to carry out Your mission."

Lokanātha stood up, then again offered his *daṇḍa-vats*. Again and again he offered his obeisances, all the while praying fervently.

Astounded by his spiritual master's humility, Narottama's heart blossomed with profound respect and appreciation.

Finally, his prayers complete, he turned to Narottama and said lovingly, "Come sit on my left side, and I will recite the *mantra* in your ear."

With a sense of his own unworthiness, Narottama did as he was bid. He listened intently as Lokanātha Gosvāmī recited the sacred *mantras* into his ear, his heart overflowing with love for his spiritual master.

Once the *mantra* had been given, Śrī Lokanātha Gosvāmī elaborately described to Narottama a wealth of ways he might serve Their Lordships Śrī Śrī Rādhā and Kṛṣṇa. "Always meditate on the lotus feet of Rādhā and Kṛṣṇa," he said. "In due course of time, all the processes of devotional service will automatically be revealed to you. Keep your *sādhana* strong, as only one who is greedy to attain Kṛṣṇa's lotus feet actually attains perfection. When you chant the holy name, know that the holy name and the Lord Himself are identical. Carefully guard against obstacles in devotional service, and, especially, never offend any Vaiṣṇava." He concluded, "Śrī Caitanya Mahāprabhu is extremely merciful to me. His sending you to me is like offering profuse riches to a poor man. By Mahāprabhu's order I have accepted you as my disciple. You, however, are the only disciple I will ever make in this life. Now go and continue your studies with Śrī Jīva Gosvāmī."

Narottama, effulgent and decorated with sandalwood paste and garlands, fell flat before his spiritual master. His heart erupted with gratitude and love, and he took the dust from Lokanātha's feet. Then, circumambulating the *kuñja,* he humbly offered his obeisances to each of the *sādhus* present. A rain of happiness poured into the *kuñja* as everyone showered their blessings on young Narottama.

Meeting at Govardhana Hill

Śrīnivāsa and Narottama sprinkled a few drops of water from the sacred Kusuma Sarovara on their heads. "Śrīmatī Rādhārāṇī and her *sakhīs* used to pick flowers along these banks," Śrīnivāsa said.

Narottama stood silently for a few minutes, drinking in the beauty of the spot.

"Come, let's carry on," Śrīnivāsa said, walking back toward the *parikrāma* path. "Soon we'll be able to see Govardhana Hill."

Reveling in each other's company, the two friends headed south toward Manasi Gaṅgā. Over the years Narottama and Śrīnivāsa had become practically inseparable: they studied together, chanted together, and relished the peaceful atmosphere of the holy *dhāma* together.

Rounding a slight bend in the path, they caught sight of the lustrous, reddish brown rocks of Govardhana Hill abruptly rising from the flat expanse. Both immediately fell to the ground to offer their respects. Then sitting up on their knees, they stared with awe at the sacred hill. A warm, rich glow seemed to radiate from the stones.

Śrīnivāsa reflected, "Kṛṣṇa is so protective of His devotees. He picked up this hill with one hand, just as a child plucks a mushroom. Then He held it over all the Vrājavāsīs like a great umbrella, shielding them from Indra's torrents of rain."

Narottama nodded. "Yes, and even though the rains of death poured all around them, the Vrājavāsīs and their cows were not disturbed. They had complete faith that Kṛṣṇa would protect them."

Śrīnivāsa and Narottama continued walking, each one silently relishing the atmosphere. The only sounds to be heard were the cries of peacocks, the chirping of parrots, and the cooing of pigeons. Sometimes they heard a drum or gong in the distance, or the occasional "Rādhe-Śyāma!" Groups of monkeys scampered across their path every now and then, and once, a herd of white cows decorated with red *sindhur* handprints passed them, stirring up the dust. Occasionally they shared the path with village women carrying baskets filled with cow dung patties.

"When Lord Kṛṣṇa was here in Vṛndāvana," Śrīnivāsa said, breaking their silence, "Govardhana Hill was twenty-four miles high. Now it's less than a hundred feet because of Pulastya Muni's curse. Every day the hill sinks into the earth by the measurement of one mustard seed."

Narottama looked at the sacred hill, calculating how this curse was affecting the hill now and into the future. "The time may come," he said, "when Govardhana Hill will no longer be visible to the unfortunate people of the world."

Śrīnivāsa nodded, and was about to reply, but their discussion was interrupted by the sound of the most enchanting music. Both stopped abruptly, listening intently.

The extraordinary sound made Narottama lightheaded, and he almost lost his balance. "What is it?" he gasped. "I've never heard anything so beautiful!"

Spellbound, Śrīnivāsa whispered, "It's a flute . . . but not an ordinary flute."

Narottama nodded. "I think it's coming from that cave over there."

Drawn by the mesmerizing music, Narottama and Śrīnivāsa crept toward the cave. As they stepped through the cave's mouth, they were overwhelmed by a fragrance so extraordinarily sweet and intoxicating that both of them fainted.

When Narottama came to, a charming cowherd boy was standing before him. The boy held a herding stick and wore a colorful turban.

Narottama looked in astonishment at the boy, and then turned to Śrīnivāsa to make sure he wasn't dreaming. Śrīnivāsa was as stunned as Narottama. The two boys sat up, and Śrīnivāsa managed to stammer, "My dear boy, wh . . . who are you? What are you doing here?"

The boy smiled enigmatically and gently replied, "I have come to protect you two. You aren't aware of the many dangers here, but we cowherd boys know everything about these hills and forests. From the distance I saw you lying on the ground unconscious. So I left My friends and quickly came here. I've been standing here for a long time, waiting for you to wake up. I'm relieved to see that you're all right. Now I will return to the pasture." The boy then turned and swiftly disappeared.

"Where did he go?" Narottama gasped.

"He went outside," Śrīnivāsa said, scrambling toward the cave's entrance. Narottama was close at his heels, hoping to catch the mysterious cowherd boy. They searched frantically in every direction, but the boy seemed to have vanished. Finally, exhausted, Narottama and Śrīnivāsa dropped down in the shade of a large neem tree, where they sat in stunned silence for several long minutes.

Narottama broke their silence with a whisper. His voice was quivering as he spoke. "That boy – he was no ordinary cowherd boy. The sound of the flute . . . the wonderful fragrance . . . "

Śrīnivāsa nodded vigorously. He put words to what Narottama was hardly daring to think. "That must have been Kṛṣṇa!"

Had they truly heard the sound of Kṛṣṇa's flute – that same sound that had driven the cows, deer, and trees of Vṛndāvana mad with joy; that same sound that had forced Anantadeva to sway in ecstasy as he held all the planets on his thousand hoods; that same sound that had astonished Brahmā as he sat on his lotus flower creating the universe? Had they actually heard that same flute-song with their own ears? And that extraordinary fragrance, like a delicate lotus flower sprinkled with camphor – could it have been the sweet scent of the Supreme Lord's transcendental body?

Narottama and Śrīnivāsa trembled in ecstasy and tears flowed from their eyes. Both of them felt certain they had indeed seen the Lord of their lives face to face. Their hearts soared in happiness.

But then, remembering that they had lost sight of Lord Kṛṣṇa's charming moon-like face – perhaps for the rest of their lives – their hearts plunged into the depths of despair. Torn between the joy of meeting their Lord and the sorrow at being separated from Him, they spent the rest of the day under the tree, sighing and crying.

As the golden moon rose high over Govardhana Hill, the two devotees fell asleep. In each of their dreams the same enchanting cowherd boy returned. This time it was clear He was Kṛṣṇa, as His complexion was a soft, storm-cloud blue. Smiling lovingly, Kṛṣṇa said, "Today I appeared before you dressed as an ordinary cowherd boy. You were both so disappointed when I disappeared from your sight that I have returned just to satisfy you."

But then, once again, the Lord disappeared.

Narottama and Śrīnivāsa woke at the same time. As they looked at each other and saw the other's face, wet with tears of bliss, it was clear they had both experienced the same vision of the Lord. Overwhelmed, they remained under the tree until the first rays of sunlight illuminated the sky, again and again and again recalling Kṛṣṇa's exquisite beauty, His intoxicating fragrance, His charming smile, and the unlimited mercy He had shown each of them.

Boiling the Milk

As Narottama lay on his *kuśa* mat, a sense of peace and gratitude warmed his heart. "How fortunate I am to be in Vṛndāvana," he thought. "I pray I can always remain here, living in the lap of the Lord." Joyous remembrances flashed across his mind of wandering blissfully through the magical forests, sitting at Śrī Jīva Gosvāmī's feet, serving his spiritual master in the *kuñja*, visiting Raghunātha dāsa Gosvāmī and Kṛṣṇadāsa Kavirāja on the sacred banks of Śrī Rādhā-kuṇḍa and Śyāma-kuṇḍa, performing the Vrāja-maṇḍala *parikrāma*, studying music, and performing *bhajan*. "Years have passed like moments," he noted with astonishment. Pleasant memories continued to flow until his eyelids became heavy and sleep finally overtook him.

As he slipped from external consciousness, Narottama was startled by the sudden vision of a stunningly beautiful young girl. She was dressed in dazzling sapphire blue garments and had a colorful garland of wildflowers around her neck. Her exquisite, delicate face, glowed with the radiance of molten gold and was beautified by the locks of curling black hair that framed her forehead. She smiled brightly at Narottama, revealing brilliant white teeth that shone like a row of precious pearls. Her eyes were shaped like lotus petals and sparkled with compassion and love. She said, "Always take shelter of your spiritual master with faith and devotion. Follow his orders and do whatever he asks."

Her sweet voice and the radiance of her body immediately convinced Narottama that this was no woman of earthly birth or even a goddess from heaven. He wondered, "Could this be the queen of Vṛndāvana, Śrīmatī Rādhārāṇī Herself, standing before me?"

She confirmed Her identity with Her next words. "I am very pleased with your sincere devotion and austerity. Therefore, I would like to give you a special service to perform for My Lord. Every afternoon, when the *sakhīs* and I meet Śrī Kṛṣṇa in the grove, we serve Him with great care. We offer Him a special milk sweet Campakalatā expertly prepares. From now on, you shall serve under her direction. She will teach you how to boil the milk for Kṛṣṇa's sweets." Flashing another radiant smile, she added, "Remember, I become happy if Kṛṣṇa is happy." Saying this, she disappeared from sight.

Narottama woke, his mind reeling. Certainly the young girl in my dream was none other than Śrī Rādhā," he marveled. "But I dare not presume such a thing without confirming it with my spiritual master."

At dawn he rushed to Lokanātha Gosvāmī's *kuñja* and related the entire dream, explaining, "She also told me my name is Campaka-mañjarī. I was so astonished by what She said that I fell at Her feet crying. Then She disappeared and I awoke. Dear Gurudeva, please tell me what I should do now?"

Despite his old age, Lokanātha leapt up to embrace his beloved disciple. Tears filled his eyes and his voice shook with emotion. "Oh Narottama, your life is glorious! You are so fortunate to have received your worshipable Deity's direct association. You have attained the ultimate goal of your life, the goal for which we all perform service day and night. From now on, simply continue your service as you have been instructed and relish transcendental happiness."

From then on, Narottama spent time each day sitting quietly in his own *kuñja* and meditating on boiling milk for Kṛṣṇa's sweets.

One day, as he sat quietly, the image of the boiling milk fixed in his mind, he fed the fire under the milk pot with dry wood to keep it burning. While he was doing this, the milk began to overflow. Distressed that he was not doing his service properly, Narottama tried to save the milk by removing the pot from the fire with his bare hands. Although his hands were scorched, he paid no heed and mentally handed the milk over to the *sakhīs*.

Narottama's meditation broke at this point. When he looked at his hands, he was shocked to see they were covered with burns! Fearing the honor and recognition that would come to him if his intimate relationship with the Lord was revealed, Narottama quickly covered his hands with strips of cloth to conceal the burns.

As soon as Jīva Gosvāmī saw Narottama, however, he understood what had happened. And eventually, all the residents of Vṛndāvana came to know how Narottama had obtained his unusual burns. Thus, his fame as a highly elevated devotee spread far and wide.

gandharva-garva-kṣapaṇa-svalāsya-
vismāpitāśeṣa-kṛti-vrajāya
sva-sṛṣṭa-gāna-prathitāya tasmai
namo namaḥ śrīla-narottamāya

I repeatedly offer my respectful obeisances to Śrīla Narottama Dāsa Ṭhākura, whose dancing destroyed the pride of the Gandharvas, and who is celebrated by all the people for creating his own style of singing. The magnitude of his diverse devotional activities amazed everyone.

Narottama-prabhor-āṣṭaka, Verse 4

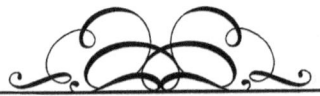

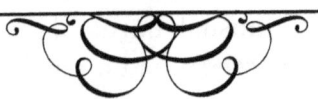

Chapter Four

The Mission

Śrī Jīva's Request

Standing before his students one day Śrī Jīva Gosvāmī announced, "Kārttika is approaching, and I want to organize a grand festival for all the Vaiṣṇavas of Vrāja. I will need your help to organize the *mahotsava* nicely in order to make it a wonderful festival of Kṛṣṇa consciousness. Narottama and Śrīnivāsa, I would like you to deliver invitations to all the devotees."

As always, Narottama and Śrīnivāsa immediately obeyed their *guru*'s request. They worked hard to prepare for the festival.

"Quick," Śrīnivāsa called to Narottama. "Bring the garlands and sandalwood paste. The devotees are beginning to arrive."

Gradually the *kuñja* began to fill with devotees. One by one, the great luminaries among Śrī Caitanya Mahāprabhu's associates arrived – Raghunātha dāsa Gosvāmī, Kṛṣṇadāsa Kavirāja Gosvāmī, Gopāla Bhaṭṭa Gosvāmī, and Jagadānanda Paṇḍita. Even Lokanātha Gosvāmī and Bhūgarbha Gosvāmī, who were rarely seen outside their *kuñjas*, were present. As devotees poured in from Rādhā-kuṇḍa, Govardhana, and Mathurā, the local villagers stood on the outskirts of the *kuñja*, staring curiously at the famous devotees. With great enthusiasm, Śrī Jīva Gosvāmī and his students warmly greeted each guest with garlands, sandalwood pulp, and the respect befitting each devotee's position.

Once the *kīrtana* began, it continued to roar throughout the day. Since it was Ekādaśī and the devotees were fasting, they feasted on the *prasāda* of *kṛṣṇa-kathā* and *kīrtana* throughout the night.

The next morning, the devotees cleaned the entire area and offered a succulent feast to the Deities. Śrīnivāsa offered each guest water to wash his hands, and Śrī Jīva ushered the guests to their seats. Śrīnivāsa expertly orchestrated the serving of sumptuous *prasāda* to the full satisfaction of all the devotees.

After respecting *prasāda* and washing their hands again, the devotees continued to celebrate with *kīrtana* and uplifting discourses through the rest of the day.

Late in the afternoon, Śrī Jīva Gosvāmī asked the devotees for their attention. Standing before the saintly gathering, he loudly announced, "Śrī Caitanya Mahāprabhu instructed all His devotees to write books explaining the science of Kṛṣṇa consciousness. He told us to distribute these books far and wide. Some of the Lord's most confidential associates, such as Rūpa Gosvāmī, Sanātana Gosvāmī, Raghunātha dāsa

Gosvāmī, and Kṛṣṇadāsa Kavirāja, have already written many manuscripts. We now have hundreds of these manuscripts in Vṛndāvana. I want these great books to go out into the world, especially to Bengal, where Lord Caitanya has thousands of followers. The time has come to fulfill Lord Caitanya's mission. These manuscripts must be taken to Bengal where they can be read, copied, and distributed throughout the land."

He paused, scanning the crowd until he caught sight of his three illustrious students. "These devotees," he said, motioning to Narottama, Śrīnivāsa, and Śyāmānanda (formerly Duḥkhī Kṛṣṇadāsa), "have studied all the *bhakti-śāstras* under my guidance for a number of years and are thoroughly trained in philosophy. I feel they are qualified and competent to fulfill this important mission. They have rightfully earned the titles, Narottama Ṭhākura Mahāśaya, Śrīnivāsa Ācārya, and Śyāmānanda Prabhu.[7] I now humbly request the masters of these disciples to give their permission so they may go out and preach."

Narottama was stunned by the unexpected announcement. His eyes flashed to the face of his beloved spiritual master to gauge his reaction.

A hushed silence fell on the assembly, as everyone waited for the response of Śrī Lokanātha Gosvāmī and Gopāla Bhaṭṭa Gosvāmī.

Though his weak legs could barely hold up his frail form, Śrī Lokanātha Gosvāmī slowly rose to speak. "The *śāstras* say that it is very difficult to get a bona fide *guru*. It is equally difficult to get a good disciple. I am very fortunate because I have only one disciple and he is the best disciple. He has given me great joy because in his association I feel ecstatic *kṛṣṇa-prema*. I wish to never give up his company, but for the mission of Mahāprabhu, I give my full blessings. He can go."

Narottama was shocked. In one short sentence, his spiritual master had dramatically changed the trajectory of his entire life. His heart sank at the thought of leaving his beloved master's personal service. At once, he was flooded with concerns: "Who will assist my Gurudeva in his service? He is so old now. Who will fan him in the summer as he does his *pūjā*? And in the winter, who will light the stove to warm him? Who will collect flowers for his worship or bring him water or wash his lotus feet?"

Then Śrī Gopāla Bhaṭṭa stood. "I too give my blessings to my disciple. Śrīnivāsa has my permission to take up this mission."

As cheers of approval rang out from among the devotees, Narottama's mind continued to reel, "But I had planned to live in Vṛndāvana for the rest of my life! I cannot bear the thought of leaving. I may never see any of these exalted Vaiṣṇavas again – not my beloved spiritual master, not Śrī Jīva Gosvāmī . . . " His heart felt as if it were being torn in two. The thought of leaving was devastating, but there could be no greater honor than to take part in the Lord's glorious mission. How could he refuse such service?

Narottama looked at Śrīnivāsa and then Śyāmānanda, and saw the same surprise and conflict etched in their faces. The approving words of both spiritual masters had sealed the fate of both Narottama and Śrīnivāsa. And certainly Śyāmānanda's participation in the mission was also inevitable. In the absence of his own *dīkṣā-guru*, he would be obliged to follow the order of his beloved *śikṣā-guru*, Śrī Jīva Gosvāmī.

The three friends exchanged knowing glances: It would be unbearable to leave Vṛndāvana, but they knew they had to. All they had experienced and learned in Vṛndāvana had been preparation for this important mission. To be chosen for such a task was truly the greatest fortune.

Śrīnivāsa stepped forward and announced to the crowd, "We are deeply honored to be chosen for this vital mission. Please give us your mercy so we may be successful."

Raising his arms over his head, Śrī Jīva Gosvāmī beamed and asked the crowd, "Bless these devotees. Give them strength so they may distribute the seed of *bhakti* far and wide."

Once more, jubilant cheers erupted from the crowd.

"*Jaya*! *Jaya*!

Sādhu! *Sādhu*!"

Narottama, Śrīnivāsa, and Śyāmānanda humbly moved through the crowd of devotees, offering their obeisances and taking the dust from each devotee's feet. Thus, the festival ended in a buzz of excited anticipation. A uniquely special mission was about to begin, with the potential for this divine knowledge to spread throughout the entire world. Not a mouth was silent, nor a heart still, as everyone discussed the task at hand. The moon rose, and night fell.

The following morning, astrologers chose an auspicious day for the commencement of the journey, and preparations began. Śrī Jīva Gosvāmī contacted a rich merchant from Mathurā and asked him to build a cart to carry the books to Bengal.

Wanting to make the most of their last few days in the holy *dhāma*, Narottama, Śrīnivāsa, and Śyāmānanda set out to bid farewell to Vṛndāvana. They visited Vṛndāvana's presiding Deities –Madana-mohana, Govindajī, and Gopīnātha– and falling flat before each Deity, humbly prayed for their mission to succeed, begging for the power to preach effectively. They wandered throughout Vrāja, visiting their favorite spots, praying at the tombs of the Gosvāmīs and bathing in the sacred kuṇḍas.

Wherever they went, the people of Vrāja came out to wish them well. Many offered them garlands or *mahā-prasāda*.

Narottama and his friends then went to offer their respects to Govardhana. They followed the sandy *parikrāma* path around the sacred hill. Upon reaching Śrī Rādhā-kuṇḍa they sought out Raghunātha dāsa Gosvāmī and found him in a secluded spot, reading beneath a tree. With great respect the three students bowed before him, touching his feet. "We will soon be leaving for Gauḍa-deśa," Śrīnivāsa said. "Please give us your blessings."

Raghunātha Dāsa rose to his feet and warmly embraced each of them. "Your mission is of vital importance," he said soberly. "You will be carrying the most valuable cargo in existence – the written teachings of Śrī Caitanya Mahāprabhu. These manuscripts, which describe the science of Kṛṣṇa consciousness in great detail, took years to compile, and each precious book is a window into the spiritual world. Guard them with great care."

Raghunātha Dāsa looked affectionately from one young missionary to the next, his bright, penetrating eyes filled with tears. "Now," he said, his voice quivering with emotion, "it's up to you to have these books copied and distributed. People are rotting in material existence because they are ignorant of their relationship with God. Try to help them by spreading Śrī Caitanya Mahāprabhu's message throughout the land."

Narottama, Śrīnivāsa, and Śyāmānanda nodded gravely. "We will try our best," Narottama assured him. With great sadness, they offered their obeisances and said good-bye.

As they turned to leave, Śrī Raghunātha Dāsa called out, "May the blessings of Śrī Rādhā be with you!"

Feeling the tremendous weight of responsibility on their shoulders, they left Rādhā-kuṇḍa and headed east, back to Vṛndāvana.[8]

The night before their scheduled departure, Narottama and Śrīnivāsa went on their final pilgrimage, first to receive the blessings of Śrī Gopāla Bhaṭṭa Gosvāmī, and then to Śrī Lokanātha Gosvāmī's hermitage.

Entering Lokanātha Gosvāmī's *kuñja*, they saw him sitting before his beloved Deities, Śrī Rādhā Vinoda. Narottama threw himself at the feet of his master, unable to contain his sorrow. When he looked up, he saw Lokanātha Gosvāmī staring lovingly at him. Narottama couldn't find the words to say good-bye to his beloved *guru*. How could he express his gratitude and love? His throat ached as he choked back tears. The thought of them being separated, perhaps forever, was unbearable.

Śrī Lokanātha Gosvāmī wrapped his thin arms around his disciple and embraced him warmly. "Narottama, what you are about to do is the perfection of everything I have taught you. Always remember to serve the Deities with love, and serve the Vaiṣṇavas with the same love and devotion with which you serve the Lord. Remain vigilant to avoid all offenses, and dedicate your life fully to spreading the *saṅkīrtana* movement." Tears flowed from Lokanātha's eyes as he spoke. "Take this Vṛndāvana atmosphere with you, Narottama. Vṛndāvana is always in the devotee's heart, so carry it with you. Just chant Hare Kṛṣṇa, because wherever there is chanting, there is Vṛndāvana."

Lokanātha turned to Śrīnivāsa. "I hand over my dear disciple to you. Watch over him carefully."

Tears streamed down Narottama's cheeks. "Gurudeva, if you give this servant permission, then sometimes I can come from Gauḍa-deśa to have *darśana* of your lotus feet."

Śrī Lokanātha Gosvāmī shook his head. "Now you have to make your life successful by preaching Mahāprabhu's religion of love. I don't think it will be necessary for you to return here."[9]

Hearing these words, Narottama fell to the ground. For some time he lay at his spiritual master's feet offering obeisances, and then, without protest, he rose and left the *kuñja* with Śrīnivāsa. His *guru's* last instructions echoed heavily in his heart.

Śrīnivāsa put his arm around Narottama as they walked back to their *āśrama* in silence. In his mind,

Narottama resolved to fix his attention firmly on his spiritual master's instruction to preach Kṛṣṇa consciousness; he wouldn't think so much now about the order not to return. With this, Narottama's sorrow began to dissipate. It was replaced by a feeling of eagerness as he thought of the service he was entrusted to render with the other devotees.

That night Narottama lay on his bed, restless and unable to sleep. His happy life in Vṛndāvana flooded his mind, and in the darkness he savored his last hours in Vṛndāvana's atmosphere – he could hear the distant cries of peacocks and a faint chime of *karatālas*. Someone was singing to his Lord deep in the night. The sweet scent of night-blooming jasmine wafted into Narottama's room. His heart ached, and heaving a deep sigh he cried out, "Oh Vṛndāvana! How can I leave you? Will I ever see my spiritual master or the Gosvāmīs and other Vrājavāsīs again? Will I ever again feel the dust of this transcendental land coat my body? Will I ever see Govardhana Hill again, or bathe in the sacred Yamunā?"

In this turbulent emotional state, he composed a verse, "When shall I see the abode of mercy, Śrī Caitanya Mahāprabhu, who has distributed His potency in two ways: by investing Śrīla Rūpa Gosvāmī and others with the power to write devotional books wherein priceless treasures of spiritual knowledge shine like brilliant jewels, and empowering Śrīnivāsa Ācārya to distribute these books. Thus, I worship the lotus feet of Śrī Caitanya Mahāprabhu, who has empowered His devotees in these two ways to shower His mercy on the world."

His mind churning, Narottama lay awake until late into the night.

But when morning arrived, Narottama forgot his lamentation and his heart raced with excitement at the thought of his mission. He leapt up from his bed and quickly bathed and dressed. Gathering his scant belongings, he rushed to meet his travel companions and Śrī Jīva Gosvāmī. Together they walked to Śrī Rādhā Govindadeva's temple, where the bullock cart was waiting to be loaded with the manuscripts.[10] A crowd of devotees had gathered to witness the party's momentous departure – devotees from as far away as Mathurā, Govardhana, and Rādhā-kuṇḍa. The greatest of all the Vaiṣṇavas were present – Gopāla Bhaṭṭa Gosvāmī, Bhūgarbha Gosvāmī, Lokanātha Gosvāmī, Śrī Madhu Paṇḍita, Rāghava Gosvāmī, Kṛṣṇadāsa Kavirāja. No one wanted to miss this most important event.

Narottama stepped privately into the temple and, bowing before Śrī Govindajī, begged for His blessings and protection. When he rejoined Śrīnivāsa and Śyāmānanda, he found that Śrī Jīva Gosvāmī had already announced that the loading would begin. The crowd excitedly watched as Śrī Jīva and other devotees ceremoniously carried the priceless manuscripts to the large cart.

The crowds shouted, "*Jaya! Jaya!*" as Śrī Jīva Gosvāmī picked up each manuscript with care, held it above his head, and called out its title: "*Ujjvala-nīlamaṇi . . . Vidagdha-mādhava . . . Lalita-mādhava . . .* "

Then he wrapped each precious book in a piece of soft cloth and gently placed it into one of the large wooden crates, beautifully studded with copper and brass, that had already been loaded on the cart. When every manuscript had been securely packed, he locked the crates and covered them with a protective tarp. When the last lock was sealed, the crowd cheered.

Seeing everything ready for departure, Śrī Jīva nodded to the driver, who then prodded the backs of the huge oxen, and the heavy cart jerked to a start. Narottama's heart lurched with it. This was the first step away from his spiritual home. The cart slowly rolled forward, and the ten armed guards took their places alongside to protect the priceless cargo. Narottama, Śrīnivāsa, and Śyāmānanda walked behind with Śrī Jīva Gosvāmī, who would accompany them as far as Mathurā.

As the cart ambled down the dusty road, Narottama again and again looked back at the crowd of well-wishing devotees. Tears streamed from his eyes as he scanned their faces – the faces of his beloved teachers, friends, and acquaintances. Some of them stood silently, others wept openly, and some joyfully called out blessings. Several devotees trailed behind the cart until it was out of sight.

The Journey

The caravan spent its first night in Mathurā. As they prepared to resume their journey the following morning, Śrī Jīva Gosvāmī gave his final advice to his beloved students. "Lord Caitanya instructed Rūpa and Sanātana Gosvāmīs to distribute love of God throughout the land. These books are the result of their hard work and dedication to their beloved Lord. Therefore, it is not my order, but the Lord's order, that these books should be taken to Bengal. May your journey be pleasant and safe. Be careful, take good care of yourselves and don't forget to send reports of your preaching work." Turning to Śrīnivāsa, he continued "You're the eldest, so I am putting you in charge of this party. He then handed him the legal papers required to cross the country and money for expenses on the journey.

And suddenly it was time to say good-bye. They had all shared such a deep love; separation was unbearable. Narottama, Śrīnivāsa, and Śyāmānanda cried openly as Śrī Jīva tightly embraced each of them.

As the bullock cart again began to roll forward, the three missionaries took their places behind it. They knew there could be no turning back.

The transcendental caravan made its way across the country smoothly and peacefully despite potential threats of dacoits, government officials, and bad weather. Each night the guards took turns to watch over the cargo while the others slept. By Kṛṣṇa's grace, all was well.

Narottama felt no fear as they passed through dense forests and jungles. He was confident the Lord was guiding and protecting them. He chanted happily with Śrīnivāsa and Śyāmānanda and together they discussed Śrī Caitanya Mahāprabhu's wonderful pastimes. Despite the dangerous animals roaming the forest, they were never disturbed.

After months of exhausting travel, the caravan finally arrived at the Bengal border in the district of Viṣṇupura. They stopped for the night on the outskirts of Gopālpura. Tired, Narottama spread his blanket on the ground and lay down. Gazing up at the brilliant stars shining in the clear night sky he thought, "Soon our journey will come to an end and part of our mission will have been successfully accomplished." Content with this thought, he fell asleep.

Narottama was awakened early the next morning by loud shouts. Fear clutched at his heart as he leapt to his feet to see what was wrong.

Śrīnivāsa's horrified cry rent the air and pierced Narottama's heart. "The books are gone! How could this be? Narottama! Śyāmānanda . . . the books . . . they're all gone! Someone has stolen them!"

Narottama's body surged with adrenaline. Shafts of early sunlight illuminated the empty spot where the cart had stood the night before.

Śrīnivāsa frantically turned to the guards. "Don't just stand there! Find them!"

Thunderstruck, Narottama stood paralyzed as he watched everyone begin a frenzied search for the lost treasure. His mind whirled. This was a nightmare. It surely couldn't be true. How could this be possible? All the books from Vṛndāvana– gone! It just couldn't be true! How could the precious works of the Gosvāmīs – works they had spent their lives preparing – be stolen?

Suddenly Narottama snapped into action and joined the desperate search for the manuscripts.

The devotees scoured every hill, forest, and riverbank in the area, but in vain. Slow, sorrow-laden, and exhausting hours crawled by as the devotees searched, but there were no clues.

They questioned the villagers in Gopālpura, who told them about a band of dacoits who often attacked and looted travelers, but no one would provide details of the thieves.

Narottama suspected the villagers knew more than they were willing to say, but it was already late, and the devotees were forced to return to their camp empty-handed and with heavy hearts.

They sat together that evening in utter despair. Tears streamed down the pallid faces of Śrīnivāsa and Śyāmānanda. Narottama was both sickened and frustrated. He let out an anguished cry and hit his head with his hand again and again. "Is this how our glorious mission is to end?" he shouted. "What can it mean? We were so careful to protect the books each night. What *happened* last night?"

Śrīnivāsa sighed heavily. "It's very strange," he said. "Every one of us seems to have been sleeping soundly – even the guards – and no one was watching the cart. That hasn't happened even once on this entire journey."

Śyāmānanda stood and began to pace before the campfire. "Those thieves probably thought we were carrying gold or jewels in the trunks. They're in for a big disappointment when they find nothing but manuscripts."

"They have no idea," Narottama said, shaking his head, "that they hold in their possession the most valuable treasure in existence. The writings of the Gosvāmīs are more precious than mountains of gold and silver."

"What use do dacoits have for manuscripts?" Śrīnivāsa said. "Surely they'll discard the books somewhere." With a more hopeful tone, he said, "And then we shall find them."

No one could sleep that night. Narottama tossed and turned, his mind lurching from one dreadful thought to another. He sank even deeper into the sea of sorrow as he worried about how they would tell Śrī Jīva Gosvāmī. And how would he tell his Gurudeva? Their hearts would be shattered. How would they maintain their lives after receiving such news? And what about the devotees waiting expectantly in Bengal? How could he meet them empty-handed? How could he go on living if the manuscripts were not found?"

The following morning the search continued, but without success. That evening, Narottama crumpled under a tree and cried pitifully. Śyāmānanda sat nearby, his pale face drawn. The guards, dejected, huddled together, not knowing what to say or do. Śrīnivāsa sat at a distance alone. Each one was lost in his private misery. Śrīnivāsa broke the despondent mood by calling Narottama and Śyāmānanda to come over. As they walked over to him, they observed with wonder, that Śrīnivāsa's expression bore no trace of anxiety.

"What is it Śrīnivāsa?" Narottama asked, mystified at his friend's peaceful smile.

"I've been thinking," Śrīnivāsa said, "throughout this journey we have passed safely through many dangerous places without a single mishap. Why is it that now, at the very end of our journey, the cart was so easily stolen?"

Narottama and Śyāmānanda shook their heads. They too had been trying to make sense of this terrible disaster.

Śrīnivāsa looked up to the star-studded heavens. "There is definitely some special meaning behind this robbery," he said. "The Gosvāmīs' books have the inconceivable power to generate love of God in the heart of those who touch, study, or even simply see them. So, I can only surmise that the theft of the books must be the divine arrangement of the Supreme Lord. Kṛṣṇa must have a plan to bestow His special mercy on someone in this area. We must take heart," Śrīnivāsa said confidently. "Have faith the Lord's plan will eventually be revealed to us."

Śrīnivāsa's insight soothed Narottama's heavy heart; he knew his friend was right.

"Yes," Śyāmānanda said softly, nodding. "What you say is true."

"So," Śrīnivāsa said firmly, "we must stop lamenting. We must carry on with our service. I was put in charge of this mission and so I have decided on a course of action. I will write to Śrī Jīva Gosvāmī to tell him what has happened. Then I will continue to search for the books. I'm confident they'll be found."

This sounded reasonable to Narottama and Śyāmānanda, and they nodded their consent.

Śrīnivāsa continued without a pause. "There's no reason for all of us to remain here. It's better the two of you bring the teachings of Śrī Caitanya Mahāprabhu to Bengal and Orissa."

Stunned, Narottama protested, "That's unthinkable! We must help you search for the books! We've got to find them! How can I go on living without knowing whether they've been found?"

"Yes, we need to stay and help," Śyāmānanda added firmly.

"No." Śrīnivāsa insisted. "It's my responsibility to find the books and yours to carry the preaching mission forward." To pacify his friends, Śrīnivāsa put an arm around each of their shoulders. In a softer tone he assured them, "Don't worry, I'll notify you as soon as the books are found."

Struggling to digest what his best friend had just said, Narottama did not reply. No matter how excruciating it would be to leave his dear companion in the midst of this ordeal, he knew he had to obey Śrīnivāsa.

"Please believe me Narottama," Śrīnivāsa said. "Everything will be all right. Go back to your hometown and preach." He then turned to Śyāmānanda and said,

"Go with Narottama as far as Kheturi, and then go to your own hometown in Orissa."

Narottama fought back his tears and nodded at Śrīnivāsa's order.

The next morning, despite their reluctance, Narottama and Śyāmānanda gathered their belongings. Their departure was an emotional one, but they headed off together for the Padmavatī River.

Return to Kheturi

Narottama stepped from the sandy riverbank into the rickety wooden boat, joining Śyāmānanda on the boat's damp floorboards. Śyāmānanda heaved a deep sigh and said, "My body is here . . . "

"But your heart is with Śrīnivāsa," Narottama said. "I know. I can't stop wondering whether he has found the books yet either."

Śyāmānanda nodded. "Until we hear from him, we will have no peace of mind."

The boatman pushed off from the bank and the two friends fell silent. Narottama peered across the vast Padmavatī. Squinting in the sunlight, he saw the faint outline of Kheturi on the horizon, and memories flooded his mind – of his childhood in the palace, his devoted parents, the doting villagers. How long ago it all seemed now – like a dream or a previous life. "I wonder what we will find in Kheturi now," Narottama mused.

"Did you receive news from Kheturi while you were in Vṛndāvana?" Śyāmānanda asked.

Narottama pulled his eyes away from the horizon. "No. For me, entering Vṛndāvana was like taking another birth. I left behind all connection with my former life."

Narottama sat pensive for a few moments and Śyāmānanda didn't interrupt his thoughts. "Yet now," Narottama said, "I realize how fortunate I was to have such kind parents. A wave of gratitude filled his heart as he remembered how as a child he sat next to his father listening to scriptural discourses. "My father always insisted I sit quietly and listen to all the *pravachans*. He made sure every *sādhu* gave me his blessings. He was a simple man, not very philosophical, but he had a wonderful service attitude. By his example he taught me the importance of serving the *brāhmaṇas* and Vaiṣṇavas."

"He must have expected you would succeed him as king of Kheturi?"

"Of course," Narottama said. "But that was partly due to his strong sense of responsibility. He wanted to insure Kheturi remained a place where people could maintain their spiritual culture and practice their religion unimpeded. My father knew that wherever a pious Hindu king rules, God conscious principles could be protected, and that such kingdoms are essential, especially under Muslim rule."

Śyāmānanda nodded, "I've heard that many devotees used to stop in Kheturi on their way to Ratha-yātrā."

"Oh, yes," Narottama said, "many of Mahāprabhu's devotees regularly passed through our town, and my father and uncle Puruṣottama accommodated them with enthusiasm. When I was young, Kheturi was bustling with *sādhus*, devotional singers, storytellers, and scholars, all eager to accept the patronage of the pious Rāja Kṛṣṇānanda." Narottama paused, then added, "My mother was also exemplary. Though a queen, she remained humble and sweet-natured." Narottama fell silent, then took his *japa* beads in his hand and began to chant softly.

Śyāmānanda joined him in *japa* meditation as the small boat plied across the glistening Padma, swept along by the strong current and gentle breeze.

As they neared the opposite shore, the boatman jumped into the shallow water and pulled the boat onto the riverbank. Narottama caught sight of the exact spot on the bank where many years ago his life had been transformed. His heart beat rapidly as he stepped out of the boat onto the shore. He shivered at his remembrance of the golden boy who had danced before him, that extraordinary form of Śrī Caitanya Mahāprabhu who had entered his heart and changed his life forever.

Overcome with ecstasy, he turned to Śyāmānanda. "This is where . . . " Narottama was so choked with emotion that he couldn't speak. Tears streamed from his eyes. "Who can understand . . . " he said. "Who can possibly fathom the depth of Mahāprabhu's mercy?"

Composing himself, Narottama headed down the path to the village, Śyāmānanda following. An old man stopped to greet them. "I see you are Gauḍīya Vaiṣṇavas," he said cheerfully. "You must be coming from Navadvīpa. Well, you will be welcomed warmly here." His voice was proud. "Our Rāja Santosh Datta serves all visiting *sādhus* very nicely, but he is especially eager to serve the Gauḍīya devotees. If you continue down this path, you will arrive at the palace."

"Why does your king favor Gauḍīya Vaiṣṇavas?" Śyāmānanda asked.

The man smiled broadly. "It's because his beloved cousin, Rāja-kumāra Narottama, left home at a very young age and took shelter of the Gauḍīya devotees."

Narottama quietly asked, "What has become of the former Rāja and Rāṇī of Kheturi?"

"Oh, King Kṛṣṇānanda and his Queen are in the palace, but they handed over responsibility for the kingdom to their nephew Santosh years ago.[11] After their only son left home to become a *sādhu*, they were too devastated to manage the kingdom." The old man sighed. "The poor Rāja and Rāṇī never fully recovered from the loss. Still, they are proud of their saintly son. So whenever Gauḍīya Vaiṣṇavas come to Kheturi, they rush to find out if they have any news about the Rāja-kumāra. And they carefully serve each and every one of those devotees. They think that since their son is with Śrī Caitanya's followers, if they serve the devotees who serve Him, they will be serving their dear Narottama."

Narottama lowered his eyes, humbled by the villager's words. The old man continued. "I was told that our revered Rāṇīji never stops thinking of her beloved son – even after all these years. She has never given up hope of seeing him again." The old man shook his head. "How that young lad could leave such loving parents is a mystery to me."

"Such a son is sinful," Narottama said vehemently. "He's a thief who has robbed the Rāja and Rāṇī of their joy." Then in a meeker tone he added, "I am that thief. I am Narottama."

The old man gaped, his narrow eyes almost popping with astonishment. After a moment, he scrutinized Narottama's face in disbelief. Then his wrinkled brown face lit with recognition. "Naru? It's you! I heard you were a big *sādhu*, but . . . but I never thought we would see you again . . . Oh! How wonderful! We are blessed! Rāja-kumāra Narottama . . . " Barely able to contain his excitement, the old man turned and ran as fast as he could toward the town.

Narottama and Śyāmānanda could hear him shouting in the distance. "The prince is back! Narottama has come home! Come, come and see! Narottama is back!"

By the time Narottama and Śyāmānanda reached the center of town, Kheturi was in chaos. Excited residents had already congregated to greet them, and more were rushing out from their shops and homes, anxious to catch sight of their prince who had vanished so long ago.

Making their way to the palace, Narottama and Śyāmānanda saw the huge ornate doors burst open. Holding onto his colorful turban, Rāja Santosh flew down the stairway, followed by Kṛṣṇānanda and Nārāyaṇī, moving as quickly as their aged feet could carry them. Delirious with joy, they cried out, "Narottama! Narottama!" Narottama's heart swelled with affection at the sight of his now white-haired parents.

Tears streamed from their eyes as they rushed with outstretched arms to greet their long-lost son. But within a few meters of Narottama both of them suddenly slowed, then stopped. Their son was radiating with the glow of a self-realized soul. He was dressed only in a *kaupīna* and *chādar*, and his hand was in his bead bag. This was not their Naru but a powerful *vairāgī*. With reverence, Narottama's parents slowly placed their palms together and offered their son their *prāṇaṁs*.

In the meantime, Rāja Santosh Datta fell to the ground in prostrated obeisances. The townspeople followed his lead. Then everyone rose and stood in a hushed silence, unsure what to do next. How should they greet this loved one, absent for so many years? Narottama was clearly no longer the beloved young prince of their town but an exalted Vaiṣṇava – Narottama Ṭhākura Mahāśaya.

The crowd watched expectantly, their eyes darting from Narottama, to his parents and Rāja Santosh.

Narottama's heart went out to his relatives and the people of the town. Understanding their confusion, he stepped forward and reverently touched his parents' feet. "Mātā, Pitā," he said simply, in a gentle voice filled with affection, "your Naru has returned."

This was too much for the simple-hearted Nārāyaṇī. Overcome with emotion she burst into sobs. The sight of her son filled her with boundless joy, yet her heart wrenched to see his scant dress, and handsome golden face gaunt and dusty. Struggling between extremes of joy and grief, she wailed uncontrollably.

Kṛṣṇānanda tried to speak, but his voice choked and instead he pulled Narottama tightly to his chest.

Narottama's eyes too were filled with tears. It pained him to think of the suffering he had caused his parents. He didn't want any living being to suffer, so what to speak of such kind and devoted souls as his father and mother. Yet he knew he could not have lived his life otherwise. He also knew his parents would share the beneficial results of all his spiritual activities. This, he felt, was the greatest gift he could offer them.

After several awkward minutes, Rāja Santosh, stepped forward and said, "You must be very tired after your long journey. Please come into the palace, and let us serve you."

"Thank you," Narottama said softly, "but why don't we sit in the temple courtyard instead?" Narottama was eager to pacify his relatives' hearts, but he knew he must make it clear that although he had returned, he did not plan to take up his old life again. Rather, he would continue to maintain the strict vows of a renunciate.

"Yes, yes, Narottama, wherever you want," Santosh said.

Surrounded by Narottama's parents, relatives, and the curious onlookers, Narottama and Śyāmānanda walked to the nearby temple. Rāja Santosh Datta affectionately ushered everyone into the courtyard and respectfully sat them down.

The villagers crowded in. Straining to get a better view, they stared in awed silence.

Kṛṣṇānanda and Nārāyaṇī, bewildered and hesitant, also remained mute, gazing at their extraordinary son with wide eyes. For years they had dreamed of this blessed moment, but now that it had come, they didn't know what to say.

Narottama broke the silence. "This is my very dear friend, Śyāmānanda Prabhu. We spent many years together in Vṛndāvana studying the scriptures under Śrī Jīva Gosvāmī's guidance."

Rāja Santosh, and Narottama's parents smiled graciously and offered reverential *prāṇaṁs* to Syamananda, then turned again to Narottama.

Attempting to heal years of heartbreak, Narottama spoke to his bewildered parents in a sweet voice. "You should see Vṛndāvana, Pitā. It is such a wonderful place, full of temples and saints."

As Narottama talked, his relaxed mood gradually put everyone at ease. Kṛṣṇānanda and Nārāyaṇī nodded their heads as they listened to him, and Kṛṣṇānanda, trying to enter the casual conversation, said, "I had heard that Vṛndāvana is mostly forest."

"Yes, formerly it was. But since my Guru Mahārāja and the Gosvāmīs have been there, Vṛndāvana has become filled with devotees, and now there are many temples, ponds, and bathing ghats. And in every temple they make many offerings to the Deities each day, so there's plenty of milk, yogurt, and butter. I've been fed well!"

"I see," Kṛṣṇānanda said. "We heard you were eating practically nothing and hardly sleeping."

"Well, I was busy studying and serving my Guru Mahārāja," Narottama said gently. "But everything was wonderful in Vṛndāvana. I was taken care of so nicely."

Nārāyaṇī spoke up in a trembling voice. "But, Naru, why are you so skinny?"

"Oh, that's just because I've been traveling for a while. We were carrying the Gosvāmīs' books from Vṛndāvana, but they were stolen along the way. I've been in a lot of anxiety since then. That's why I'm so thin now. Usually I'm quite strong and healthy."

Kṛṣṇānanda beamed at his son. "Narottama you have brought life back to us in our old age. Words cannot describe how happy we are to see you. Now that you are back, what do you plan to do?"

Santosh Datta, suddenly spoke up. "Narottama, in your absence your father placed me in charge of the kingdom, but the throne belongs to you. I have simply been taking care of Kheturi on your behalf. Now that you're back, please take your rightful place."

Narottama's brow furrowed. "No, no, no," he protested, his voice grave. "I have nothing to do with such things anymore. I have taken strict vows of renunciation." Narottama knew that living in Kheturi would be challenging. As a renunciate, he needed to remain firmly fixed in his vows, yet, he equally felt impelled to reciprocate the love of his relatives and friends. It was a delicate situation, and he wanted to make his intentions clear from the beginning. "If anyone even mentions royal responsibilities or marriage," he said firmly, "I will be forced to leave Kheturi at once. Actually, it's not right for me to stay in my hometown, but Śrī Jīva Gosvāmī's order and your love have brought me here. If you want me to stay, please protect my *dharma* and help me keep the lifelong vows I made to my spiritual master."

"Oh, don't worry," Santosh quickly assured him. "We won't discuss anything that displeases you or ask you to do anything you deem inappropriate. Whatever you want, you can do. We won't interfere. If you want me to remain king, then it shall be so."

Narottama smiled warmly. "Yes, you rule the kingdom and I will preach and perform *bhajan*."

Seeing a glimmer of pain in his father's eyes, Narottama gently added, "But I will stay near the palace and every evening come to offer respects to my parents."

Now it was clear to Kṛṣṇānanda and Nārāyaṇī. Their son would never enter their world again, but at least he would remain in Kheturi and they would be able to see him at least briefly each day. Kṛṣṇānanda smiled lovingly. "It will give us the greatest joy to see you, Narottama."

Rāja Santosh bowed respectfully. "I am your humble servant, Narottama," he said. "I will do whatever you ask."

"Then I ask you to arrange a festival for tonight. Call the villagers. We shall have *kīrtana* and *pravachana*!"

"Oh yes!" Santosh said enthusiastically. "We must celebrate! I will arrange everything."

"It's getting late," Narottama said, "and I have to do my evening *sādhana*." He respectfully touched his parents' feet again. Then he and Śyāmānanda walked toward the Padmavatī to bathe.

Evening arrived, and the temple overflowed with people dressed in their finest in honor of this special occasion. Oil lamps burned brightly in every corner and colorful festoons of leaves and flowers had been strung from the ceiling and pillars. Narottama and Śyāmānanda sat down before the crowd. Narottama closed his eyes and began to sing. His deep, melodious voice echoed through the courtyard, melting the villagers' hearts. By the time he had finished singing, many in the hall were shedding tears.

As Narottama began to speak, explaining the goal of human life and the glories of devotional service, the audience sat spellbound. Not one fidgeted or stirred. Even the children listened attentively. Only the crickets' evening song, and the gentle breeze rustling in the trees accompanied Narottama's nectarean speech. When it was close to midnight Narottama said, "Please go and rest. You have your duties to perform in the morning."

As the crowd reluctantly dispersed, Narottama went to his parents and spoke sweetly with them for a few minutes. Then he offered his respects and said, "Now I will go and finish my prescribed meditation."

"But, Narottama, it is so late," Nārāyaṇī protested. "It's time to sleep. Can we arrange beds for you and your esteemed friend?"

"Don't worry, Mā. Śyāmānanda and I will stay in the Chandi-maṇḍapa."

"No, that's not a suitable place. There's nothing there but a little cloth-covered stage – not even a bed to lie on. Why don't you – "

"Let him stay wherever he likes," Kṛṣṇānanda interrupted.

"Please don't worry about me," Narottama said, smiling warmly at his mother. "I will be fine." With this, he rose and respectfully left.

Kṛṣṇānanda and Nārāyaṇī returned to the palace, emotionally exhausted from the day's events yet bubbling with excitement at Narottama's return.

"Did you see how radiant his face was?" Kṛṣṇānanda marveled.

Nārāyaṇī smiled and nodded. "He didn't even look tired," she said. "After such a long journey I would have thought he would be exhausted."

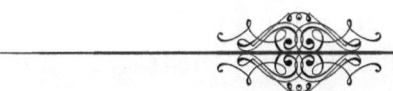

"Our son is not an ordinary person," Kṛṣṇānanda said proudly. "He seems to have completely conquered the demands of his body. And simply by listening to him, the village people forgot their bodily existence as well."

After a few moments of thoughtful silence, Nārāyaṇī sighed deeply. "He will never live with us again," she said softly. "The temple is his home now."

"That's true," Kṛṣṇānanda agreed. "He has become the son of everyone in this world. We can't tie him up and keep him in our house. What a sin that would be! The world would be bereft of his wonderful association. We should simply be happy that he is here with us again."

Comforted, Nārāyaṇī smiled gently. "I know you're right," she said. "I am very proud of him."

Everyone in Kheturi came to know about the theft of the manuscripts. But Narottama and Śyāmānanda had agreed that they shouldn't discuss the tragedy. It was too devastating to talk about. To distract themselves from their own turmoil about it, Narottama and Śyāmānanda threw themselves into their preaching work. Swarms of people now crowded around them every day, eager to hear their lectures and *kīrtanas*. News of Narottama's return had also spread, and now people from neighboring villages flocked to Kheturi for his *darśana*. The seeds of *bhakti* sprouted quickly.

One afternoon, as Narottama sat with Śyāmānanda chanting *japa*, they saw King Santosh and another man hurriedly walking toward them. Santosh excitedly called out, "A messenger has come from Viṣṇupura with a letter for you."

Narottama's heart leaped – it must be from Śrīnivāsa Ācārya! He jumped to his feet to greet the man.

The messenger fell at the feet of the two saints, then stood up and handed Narottama the letter. Trembling, Narottama opened the envelope and read aloud, "I am happy to inform you that the books have been found undamaged." An immense wave of relief surged through Narottama's body and he heaved a great sigh.

"They are safe! The books are safe!" Śyāmānanda cried out in delight. "*Jaya! Jaya! Haribol!*"

A broad smile broke over King Santosh's face and the messenger clapped his hands in delight.

Narottama's face beamed as he continued reading, "After some careful investigations, I began to suspect that King Birhambir of Viṣṇupura had something to do with the theft, so I went to his court. What happened there is a long story, but I eventually found out that the king was indeed the culprit. His astrologer had informed him that our traveling party was carrying immense wealth. Believing we were carrying jewels or gold, he sent dacoits to steal the trunks. The king realized his mistake when he opened the trunk and found only manuscripts. On closer inspection he understood they were sacred scriptures and became fearful of the grave sinful reactions he would incur from stealing them. The king is basically pious, and he was relieved to return the books to me when I arrived at his palace."

"Kṛṣṇa's grace," Śyāmānanda sighed.

"Listen, there's more," Narottama said. "Since then, the King as well as his wife and son have become my disciples. As a result, most of the residents of Viṣṇupura have accepted the path of *bhakti.*"

"Śrīnivāsa was right," Śyāmānanda said. "The manuscripts were stolen because the Lord wanted to bestow His mercy on the fortunate residents of Viṣṇupura."

Raising his hands in the air, Narottama began to sing in jubilant celebration, and Śyāmānanda danced joyfully.

Their excitement was contagious, and the messenger joined Śyāmānanda in twirling about happily.

Tears of joy trickled down the face of King Santosh as he watched their delightful display of relief and happiness.

The black clouds of devastation that had hung over Narottama's and Śyāmānanda's heads since the theft of the manuscripts dispersed and the bright sun of Śrī Caitanya Mahāprabhu's glorious mission shone brilliantly again. Narottama turned to Santosh. "Please arrange a five-day festival to celebrate this wonderful occasion."

"It will be my greatest pleasure," Santosh replied happily.

"And now," Narottama said, "I shall write a letter to Śrīnivāsa Ācārya and one to King Birhambir as well.

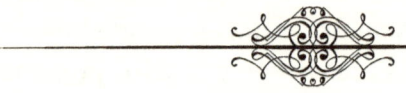

Narottama was chanting alone in a secluded grove a few days later when Śyāmānanda quietly approached him, his face downcast. "Is something wrong?" Narottama asked.

"The books are safe," Śyāmānanda said.

"Yes," Narottama said, "but that's cause for celebration, not for feeling glum."

"I feel it's time for me to leave for Orissa," Śyāmānanda said. "I have already overstayed my visit in Kheturi, and yet I can't bear the thought of being apart from you."

Narottama's heart went out to Śyāmānanda. He too dreaded the thought of parting with his dear friend. They had been close companions for so many years that a deep bond of spiritual affection had grown between them. But Śyāmānanda was right – it was time for him to carry Mahāprabhu's message to the people of Orissa.

"Yes," Narottama clasped his friend's hand reassuringly, "you should not delay any longer. I will miss your company immensely, but perhaps, by the Lord's grace, we will meet again soon." Then, with a broad smile, he added, "Don't worry. Kṛṣṇa will give you the strength to carry out your preaching mission."

Śyāmānanda's face brightened, and he said, "I'll leave tomorrow."

News of Śyāmānanda's imminent departure spread quickly. The following morning the entire village, including King Santosh and his guards, showed up at the Chandi-maṇḍapa to bid Śyāmānanda farewell.

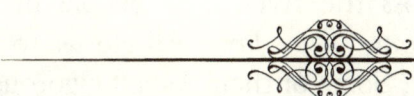

Although a few people tried to convince him to stay in Kheturi, Śyāmānanda was resolute. He left the Chandi-maṇḍapa with Narottama by his side, heading toward the Padmavatī River. The residents of Kheturi followed them all the way to the riverbank.

Reaching the boat that was to ferry Śyāmānanda, Narottama handed his friend a small pouch. "Rāja Santosh sent this for you for your travel expenses. He also sent a man to escort you to Orissa."

Śyāmānanda nodded, humbly accepting the arrangements King Santosh had made. He then knelt and then prostrated himself at Narottama's feet. Narottama immediately dove to the ground to return the obeisances. When the friends rose to their feet, they embraced tightly. Turning to the affectionate crowd of onlookers, Śyāmānanda bowed his head and pressed his palms together, offering *prāṇaṁs* to them all.

Everyone present, including King Santosh, then offered their prostrated obeisances to the *sādhu* for the last time. The King took hold of Śyāmānanda's arm and helped him into the boat. When Śyāmānanda and his escort were comfortably seated, the boatman planted his pole in the riverbed and heaved the boat away from the shore.

Tears rolled down Narottama's cheeks as the small craft glided out across the river. The people lining the riverbank called out, "*Jaya*! *Jaya*! All glories to Śrī Śyāmānanda Prabhu!" Some of them waved vigorously, while others simply cried. Narottama stood motionless, his heart aching as he watched his beloved friend disappear from sight.

After Śyāmānanda's departure, Narottama preached vigorously in Kheturi and the surrounding villages. He gathered a group of expert Vaiṣṇava musicians, and together they flooded the area with melodious *kṛṣṇa-kīrtana.*

Narottama also spent time composing his own songs, expertly conveying the profound philosophy of Kṛṣṇa consciousness in a way even the common man could understand. Each of his songs, though written in simple Bengali language, was like a condensed *Veda* – filled with the deepest wisdom and the highest devotional sentiments.

Drawn by Narottama's enchanting *kīrtana*, gentle demeanor, and profound spiritual insight, people began to flock to Kheturi, eager to take shelter of Ṭhākura Mahāśaya. Thus, within a short time, Narottama gathered many followers and disciples. His fame spread even further when his cousin, the powerful and influential King Santosh Datta, took initiation from him.

Despite all his apparent success, a desire to visit Navadvīpa dhāma began to grow in Narottama. Apprehensively, he approached his parents, his palms joined in supplication. "I would like to go on a pilgrimage to visit Śrī Caitanya Mahāprabhu's pastime places. I want to see the Lord's house and meet whichever of His associates are still alive. If you give me permission I will go; if you do not, however, I will stay here in Kheturi."

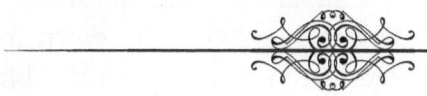

Narottama carefully watched his parents' reaction to his request. He noticed that his father waited to see how his mother would respond.

Nārāyaṇī sat pensive for a few moments, then gently smiled. "Yes, of course you can go. We cannot hold you here like a prisoner. But please, this time, come back soon."

"Of course, I also agree, Narottama," Kṛṣṇānanda said. "But I would like to send some escorts with you."

"That is kind of you to offer," Narottama said, "but there is really no need."

"Just a few soldiers and guards for protection," Kṛṣṇānanda said.

Narottama laughed lightly and said, "Kṛṣṇa is the only protection I need. I want to go alone."

"All right," Kṛṣṇānanda relented. "Just hurry back soon."

Though this time there was no need for secrecy, the following morning, with the moon still hanging full and low, Narottama silently slipped out of Kheturi. This was his first time travelling alone in many years, and he savored the bittersweet memory of his solitary journey to Vṛndāvana, all those years ago. Pre-dawn mist covered the acres of green paddy fields, and the birds were silent. With anticipation illuminating his heart, Narottama smiled, and walked on toward Navadwipa.

ānanda-mūrcchāvanipāta-bhāta-
dhūlī-bharālaṅkṛta-vigrahāya
yad-darśanaṁ bhāgya-bhareṇa tasmai
namo namaḥ śrīla-narottamāya

I repeatedly offer my respectful obeisances to Śrīla Narottama Dāsa Ṭhākura, who would faint in bliss and fall to the ground, decorating his body with great quantities of dust. To have *darśana* of him in this way is the summit of good fortune.

Narottama-prabhor-āṣṭaka, Verse 5

Chapter Five

Pilgrimage

Navadvīpa

Perspiring under the midday sun, Narottama made his way down a forest path, following the course of the Ganges. After many long hours, he pushed through the thick leaves into a clearing. He scanned the horizon carefully. In the distance, he spotted the faint outline of a town, a hazy glimmer above the acres of brilliant green paddy fields. His heart pounded as he realized that it must be the crest jewel of all holy places, Śrī Navadvīpa-dhāma. His body quivered and tears came to his eyes. Dropping to the ground he offered his obeisances and called out, "All glories to the residents of Navadvīpa, the associates of Lord Gaurāṅga!"

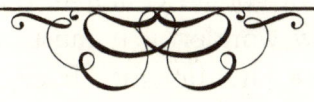

Rising to his knees and joining his palms in prayer, he gazed at the distant temple spires and towering date palms. He remembered how many nights he had lain awake in bed, dreaming of visiting the pleasure grounds of Lord Gaurāṅga's pastimes. Suddenly anxiety gripped his mind: "Even the greatest of demigods are unable to comprehend the glories of Navadvīpa, so how can I, an insignificant and fallen living being, possibly understand Mahāprabhu's sacred *dhāma*?

"Oh Nadia!" he pleaded, "give me your mercy, for without your mercy I cannot understand anything about the transcendental nature of Śrī Caitanya Mahāprabhu's appearance and activities."

With eagerness and trepidation, Narottama rushed toward the town, his heart pounding in his chest. The sweet fragrance of golden champak flowers drifted on the breeze. "How wonderful it must have been when the Lord was here," he thought. "Every day would have been a festival for the fortunate residents of Navadvīpa because they would have seen Śrī Gauracandra daily."

As he came closer to the outskirts of the town, Narottama suddenly slowed. His face darkened, and the sandy path suddenly felt hot and harsh beneath his feet. "What am I rushing for?" he called out to the wind. "What do I expect to find in Navadvīpa now? What joy will I find here? The Lord of my life is no longer present!"

Tears burned at the corners of Narottama's eyes. "Baby Nimāi no longer crawls in Jagannātha Miśra's courtyard," he lamented, "and Śacī-mātā will not be cooking for her beloved Nimāi. I won't see Nimāi Paṇḍita teaching his students grammar or bartering with Kholāvecā Śrīdhara for banana leaves. The waters of the Gaṅgā must now be bereft of the sporting and splashing of moon-like Śrī Nityānanda Prabhu. And oh! That oasis of ecstatic *saṅkīrtana* –the house of Śrīvasa Thakur– will be silent!"

Anguished, Narottama bellowed, "I missed everything! All these treasured scenes have vanished! Oh, why was I born too late? If only I would have taken birth a few years earlier I could have witnessed all these glorious pastimes with my own eyes. I could have taken the dust of the Lord's lotus feet on my head! Oh most merciful Śrī Caitanya Mahāprabhu, why have you sent me into this world now? Why have you brought me here? What can I see in this place now that You are gone?"

Although Narottama grieved, his feet did not turn back. Crying pitifully, he continued his slow pace toward the town, his cascading tears falling all over the path as he walked.

Suddenly his reverie was broken by the tumultuous sound of chanting. Startled, he looked up and saw a massive *saṅkīrtana* party ecstatically dancing down the street before him. Devotees bustled here and there, some jubilantly dancing and singing, and some talking with wide smiles, about Śrī Gauracandra. The people of Navadvīpa appeared to be floating in an ocean of happiness!

The dark cloud in Narottama's heart dissipated as he stared with wide open eyes at the astonishing scene. Two men passed in front of him, talking about the exquisite dancing of Śrī Gaurahari. Then a group of people rushed by. "Hurry," he heard one say. "I want to get to Jagannātha Miśra's house quickly."

"Jagannātha Miśra's house?" Narottama asked aloud, his heart soaring at the mention of this holy place. Swept up by the devotees' ecstasy Narottama called out, "Wait for me!"

But the moment he uttered these words the scene transformed. The joyful devotees disappeared and the chanting dissolved on the breeze. What had been a bustling town a moment before now appeared desolate, as if enveloped in the darkness of a moonless night.

Narottama gasped. He was rooted to the spot. Solemn villagers passed him as he stood paralyzed, a crushing realization dawning. "My cruel eyes have deceived me. What I saw a few moments ago, must have been the joyful Nadia of Mahāprabhu's time, and now, I see the terrible reality – this is a town of ghosts in his absence."

Narottama stumbled forward, finally sinking to the ground beneath a massive fig tree. "Oh my Lord," he cried out. "Why do You tease me so? If only I could see that incredible vision again. If only I could enter into it – become part of it."

Narottama added a silent prayer: "Please forgive me, Lord. How ungrateful I am to beg for more when You so kindly gave me a precious glimpse into the true nature of Your sacred *dhāma*. I realize that Navadvīpa is immersed in separation from You, yet by Your internal potency You kindly lifted the curtain for a moment so I could see the eternally joyous Nadia."

Narottama sat for a while beneath the tree, contemplating the extraordinary *darśana* he had been given. Meanwhile, a very old *brāhmaṇa* shuffled toward him. He stared at Narottama curiously, then came closer and asked, softly, "Who are you? You must be a devotee of Nimāi because simply by glancing at you my body has become cooled from the sun's scorching heat."

His reverie broken, Narottama bowed respectfully to the *brāhmaṇa* and introduced himself.

The old man's face lit up when he heard the name Narotttama. He eased his aged body down to sit beside Narottama. "Everyone in Gauda has heard of you and your journey from Vrāja with the Gosvāmīs' books," he said. "Is this your first visit to Navadvīpa?"

"Yes," Narottama answered. "I've come to see the pastime places of Śrīman Mahāprabhu. It would be the greatest honor to meet any of His associates."

"I suppose you're wondering what this place was like when Nimāi was here?" the old *brāhmaṇa* said, as he looked around.

Narottama nodded.

"I couldn't possibly describe the ecstasy permeating Nadia when Nimāi was here even if I talked for months."

The old man leaned back against the tree and stared up at the bright blue sky. He let out a long, deep, anguished breath. "Ah, what a fool I was," he said.

"I knew Nimāi from His very childhood, but I didn't understand that He was the Supreme Lord until much later." Tears welled up in his eyes as he reminisced. "But I always adored that boy. He was fascinating to look at with his luminous golden face, pinkish lips and beautiful elongated eyes. You could not help but be captivated by Him.

Narottama stared at the old man with amazement. "You actually knew Mahāprabhu?"

"Ah, yes, yes," he said, smiling brightly. "What a mischievous boy He was too. Every day He would enter a neighbor's house and steal something. He drank milk in one house, ate rice in another; and if He couldn't find anything to eat, He would break the clay pots. If there was a baby in the house Nimāi would pinch it and make it cry. If anyone saw him He ran away. If He was caught, He would grasp that person's feet and plead, 'Please let me go this one time. I promise I will never come back and steal anything. Please be merciful.' The *brāhmaṇa* chuckled as he added, "With that sweet smile, no one could be angry with Him for long."

Fascinated, Narottama listened with his heart and eyes overflowing. The old man seemed oblivious to his surroundings, so immersed was he in his joyful remembrance of Mahāprabhu's transcendental *līlā*.

"He was such a rascal," the man said, "that sometimes He would hide one of His friends and then tell the boy's father that his son had been kidnapped. While the family members were out searching for the boy, Nimāi would sneak into their homes and steal sweets for His friends."

Narottama laughed.

The *brāhmaṇa* continued. "Once," he said, his eyes twinkling with delight, "Nimāi heard Murāri Gupta giving an impersonal explanation of *Śrīmad-Bhāgavatam* to his disciples. Nimāi openly laughed at Murāri, who got angry and went home. But Nimāi made Murāri even more angry by following him home and passing urine where he ate. Then Nimāi told Murāri, 'According to your impersonal philosophy, everything is Brahman, so urine is nothing but Brahman!' " The old man slapped his thigh and laughed until tears streamed from his eyes.

"And what havoc He would wreak at the Gaṅgā! He would splash people on the shore and break their meditation. Or he would spit water at them, forcing them to bathe repeatedly for purification. Once, He stole someone's Śiva-liṅgam, and on another occasion, after one *brāhmaṇa* had made an *āsana* for Viṣṇu worship, Nimāi sat on it and ate all the offerings."

Narottama laughed heartily, greatly relishing the Lord's transcendental antics.

"Śacī-mātā tried her best to reform Nimāi, but He ignored her and continued making mischief with everyone in Navadvīpa. Even though He was a notorious tease, He was still the joy of Nadia. Everyone loved Him even more than their own children."

Narottama urged the *brāhmaṇa* to continue: "And later, when Nimāi grew up, what was He like then?

Please tell me everything! Your words are as sweet as water to my parched lips."

"Oh," the old man said, "then the people in Nadia saw Him as a proud and arrogant scholar. We called Him 'The Scholarly King of the City of Learning'."

"Why was that?" Narottama asked.

"Because He spoke with eloquence and His voice was musical. His speech was poetic because He interspersed it with the sparkling gems of His profound and imaginative thought. But after he went to Gaya and accepted initiation from Śrī Īśvarī Purī, He was a different person. His arrogance was gone along with the pride in His scholarship. He was extremely humble and would fall at the feet of any *kṛṣṇa-bhakta* and offer him menial service. Nimāi would carry their offerings for their *Gaṅgā-pūjā* or wring out their wet garments after they had bathed. He seemed always absorbed in trance. Whenever he met a Vaiṣṇava He would ask, 'Where is Kṛṣṇa? Where is Kṛṣṇa?' "

"How did that affect the villagers and His family and friends?" Narottama asked.

"His unparalleled humility surprised and moved both the *bhaktas* and the materialists. Even the jealous among Nadia's intelligentsia gave up their envy on seeing His piety, sincerity, and humility."

The old *brāhmaṇa* suddenly frowned, the smile fading from his lips as he shook his head. "And then He . . . He shocked us all. None of us could understand what drove Nimāi to accept the life of an ascetic." The *brāhmaṇa* shuddered. "I cannot bear to think of Him like that, with his head shaven and wearing a *kaupīna*. Everyone in Navadvīpa became miserable when young Nimāi left for Nīlācala. It seemed impossible to tolerate his separation. To mitigate our suffering, we found ourselves crying out His name constantly, and we talked continuously about His divine character. Even the wicked were disheartened by His absence. We were only consoled when we received news of Him from pilgrims coming from Nīlācala."

Narottama nodded. He understood the pain of separation.

A flush of gloom shadowed the *brāhmaṇa's* somber face. "Then the terrible day came when we heard about Nimāi's sudden disappearance in Nīlācala. It was an intolerable shock for all of us living in Nadia. The misery of the devotees here was beyond description. Unable to bear His separation, many of His companions left this mortal world or moved away – Śrīvasa Paṇḍita, Advaita Ācārya . . . Day by day since then, Nadia has sunk deeper into despair. Now this same Nadia, which was flooded with love of God during Mahāprabhu's time, is flooded only by the tears of His devotees, who are lost without His association." Choked with emotion, the venerable *brāhmaṇa* could no longer speak.

Narottama and the elderly *brāhmaṇa* sat silently side-by-side, crying softly, deeply immersed in thoughts of their beloved Lord.

After some time, the old *brāhmaṇa* shook off his despondent mood. Sitting straighter he smiled brightly and turned to Narottama, "Under this very tree Nimāi studied the scriptures encircled by His companions, like the moon surrounded by the stars." Lowering his voice, he confided, "One day not long ago, I actually saw Nimāi sitting right here beneath this tree surrounded by many disciples. I was so overjoyed that I fainted. When I regained consciousness, He was gone. From that day, I understood that Nimāi and His companions are always here in Navadvīpa and can reveal themselves whenever they desire. Now I come to this fig tree every day in hopes of seeing Him again."

Narottama nodded gravely, deeply touched by the *brāhmaṇa's* confidential disclosure.

"Now, my son," the old Vaiṣṇava said cheerfully, "you must go to Jagannātha Miśra's house. There are still a few intimate companions of the Lord living in that area, and they will be overjoyed to meet you."

"Is Mahāprabhu's house nearby?" Narottama asked softly.

"Not far. Just go straight down this road," he said, pointing to a sandy path.

Narottama hesitated. Though only moments before, he and the old *brāhmaṇa* had been utter strangers, a profound affection had sprung up between them. Filled with grateful love, Narottama fell at the feet of the *brāhmaṇa*. "It's not possible to thank you for the supreme joy you have brought me. Please give me your blessings so I may one day become a genuine devotee of Śrī Caitanya Mahāprabhu."

Smiling affectionately, the elderly Vaiṣṇava embraced Narottama warmly and sent him on his way.

Narottama hurried down the road, following directions other residents gave him, until he found Jagannātha Miśra's house. Arriving before the small thatched cottage, he stared in awe, not sure whether he felt qualified to take another step forward. He reverentially touched the old bamboo gate in front of the house, silently marveling: "This is the actual place! Śrī Caitanya passed through this gate every day! And there is the veranda where He sat with Murāri and Śrīvasa." Tears streamed from his eyes and the hairs on his body stood on end. Shivering with ecstasy, he stood motionless with his hand on the gate, calling out, "Gaurāṅga, Gaurāṅga!"

Narottama felt a hand on his shoulder and turned to see an aged *brahmacārī* smiling at him, his face bright with the light of a long saintly life. In a voice filled with emotion, the *brahmacārī* asked "Are you Narottama?"

Shocked to be recognized, Narottama nodded. "How did you know?"

"When I saw the transcendental symptoms of ecstasy that manifest in your body when you simply looked at Mahāprabhu's house, I knew you must be the disciple of Lokanātha Gosvāmī we've heard so much about." The old *brahmacārī* drew Narottama into an embrace. "My son, we have been waiting for years to meet you."

Narottama was astounded to learn that devotees in Navadvīpa were expecting him. "Who are you? And who told you I was coming?"

The old *brahmacārī* smiled again and said, "Long ago, when Śrī Caitanya Mahāprabhu traveled to Rāmakeli, He fell into an ecstatic trance and loudly called out your name. At that time, He predicted your arrival here. At last you have come. I am Śuklāmbara Brahmacārī."

When Narottama heard the name of one of Śrī Caitanya Mahāprabhu's most intimate associates, he fell to his knees in awe. Sweeping up dust from the spot where Śuklāmbara Brahmacārī stood, he sprinkled it on his head.

As Narottama rose, Śuklāmbara took him by the arm. "Come with me," he said, excitedly ushering him toward the house. "I will show you Mahāprabhu's house."

Trembling uncontrollably, Narottama followed Śuklāmbara. As soon as they entered the sacred residence

Narottama dropped to his knees, crying, "*Ha* Gaurāṅga!" With great reverence he rubbed his palms along the floor, gathered dust, and smeared it all over his body.

He was filled with wonder as he gazed around at the bare, darkened room. "It's impossible to comprehend what's before me," he whispered, his dark lashes brimming heavy with tears. "This is where Śrī Caitanya Mahāprabhu lived, walked, and played. These fortunate floors felt the touch of my beloved Lord's lotus feet."

Standing up, he shuffled forward a few steps, and placed his forehead and hands against the wall. "And these walls witnessed everything."

Narottama's hair stood on end and his body shivered as he remembered the transcendental pastimes that had taken place there. He said, "But now there is only silence . . . If only I could have seen . . . If only I could have been here . . . " His heart burned with regret and longing.

He suddenly realized there was someone else in the room. Stepping closer, he saw a hunched old man in a corner. Slow desolate tears ran from his unblinking eyes and dripped steadily onto the dusty floor, yet he shone with a brilliant effulgence. Narottama could hear the heavy sighs that were escaping his lips as he whispered, "Mahāprabhu, Mahāprabhu," again and again.

"This is Śrī Īśāna," Śuklāmbara said. "He was Śacī-mātā's servant. No one can understand his fortune. He lived in this house with the Lord, sharing in all His childhood pastimes. Nimāi was so attached to Īśāna that He wouldn't go anywhere without him. Nimāi was also Īśāna's life and soul. After Śacī-mātā left this world, Īśāna humbly served Śrī Viṣṇupriya Devī for many years."

Narottama's knees buckled, and he nearly fainting at the thought that he was now in the presence of Śacī-mātā's personal servant. Falling flat, he lay on the ground at Īśāna's feet for a long time. Eventually he pulled himself up to his knees. With immense reverence he stared speechlessly at Īśāna Ṭhākura's radiant, wrinkled face.

Śuklāmbara spoke softly into Īśāna's ear. "Narottama of Kheturi has come."

Śrī Īśāna opened his eyes. Raising his aged, stooped body, he extended thin arms to embrace Narottama tightly. His penetrating eyes glistened with tears. "My dear son," he said in a quivering voice, "today my desires have all been fulfilled, for I have had the opportunity to meet you. I have lived in hope that I would see you one day. Otherwise, I would have given up this body long ago."

Placing his soft palms on Narottama's cheeks Śrī Īśāna affectionately studied Narottama's face. "You remind me so much of Nimāi with your lotus eyes and golden complexion," he said lovingly. "We have been burning in a fire of separation from Śrī Caitanya. Now you have come to soothe our aching hearts."

"Soothe you?" Narottama was aghast. "You are the personal servant of the Lord! How dare I stand in your presence! I am so low. You should not even touch me." Saying this, Narottama bent low in reverence.

"Come here, Narottama," Śuklāmbara said, walking toward the adjoining room. "See? These are Mahāprabhu's shoes."

Narottama's body quivered at the sight. Wracked beyond bearing between the extremes of joy and grief, he took hold of the shoes and pressed them to his chest, wetting them with his tears.

"And here is His *chādar*, and these are His ankle bells." Śuklāmbara led Narottama through the house, showing him everything. "This is the bed where He used to sit, and this His drinking cup." Śuklāmbara's voice trembled with emotion, "We have left everything exactly as it was when the Lord was here."

"Over here is Mahāprabhu's sleeping place," he said, gesturing to a corner of the room. "And over here is where Viṣṇupriya would chant *japa*. After Mahāprabhu left home, she would sit here for hours every day, fully immersed in calling out the name of her beloved Lord. For each round she chanted, she would set aside one grain of rice. When she had finished chanting, she would cook that tiny pile of rice and offer it to Mahāprabhu. That is all she would accept for *prasāda*. When Śacī Mātā left this mortal world, Viṣṇupriya would not leave this room. The door was always closed. Īśāna would hand her water through a gap in the door."

Listening intently, Narottama followed Śuklāmbara through the house, moving silently and slowly, as if to avoid disturbing the sanctity of the place. Knowing the Lord's personal paraphernalia to be nondifferent from Him, Narottama gently touched and bowed to each sacred item with great devotion.

As they completed the tour, another elderly devotee entered the room and was introduced as Dāmodara Paṇḍita. Eager to show Narottama around the Navadvīpa area, Damodara Paṇḍita and Śuklāmbara escorted their guest outside and led him down a path two hundred meters to the north, to the house of Śrīvasa Ṭhākura.

The two brothers of Śrīvasa Ṭhākura, Śrīpati and Śrīnidhi, greeted Narottama with enthusiasm. They took him to the courtyard where the *saṅkīrtana* movement began.

Standing in the now-silent courtyard, Narottama felt his heart erupt with emotion. "Oh, why couldn't I have taken birth a little earlier?" he cried. Falling on the ground he lamented, "If only I could have been here. If only I could have seen the ecstatic *kīrtana* performed in this spot." Overcome with intense feelings of separation, Narottama cried uncontrollably. "But I am so unfortunate," he sobbed. "I was not allowed entrance to these precious moments."

Understanding Narottama's emotional state, Śrīnidhi gently took him by the hand and lovingly guided him to a seat in the shade. After giving Narottama a drink of water, he described the extraordinary *kīrtanas* that had taken place at that spot. "It was unlike anything we'd ever known," Śrīnidhi said, his voice trembling. "Mahāprabhu was the soul of the *kīrtana*. The tunes we sang were simple, yet indescribably sublime. When Mahāprabhu stood up and started to dance, His companions, electrified, would leap up to join Him. Dancing with His arms extended and His eyes turned upward, Nimāi would cry out, '*Hari bol! Hari bol!*'

During the *kīrtana* the devotees were often unable to suppress their deep emotions," Śrīnidhi said. "They would roll on the ground or embrace one another. Sometimes they would cry and then laugh and then cry again, or loudly call out in unison, '*Hari bol! Hari! Hari!*' Sometimes they even fell unconscious. Everyone swam in a sea of *bhakti*."

Captivated, Narottama envisioned each wonderful pastime in his mind.

"Once," Śrīpati said, "while Śrīvasa was worshiping the Deity in the temple here, Śrī Caitanya Mahāprabhu knocked on the door. 'Who are you meditating on?' He called out in His booming voice. 'He whom you are worshiping is standing here before you.' When my brother opened the door he saw the resplendent form of Lord Viṣṇu before him. Currents of joy ran through his body and he fell into a trance of ecstasy. Barely able to catch his breath in his excitement, he yelled for the rest of the family members to come, and after gathering together the articles for worship, he performed *ārati* to the Lord while offering continuous prayers."

Finding comfort in expressing both their love and their grief, the two brothers recounted one incident after another that had taken place in the house of Śrīvasa Ṭhākura. Narottama, Śuklāmbara, and Damodara Paṇḍita relished every detail. The group spent the entire day absorbed in delightful pastimes, barely noticing that the sun had set.

That evening, after returning to Mahāprabhu's house with Śuklāmbara and Dāmodara Paṇḍita, Narottama lay on the floor inside and stared up at the underside of the thatched roof, rapt in thoughts of Śrī Caitanya until even the night birds calling in the trees had fallen silent. His heart swelled with gratitude as he pondered how merciful Śrī Caitanya Mahāprabhu was to allow such a fallen soul to enter His holy *dhāma*. He yearned for the Lord's association with an unprecedented passion. "What could be more painful than to see these pastime places without seeing the Lord Himself here? It's like looking at an empty stage without the actors." Narottama eventually drifted off to sleep, these thoughts on his mind.

Late in the night, to appease Narottama's lamenting heart, Śrī Caitanya Mahāprabhu and His associates appeared in a dream. They were chanting and dancing ecstatically, just as they had done in the house of Śrīvasa long ago. Śrī Caitanya Mahāprabhu spun like a golden whirling firebrand. Śrī Nityānanda leapt ecstatically by His side, surrounded by Śrī Gadādhara, Śrī Advaita Ācārya, Murāri Gupta, and many other exuberant devotees.

Having witnessed this extraordinary vision, Narottama felt that his heart, which had been burning in the fire of separation, was cooled and soothed. When he awoke, he was filled with the joy of meeting his beloved.

The following morning, Narottama met many more devotees. He visited numerous places where Śrī Caitanya Mahāprabhu had played, sat, wandered, and performed *kīrtana*. Hours passed like minutes as he listened to descriptions of Mahāprabhu's pastimes from the mouths of the devotees who had personally witnessed them. Narottama marveled at the depth of attachment he saw in their timeworn but animated faces. He was reminded of the wonder Uddhava experienced when he saw the love the *gopīs* had for Śrī Kṛṣṇa. The devotees of Navadvīpa, who had once danced and conversed personally with Śrī Caitanya, were now barely alive in His absence. The only panacea for their burning hearts was constant remembrance and glorification of the Lord.

Narottama understood their pain all too well, and reverence and respect swelled in his heart. He knew that their lamentation and tears had nothing to do with mundane feelings of sorrow but were due to profound, ecstatic love for God. Such feelings of separation appear like severe tribulation, but internally they fill the heart with sublime joy.

Narottama could have listened endlessly to their accounts, but the Navadvīpa devotees were equally anxious to hear from him. They had waited years to meet this effulgent young devotee overflowing with *prema* whom Mahāprabhu had once glorified. They peppered him with questions about his life in Vṛndāvana, about the writings of the Gosvāmīs, and about his preaching.

Narottama carefully answered their enquiries and described as far as possible the deep secrets contained in the Gosvāmīs' *bhakti* literature.

The devotees listened attentively, finding incredible relief and happiness in Narottama's company. They said his radiant features and ceaseless outpouring of profound spiritual emotions reminded them of Śrī Caitanya Mahāprabhu. They claimed that in his presence it seemed as if the clock had turned back and Śrī Caitanya was again enacting His pastimes, bringing them the joy of union once more. The only difference they saw was that Narottama was crying for Śrī Caitanya whereas Śrī Caitanya had been crying for Kṛṣṇa.

As Narottama and the residents of Navadvīpa bathed in the delight of one another's company, days passed rapidly. Though his heart beat wildly at the thought of leaving Navadvīpa, Narottama approached Śuklāmbara Brahmacārī and humbly asked for his permission to continue his pilgrimage to Jagannātha Purī.

Śuklāmbara's kind eyes reflected both the love and sadness in his heart. "Mahāprabhu kept us alive only to see you, and now your visit has given us great consolation. It's made us forget our grief for a while. But there are many more devotees waiting to meet you, so it's right that you should go. By Śrī Caitanya's wish you will certainly execute His plans and perform wonderful service."

Narottama blinked back tears.

One by one, other devotees gathered to bid Narottama good-bye. A painful lump grew in Narottama's throat and his eyes burned as he bent reverentially to touch each devotee's feet. As he said farewell to the last devotee, he collapsed in the courtyard of Mahāprabhu's house and cried uncontrollably. Leaving was unbearable.

But he had to go. A gentle breeze blew, reminding him of the ocean at Purī that awaited him. Checking his emotions, he picked himself up and began to walk along the road that led south toward Śāntipura. After a few minutes, the road began to curve, and the villagers that stood watching him leave would soon disappear from sight. He cast one last glance over his shoulder, as the sad faces of Navadvīpa followed him with tear-filled eyes.

Jagannātha Purī

Narottama's pilgrimage took him through the charming village of Śāntipura, where he worshiped the feet of Advaita Ācārya's son, Śrī Acyutānanda. After relishing the association of Advaita's many followers, he proceeded to Harinadī, where he crossed the Ganges and entered the village of Ambikā Kālnā. There he met Śyāmānanda's spiritual master, Hṛdaya Caitanya, and was fortunate to receive the *darśana* of his famous Gaura-Nitāi deities. From there Narottama went to Kardaha, where he was greeted with great love and enthusiasm by Śrī Vasudhā and Śrī Jāhnavā Mātā, Nityānanda Prabhu's wives, and their son, Śrī Vīracandra Prabhu.

Thus, traveling from one village to another and meeting many of Mahāprabhu's associates Narottama remained in a continual state of divine ecstasy. He cried, shouted, laughed, and even fainted as he listened to the great souls recount their pastimes with the Lord. With every anecdote, Narottama's feelings of separation from Śrī Caitanya Mahāprabhu deepened, and he found himself breaking out in spontaneous songs of lamentation and hankering for the Lord's association.

Lost in thought of Śrī Caitanya, Narottama then headed toward Jagannātha Purī, following the same path Śrī Caitanya Mahāprabhu Himself had taken years before. At night, he stopped in the same villages the Lord had chosen to rest in, and in each place he discussed *kṛṣṇa-kathā* with the local people just as Mahāprabhu had done.

The simple village people were quickly taken by Narottama's magnetic spirituality and handsome features, and they often tried to convince him to remain with them. Each morning when Narottama prepared to resume his journey, crowds of people swarmed around him, following him as he walked. Narottama often found it difficult to disperse these crowds, but eventually, with sweet words, he would manage to bid them farewell and continue on his way alone.

In one village, Narottama met an elderly gentleman who had met Śrī Caitanya Mahāprabhu. The man invited Narottama to sit with him. "Come, my boy," he said enthusiastically, "let me tell you about the wonderful things I saw with my own eyes."

Eagerly Narottama took a seat next to this fortunate soul and listened as the old man shared his remembrances.

"When Śrī Caitanya Mahāprabhu and His associates came to this village on their way to Jagannātha Purī," the man said, "I was amazed to see that the Lord walked with the gait of a stalking, maddened lion. I couldn't take my eyes off His beautiful golden form. He appeared oblivious to his surrounding – as if the land, water, and paths were of no consequence. His devotees – Nityānanda, Gadādhara, Mukunda, Govinda, Jagadānanda, and Brahmānanda – stayed by His side to protect Him from harm. When He sat with the devotees to respect *prasāda*, I saw that He ate hardly a morsel. He was so anxious to reach Purī that in the middle of the meal He got up and, with a thunderous roar, yelled, 'How far is Jagannātha Purī? How far is Jagannātha Svāmī?' Seeing the Lord's impatience, Mukunda started to sing, and the Lord began to dance."

Narottama's smile broadened when he heard of the Lord's eagerness to reach Jagannātha Purī.

The man's face beamed as he remembered the sight. "The residents of our village then had the rarest treat – the Supreme Lord, the hero of Vaikuṇṭha, dancing before our eyes. As He spun around and around, tears gushed from His eyes like the rushing currents of the Gaṅgā during the monsoon. We were all drenched by them."

Narottama suddenly cried out, "Why couldn't I have been here to see such a sight?" Then, bowing at the feet of the man, Narottama murmured, "You are the most fortunate person."

The old man gently lifted Narottama and continued his narration with barely a pause. "Just a few miles down this road," he said, pointing to a nearby path, "Śrī Caitanya Mahāprabhu and his associates were stopped from proceeding toward Nīlācala. A man at the tollgate demanded a tax, and he wouldn't let them pass if they didn't pay it."

Narottama's face must have registered his incredulity that anyone would dare to stop the Lord, for the old man added, "But when the tax collector saw the Lord's grave, imposing figure, he was impressed and asked, 'How many men are with You?'

"The Lord replied, 'I do not have anyone in this world, and I do not belong to anyone. I am all alone. The entire world is mine.' Saying this, the Lord began to shed incessant tears, which flowed in streams down His cheeks.

"The taxman said, 'Oh master, You may kindly leave. But I will not release the others until I have received full payment."

"What did the Lord do?" Narottama asked.

The old man's voice shook with emotion. "He left the devotees and, after traveling a short distance alone, sat down. He hung His head and tears welled in His eyes. The devotees watched him from the other side of the tollgate, desperately worried that they would be separated from their Lord. The taxman watched with them, and even his stone-like heart couldn't fail to be melted by the Lord's weeping. In wonderment, the taxman said, 'That *sannyāsī* is certainly no ordinary person. It's impossible for an ordinary human being to shed so many tears!'

"He looked again at the devotees and asked, 'Tell me clearly who you are. Whose associates are you?'

"They replied, 'That *sannyāsī* is our master. You must have heard of Him. His name is Śrī Kṛṣṇa Caitanya. We are His servants.' They all then began crying tears of divine love for their Lord.

"The tax collector was now dumbfounded. Overwhelmed by the depth of their mood and purified by their association, he also began to cry. He hastened toward the sitting figure of the Lord and threw himself on the ground like a rod before the Lord's lotus feet. Humbly he said, 'The great fortune of seeing You is the result of many millions of lifetimes of pious activities. Kindly forgive me for my offenses at Your feet. I pray You and your devotees will arrive safely in Nīlācala.'

"Lord Caitanya blessed the tax collector, and the party continued on its way."

Narottama touched the old man's feet with great reverence. He thanked him again and again for sharing the wealth of Mahāprabhu's transcendental *līlā*. Then he too eagerly resumed his journey.

Arriving at the Bhārgī River, about six miles north of Jagannātha Purī, Narottama took a refreshing bath in the crystal-clear water before entering the nearby village.

Many villagers gathered around to greet Narottama. Understanding him to be a follower of Śrī Caitanya Mahāprabhu, one of the village elders invited Narottama to hear the story of Lord Caitanya's visit there. Eager to know all the details of the Lord's travels, Narottama sat among the villagers and listened attentively as the man described how the Lord of Vaikuṇṭha had showered His merciful glance on these fortunate villagers.

"When Śrī Caitanya Mahāprabhu and his devotees arrived here, He went to bathe in the river, leaving His *sannyāsa* staff in Lord Nityānanda's hands. While He was gone, Nityānanda Prabhu broke the staff in three parts and threw it into the river. For this reason, we call the Bhārgī River *daṇḍa-bhaṅga-nadī* – the place where Śrī Caitanya's *sannyāsa* staff was broken. At the time, we couldn't understand why Nityānanda Prabhu would do such a thing, but later, a devotee of Mahāprabhu explained that Nityānanda Prabhu knew that Śrī Caitanya Mahāprabhu was the Supreme Lord Himself. He therefore considered His acceptance of *sannyāsa* to be useless. That's why he relieved the Lord of the trouble of carrying the staff. Nityānanda Prabhu reasoned that the Supreme Personality of Godhead is automatically a *parāmahāṁsa* – he doesn't need to carry a *sannyāsa-daṇḍa*."

Narottama offered his respects to the Bhārgī River, expressed his gratitude to the village elder, and continued along his way, eager to reach Jagannātha Purī as quickly as possible.

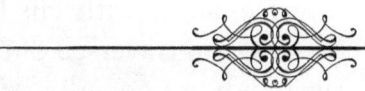

Narottama's heart raced as he entered the sacred township of Puruṣottama-kṣetra (Jagannātha Purī), the abode of the Supreme Person.[12] He shivered with delight to think that this tract of land, spreading over eighty square miles, was the Lord's eternal residence. It had always remained intact, unscathed – even during cosmic annihilations. Steeped in profound humility, Narottama regarded everything he saw there –the trees, birds, animals, and people– with awe and respect, remembering that all living beings, by the influence of the place, possess four-armed forms, though these are visible only to the most highly elevated beings.

Narottama offered silent prayers of appreciation for the sacred *dhāma*, which lies outside the jurisdiction of Yamarāja. In this place, even the simple act of sleeping is equivalent to deep meditation, or *samādhi*, and lying reposed offers one the same result as offering obeisances to the Deity.

Turning on to the wide Grand Road, Narottama caught sight of the towering red sandstone spire of the ancient temple of Lord Jagannātha. Collapsing to his knees, he stared in wonderment at the massive red flag waving above the famous eight-spoked Nīlācakra crowning the top of the temple dome. What a glorious sight!

Heart pumping with excitement, Narottama got up and rushed along the sandy avenue towards the huge temple complex. He was acutely aware that his feet now tread upon the same sanctified road that for centuries the Lord of the Universe, along with His brother Baladeva and sister Subhadrā, had traversed during the yearly Ratha-yātrā festival, riding upon their massive chariots, pulled by a multitude of loving devotees.

Approaching the main gateway to the temple, Narottama saw two huge statues of crouching lions on either side of the entrance: the Siṁha-dvāra. To the right, stood a stunning form of Lord Jagannātha, with a sign next to Him stating: *Patita-pāvana* – the saviour of the downtrodden and fallen. Narottama fell prostrate before the smiling Lord.

Rather than visit the temple, Narottama first sought directions to the house of Gopīnātha Ācārya,

Mahāprabhu's beloved associate and brother in-law of Sārvabhauma Bhaṭṭācārya.

Arriving at the house, Narottama called inside to announce his arrival. At once, the elderly Gopīnātha Ācārya leapt up to welcome Narottama with a warm-hearted embrace. With tender words, that venerable Vaiṣṇava invited Narottama to sit peacefully by his side.

"Narottama, everyone here is greatly eager to meet you. But, first take some rest, and after you can meet the devotees."

News of Narottama's arrival spread rapidly, and Gopīnātha Ācārya's house quickly filled up with devotees who had long hoped to meet Narottama. Everyone had questions to ask him, and he humbly answered them all, reporting everything about Vṛndāvana and details of his travels. Gopīnātha Ācārya arranged for *prasāda* to be brought from the temple. After respecting that succulent *mahā-prasāda,* Gopīnātha Ācārya asked-Kānāi Khuntia, his dear associate, to take Narottama for *darśana* of Lord Jagannātha.

Passing through the massive doorways of the ancient stone temple, Narottama was overcome with ecstasy and his whole body trembled. He broke ahead of his escort and ran toward Lord Jagannātha's main *darśana* hall. Catching sight of the massive forms of the Lord glowing before him, Narottama fainted. A knot of people quickly formed around him, both curious and concerned about this handsome young *sādhu* sprawled on the floor.

A few moments later Narottama opened his eyes. Oblivious to the people gawking at him, he sat up and his gaze fell on the Garuda *stambha.* Jumping up he ran to the *stambha,* where he stared entranced at the stone column topped by Garuda. "This is the very spot," he marveled, "where Śrī Caitanya Mahāprabhu stood day after day, taking *darśana* of the Lord." Narottama ran his fingers over the rough stone, envisioning how Śrī Caitanya had draped His long golden arms around the column as He gazed at Lord Jagannātha's exquisite form. Narottama looked down at the column's base. "And here is the crater created by the tears that continuously coursed down Śrī Caitanya Mahāprabhu's cheeks as he gazed lovingly at the Deities." Narottama touched the groove in the floor and then saw the imprint of Mahāprabhu's hand on the wall. He rested his head against that sacred impression. All this was unfathomable – too much for his mind to comprehend.

By now, a crowd had formed around Narottama, but he saw none of them. Wrapping his arms around the sacred column the way Śrī Caitanya Mahāprabhu had done previously, he gazed at the beautiful forms of Śrī Jagannātha, Baladeva, and Subhadrā. Tears flowed from his eyes in a constant stream, filling the bowl at the bottom of the *stambha* just as Śrī Caitanya's Mahāprabhu's tears had done long ago. Though staring intently at the Deities, Narottama could think of nothing but Śrī Caitanya Mahāprabhu. A simple phrase ran through his mind again and again: "I was unable to have the privilege of being with You when You stood here. Had I been born earlier I could have seen You! Why have You brought me here? What have I come to see?"

All the people who *had* seen Śrī Caitanya Mahāprabhu – both the local people and Lord Jagannātha's *pūjārīs* – were overjoyed to see this extraordinary saint who so utterly resembled Śrī Caitanya Mahāprabhu. Though Narottama felt such separation, Purī's residents, who had been missing the Lord for so long now, felt as if they were again in His company. For them, it was as if Mahāprabhu's pastimes were being replayed. Everyone was ecstatic.

Narottama didn't move from his spot for the entire afternoon, observing all three *ārati* ceremonies. Finally, Kānāi Khuntia urged Narottama to return to Gopīnātha Ācārya's house.

The following morning, Narottama went to the house of Kāśī Miśra, where he entered the hallowed Gambhīra, the small room where Śrī Caitanya Mahāprabhu lived during the last years of His manifest presence. The Lord had remained in a constant state of divine love during those years, manifesting the symptoms of ecstasy in separation from Kṛṣṇa. His state of mind was practically identical to that of Śrīmatī Rādhārāṇī when Uddhava came to Vṛndāvana to see the *gopīs*.

Narottama entered the room quietly and reverently fell to the ground, offering his obeisances to the sitting place where Śrī Caitanya Mahāprabhu had chanted *japa*. Placing his head on the *āsana*, he breathed in its fragrance. With profound respect, he touched the bed of *khandali* leaves where Mahāprabhu used to lie while Svarūpa Dāmodara massaged his legs. Crying incessantly, he offered respects to each and every thing in the room. Touching the Lord by touching His divine paraphernalia, Narottama felt His presence and his feelings of burning separation eased. Overcome with ecstasy, he rolled in the dust of that sacred site.

Walking on to the Ṭoṭā Gopīnātha temple, Narottama saw a very large, enchanting Deity with a shining black complexion seated cross-legged on a throne. Ṭoṭā

Gopīnātha, he realized, could defeat the pride of Cupid. Moved, Narottama lay prostrate before Him.

The temple priest brought a garland and placed it gently around Narottama's neck as Narottama stood. Then he ushered Narottama to Śrī Gadādhara Paṇḍita's seat, where Narottama offered his obeisances and cried, "Oh Gadādhara Paṇḍita Gosvāmī Prabhu, how unfortunate I am for not having had the opportunity to see you."

Narottama was startled by a heavy sigh. When someone asked, "Who is crying?" Narottama saw a small form in the shadows. Peering closer he saw a very, very old and very radiant Vaiṣṇava hunched over in a seat.

It is Māmu Gosvāmī," the *pūjārī* whispered to Narottama. "He is the foremost disciple of Vakreśvara Paṇḍita and an intimate associate of Mahāprabhu. He has been lying in a half-conscious state for months due to separation from the Lord." Turning to the venerable saint the *pūjārī* said, "This is Narottama, arrived from Nadia."

To Narottama's surprise, Māmu Gosvāmī rose. Though the Gosvāmī's body was obviously in a precarious state, he looked exceedingly happy to see Narottama. He embraced Narottama tightly, soaking him with his tears. "By the Lord's will," he said, "I have now seen you. I heard about you from visiting Vaiṣṇavas, and I yearned to see you. Now my desire has been fulfilled." Taking Narottama's hand, he led him to a secluded place, where they sat together. "Narottama," he said gently, "just look at this beautiful garden. So many blissful pastimes took place here. Right here, in this spot, my master, Gadādhara Paṇḍita, would sit and read from *Śrīmad-Bhāgavatam*. When he explained the verses, it appeared that many rivers of blissful spiritual love were flowing from his graceful mouth. Everyone yearned to hear him speak, and anyone who heard him even once would never forget the experience.

"Lord Gaurahari, the master of Gadādhara Paṇḍita's life, would sit beside him and listen to his sweet discourses. Oh Narottama, there is no end to the descriptions of the beautiful pastimes that took place here." Speaking with great love, Śrī Māmu Ṭhākura shared many of those confidential pastimes with Narottama.

After some time, Māmu Gosvāmī placed his wrinkled hands on Narottama's head, blessing him and dedicating him to the feet of Gopīnātha.

For several days Narottama wandered in Purī from one sacred site to another. He visited Haridāsa Ṭhākura's tomb, where Śrī Caitanya had danced holding His dear devotee's dead body. He went to the beach, where the Lord had danced to the rhythmic crashing of the waves. He saw where the Lord had run through the sand dunes, mistaking them for Govardhana Hill. And he visited the small parks the Lord had mistaken for Vṛndāvana.

One night, Narottama lay awake in Gopīnātha Ācārya's house. Thoughts of the Lord's divine pastimes ran incessantly through his head and he couldn't sleep. After many hours, he finally drifted off into a vivid revelatory dream: Narottama found himself standing on the large wide Grand Road not far from Lord Jagannātha's temple. He was stunned to see coming down the road three magnificent chariots. It was the Ratha-yātrā procession! In front of Lord Jagannātha's chariot Narottama saw Śrī Caitanya Mahāprabhu, surrounded by His associates, dancing in transcendental love. Narottama's eyes drank in the beauty of Mahāprabhu's transcendental form – His beautiful wide eyes that resembled fully blossomed lotuses, His reddish lips curved in a benevolent smile, His strong neck, broad chest, and thin waist, His graceful arms that extended below His knees, and His complexion of molten gold, which illuminated all directions. His limbs were trembling in ecstasy, and rivers of tears flowed from His eyes as he loudly chanted the holy names. Śrī Caitanya Mahāprabhu danced jubilantly among His loving devotees, as their melodic *saṅkīrtana* roared throughout the universe. All the intimate associates who had disappeared from the world years ago were there, dancing along with the Lord –Śrī Advaita Ācārya, Gadādhara Paṇḍita, Murāri Gupta, Haridāsa Ṭhākura, Rūpa Gosvāmī, Sanātana Gosvāmī, Kholāvecā Śrīdhara– all sang with full heart.

Narottama Ṭhākura stood transfixed, trying to take in every aspect of the extraordinary scene. He watched Lord Caitanya dancing with such love that all the devotees could do nothing but gaze at Him or dance with Him in utter joy. Huge crowds of pilgrims eagerly pushed forward to catch a glimpse of the Lord's beautiful dancing. Some demigods showered flowers, while others disguised themselves as humans to join in the extraordinary festival. Even those who were lame, blind, or deaf stumbled eagerly towards the *kīrtana*, determined to join in. Even stonehearted people wept when they heard the Lord's melodious chanting of the holy names, and animals and birds became restless with excitement.

As Narottama watched all this from the side of the road, weeping silently, Lord Caitanya left the *kīrtana* and approached him. The Lord took hold of Narottama's hands and embraced him. Then He said, "Narottama, go back to Kheturi. It is my desire that you establish a new type of *saṅkīrtana*. Through your *kīrtana* you will reveal

My teachings, mission, and pastimes to the world. I will empower your *kīrtana* to mesmerize the hearts of all who hear it. Those who are fortunate enough to take shelter of you will receive the most precious wealth of love of God. Now go back to Bengal and establish the *saṅkīrtana* of the holy name. Soon you will meet the son of Cirañjīva Sen, Rāmacandra Kavirāja. You two will become the most intimate friends. Together you will establish *kīrtana* and deliver thousands of people from the suffering of material existence. Go and deliver these souls, Narottama. Bring them into the *sampradāya* of love of God. I will always be with you and I will protect you."

Narottama fell at Lord Caitanya's feet and bathed them with his tears. Then each of the devotees, including Śrī Nityānanda Prabhu, Advaita Ācārya, and Śrīvasa Ṭhākura embraced Narottama and encouraged him to fulfill the Lord's mission.

Narottama jolted awake. Finding himself alone in the quiet of the night, he became perturbed, vacillating between the ecstatic joy of his meeting with the Lord and His associates and the unbearable sorrow of losing their company. He could do nothing but chant the holy name intensely through the remainder of the night.

Early the next morning Narottama went to Lord Jagannātha's temple for *ārati*. Gazing at Lord Jagannātha's smiling face, he prayed for permission to leave Śrī Kṣetra and the empowerment to fulfill the mission he had been given. As he offered his sincere prayer, a garland fell from Lord Jagannātha's body. The pujari caught it. Although there were hundreds of people in the temple, he brought it directly to Narottama and draped it around his neck. Narottama considered this to be Lord Jagannātha's confirmation that he should leave for Kheturi.

Narottama didn't speak of what had transpired when he returned to Gopīnātha Ācārya's house, but

Gopīnātha Ācārya knew. He said, "Narottama, the Lord wishes you to return to Kheturi to establish *kīrtana*."

Now there could be no doubt that it was time to leave Lord Jagannātha's abode. After Gopīnātha Ācārya consulted several local *paṇḍitas*, an auspicious date was fixed for Narottama to begin his journey.

The Purī devotees surrounded him on the day of his departure. Gopīnātha Ācārya clasped Narottama's hands. "We waited for so long to meet you," he said lovingly. "And our dreams were finally fulfilled!"

Deeply moved by all the love the devotees were showering on him Narottama bade a reluctant farewell, carrying a basket of Jagannātha *mahā-prasāda* to share with the people at home.

Narottama traveled north to Nṛsiṁhapura, where happily he was reunited with his dear friend Śyāmānanda. Narottama was delighted to find that Śyāmānanda was meeting with great success in his preaching. A few joyous days later, Narottama continued his journey.

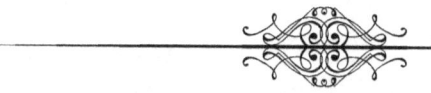

In Śrī Khaṇḍa Narottama was greeted by Śrī Raghunandana Ṭhākura and taken to meet Mahāprabhu's dear associate Śrī Narahari Sarkara Ṭhākura.[13] Though aged and usually absorbed in a solitary trance of remembering Mahāprabhu, Śrī Narahari was overhelmed with joy to meet Narottama. The other devotees of Śrī Khaṇḍa also gathered eagerly to greet Narottama, and they took him for *darśana* of the Śrī Gaurāṅga Deity.

The next morning, as Narottama was about to depart, Śrī Narahari Ṭhākura bid him farewell, saying, "I am so happy I had the chance to see you. In His absence, Mahāprabhu will distribute love of God through you. Many fallen souls will take shelter of you, and you will spread the Lord's ecstatic message by manifesting a new type of *kīrtana*. Don't worry about anything – all your desires will be fulfilled by Lord Caitanya's mercy." Then, his face becoming grave, Narahari Ṭhākura said, "Ah, how peaceful I feel to look on your face. I shall not have this opportunity a second time."

Unable to bear this sad thought, Narottama fell at the Ṭhākura's feet, tears streaming down his face. As he rose, the other devotees offered their farewell.

Ekacakrā

Narottama next passed through Katwa, where Śrī Caitanya had shaved off his beautiful locks and accepted the renounced order of life from Keśava Bhāratī. Then he went to Ekacakrā, Śrī Nityānanda Prabhu's birthplace. Meditating on the lotus feet of Nitāi, Narottama walked quickly toward that ancient town, where the Pāṇḍavas had lived during their exile and where Bhīma had slain the wicked Baka. Approaching the village, Narottama felt new energy when he was touched by the breeze rustling through the peepal trees that lined the road.

At the outskirts of Ekacakrā, an old, lame *brāhmaṇa* approached Narottama. "What is your name?" he asked, "and where have you come from?" Narottama felt a strange affinity with the old man – as if he already knew him.

"I am Narottama," he answered, "and I stay in Kheturi on the other side of the Padmavatī. I have been on pilgrimage in Gaura-maṇḍala and Jagannātha Purī for some time. Now I have come here to see the sacred places where Śrī Nityānanda Prabhu performed His pastimes."

The old *brāhmaṇa's* eyes twinkled. "Well, come along then," he said happily. "I know everything about this place. I'll show you around."

Unaccountably attracted to the wrinkled old man and pleased to have a guide, Narottama followed him into the village. At a small clump of bushes, the *brāhmaṇa* turned to Narottama. "This is where Nityānanda Prabhu and His friends used to enjoy grazing cows and calves, just like the *gopas* of Vṛndāvana."

Narottama pictured Nityānanda roaming the area with a club or plow on his shoulder. He bowed reverently, offering silent prayers to Śrī Nityānanda Prabhu.

A little further on, the guide pointed to another spot. "This is where Nityānanda Prabhu performed Rāma-*līlā*. That boy," the old man said chuckling lightly, "played the part of Lakṣmaṇa with such gusto that when He was shot down in battle, it appeared he had actually left His body. His friends called to Him, and then His elders tried to revive Him, but He remained motionless, His breath barely visible. No one could awaken him until the boy who played Hanuman in the drama realized he was supposed to bring the Himalayan herbs to rescue Him. Only when the play-herbs were brought did Nityānanda Prabhu return to consciousness." The old man seemed to delight in these memories. "Those boys," he laughed, "were constantly absorbed in reenacting the pastimes of Kṛṣṇa and Rāma. Day and night, they thought of nothing else."

The old man moved on, with Narottama following closely. "Let me show you the house of Hāḍāi Paṇḍita," he said. "This is where Nityānanda Rāya took birth."

Walking swiftly from place to place with a surprising agility, the *brāhmaṇa* animatedly pointed out one pastime site after another. "Here in this courtyard baby Nitāi used to play . . . and over here is where His *guru-karana* ceremony was performed. This is the Viṣṇu temple where He worshiped the Lord, and this is the spot where a visiting *sannyāsī* asked Hāḍāi Paṇḍita to give his son, Nityānanda, in charity. Hāḍāi Paṇḍita was forced to agree, but when the *sannyāsī* took Nityānanda away on that road over there, Hāḍāi Paṇḍita fell to the ground and rolled about in anguish. Padmavatī, Nityānanda Prabhu's mother, wailed loudly as her son departed and fell unconscious right there. The whole town followed them as they walked down the road. They were begging the *sannyāsī* not to take their Nitāi!"

The *brāhmaṇa* stopped. Turning to Narottama, whose eyes were streaming with tears, he said, "Son, these places I'm showing you are beyond the grasp of even the demigods. In this village Nityānanda Rāya still performs His pastimes, but only a fortunate few can see them." Saying this, the *brāhmaṇa* suddenly disappeared and Narottama was left alone.

Narottama looked around in confusion and shock. His guide had vanished, and despite Narottama's calls, did not return. Narottama searched the area but found no trace of the elderly man.

Devastated, he sat beneath a tree with an agitated mind. Although he tried to chant *japa* to calm himself, he couldn't stop thinking about the *brāhmaṇa*. "Why does his disappearance cause me such distress?" he wondered. "I only met him a few hours ago. If he had other business to tend to, so be it . . . but to vanish without warning?" His anxiety grew even more desperate. He felt he couldn't live if he didn't see that venerable Vaiṣṇava again.

Then, as suddenly as he had vanished, the *brāhmaṇa* reappeared. In an instant his wrinkled form transformed into an effulgent white youth dressed in brilliant blue, his hair gathered in a topknot. He carried a club and a plow, and Narottama recognized Him at once as Lord Balarāma.

Flashing a wide smile, the Lord said, "I did not intend to deceive you. You are extremely dear to Me, and that's why I came to be with you. But don't tell anyone that you have seen Me here. All your desires will be fulfilled very soon." Saying this, Lord Balarāma once again disappeared.

Narottama stood transfixed. For a long time, he remained rooted to the spot, in a trance of ecstasy. Then, falling to the ground he cried, overcome with love for the Lord.

The following morning Narottama left Ekacakrā. Singing Lord Nityānanda's glories, he proceeded toward Kheturi.

sthale sthale yasya kṛpā-prabhābhiḥ
kṛṣṇānya-tṛṣṇā jana-saṁhatīnām
nirmūlitā eva bhavanti tasmai
namo namaḥ śrīla-narottamāya

I repeatedly offer my respectful obeisances to Śrīla Narottama Dāsa Ṭhākura. Wherever he went, the splendour of his mercy eradicated people's thirst for anything other than Kṛṣṇa.

Narottama-prabhor-āṣṭaka, Verse 6

Chapter Six

The Festival

Preparations

The small bamboo craft carried Narottama swiftly across the Padmavatī. Stepping onto the bank, he set out on the familiar route to Kheturi, striding over the ground he knew so well. When he arrived, he found that news of his return had already spread. Crowds of villagers rushed forward to welcome him home, and excited cries of "Hari! Hari!" filled the air.

Narottama's parents stepped out jubilantly to greet him, and Narottama touched their feet respectfully. "Oh, Naru, we're so relieved you have returned," his mother said, breathless with excitement. "Please don't go away again. We can't tolerate being separated from you. You can go wherever you like, but please, wait until we have left this world."

Narottama smiled gently, "Don't worry, Mātā, I won't go away anymore. I just wanted to see the pastime places of Śrī Caitanya Mahāprabhu. Now that I've done that, I won't give you any more unhappiness. I plan to stay here and do *bhajan*."

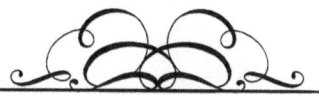

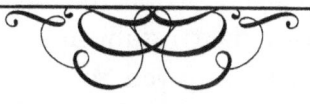

Not long after returning, Narottama received a letter from his *gurudeva*, Lokanatha Gosvāmī. News from Vṛndāvana was rare, and Narottama eagerly devoured the contents of the letter as if eating a sumptuous feast. In his letter Śrī Lokanātha Gosvāmī emphasized the importance of engaging people in Deity worship, and he encouraged Narottama to establish a temple in Kheturi.

Narottama was overjoyed to receive this instruction; it was the confirmation he needed. While on pilgrimage he had seen devotees worshiping Deities of Śrī Caitanya Mahāprabhu, and a desire had grown in his heart to worship the Lord in the same way. Now his feelings were being encouraged and approved by the one whose opinion mattered most.

Narottama was suddenly overcome with excitement as beautiful visions filled his mind's eye. "How wonderful it would be to invite Mahāprabhu's devotees from far and wide to inaugurate the temple!" His heart swelled with anticipation as a plan began to unfold within his mind. Although it had been several decades since Śrī Caitanya Mahāprabhu had completed His manifest pastimes, His birth anniversary had never been observed in a big way. Why not use the Deity installation as an opportunity to hold a grand celebration in honor of the Lord's appearance day?

Narottama's desire to bring all the Vaiṣṇavas together intensified as he thought of the many associates of Śrī Caitanya Mahāprabhu he had met while traveling. Some were barely alive due to the pain of intense separation from the Lord. How happy it would make them if they could come together for a *mahā-saṅkīrtana-yajña* just as they had done during Mahāprabhu's time.

He also thought of the diversity he had observed among Mahāprabhu's followers. With many independent communities and various lineages developing in Orissa, Navadvīpa, and Vrāja, different interpretations of Mahāprabhu's message had arisen. In the absence of their Lord, some less advanced devotees had become bewildered about Advaita Ācārya's position, for example, while others misunderstood Śrī Nityānanda Prabhu's divine character. In Bengal, which was rife with *śāktas*, *sahajiyās*, and Buddhists, the polluting effects of such association were sometimes visible even in established Vaiṣṇava communities.

Narottama noted that for the Gauḍīya devotees, whose worshipable Deity was Mahāprabhu, it was sometimes difficult to understand the primary focus of the Vṛndāvana Gosvāmīs on Rādhā and Kṛṣṇa. Narottama saw the need to unify Mahāprabhu's devotees by linking each group to the larger tradition. He was certain the devotees would benefit if they joined in a festival of glorification for Śrīman Mahāprabhu. Surely this would bring happiness to their hearts. It would also give Narottama a chance to deliver the books and teachings of the Vṛndāvana Gosvāmīs and especially to establish the *Caitanya-caritāmṛta* as the authorized biography of Śrī Caitanya and the reference point for understanding Mahāprabhu's teachings.

Convinced that all these purposes could be served by establishing Deities during a huge festival, Narottama was gripped by a burning desire to make it happen.

The next day, Narottama revealed his mind to King Santosh, who was immediately drawn in by Narottama's enthusiasm and declared, "We should hold a festival here like no one has ever seen! I will cover all the expenses. Preparations for the building of the temple shall begin at once!"

As soon as the date for the festival was set, Narottama sent a message to Śrīnivāsa Ācārya. Yet after many days, he had received no reply. Narottama became anxious. "I haven't received word of Śrīnivāsa Ācārya's whereabouts for a long time. The temple construction is underway and preparations for the festival have begun, but how can I organize this festival without his help? He has the experience to make it a success. I must reach him."

At that moment, a man approached Narottama, bowed, and announced, "I have come from Yajigrāma."

Knowing this to be Śrīnivāsa Ācārya's preaching base, Narottama eagerly inquired, "Have you seen my dear friend, Śrīnivāsa Ācārya? Can you tell me where he is?"

"He recently returned to Yajigrāma from Vṛndāvana," the man said. "I had the good fortune to have his *darśana* in Yajigrāma. He has been fully absorbed in traveling and preaching Śrī Caitanya Mahāprabhu's message."

Narottama invited the visitor to sit, and listened eagerly as the man described Śrīnivāsa's activities and travels. As they conversed, two messengers arrived with a letter. Amazingly, it was from Śrīnivāsa Ācārya.

Narottama happily read it aloud. "The bearers of this letter are Śrīdāsa and Gokulānanda, the sons of Dvija Haridāsa, one of Mahāprabhu's dear associates.

At present I am traveling and preaching. Yesterday I left Kancanagaria and started for Budhuri, where I will stay at Govinda Kavirāja's house for a few days. Since it's close to Kheturi, I hope you can meet me there. I'm eager to see you."

Narottama was ecstatic. "Oh, what a wonderful morning!" he exclaimed.

The next day Ṭhākura Mahāśaya crossed the Padmavatī with his disciples –Devīdāsa, Gokula, and Gaurāṅga– and headed toward the town of Budhuri. As they approached the village, two Vaiṣṇavas came toward them, falling on the ground to offer respects. "We are disciples of Śrīnivāsa Ācārya," one of them said, "and we have come to take you to him." Grasping Narottama's hand, the effulgent devotees ushered him down the path.

Narottama was inexplicably drawn to the bright-faced devotee who was guiding him. Intrigued, he wondered, "Who is this person whose touch fills me with such happiness?"

Just then, Narottama caught sight of Śrīnivāsa sitting with a large group of devotees. Śrīnivāsa also saw Narottama. They rushed toward one another. Narottama bent to offer his obeisances, but Śrīnivāsa pulled him up and embraced him. At last, after such a long time, the friends were reunited.

Sitting with their disciples, Śrīnivāsa and Narottama talked for hours, catching up on everything that had transpired since they had last parted. Śrīnivāsa described how he had successfully copied and distributed all the Gosvāmīs' books, and how, at the request of Narahari Sarakara Ṭhākura, he had married and settled in Yajigrāma. Then he disclosed how later, being deeply afflicted by the demise of Narahari Sarakara Ṭhākura and Gadādhara Dāsa, he had decided to return to Vṛndāvana for a visit.

Narottama listened with rapt attention as Śrīnivāsa described his recent visit to Vrāja – the joy of being in the holy *dhāma* again, the sweetness of his association with the Vṛndāvana Gosvāmīs, and the ecstasy of visiting Giri-govardhana, Rādhā-kuṇḍa, and Śyāma-kuṇḍa. Narottama was also overjoyed to hear that Śrī Jīva Gosvāmī had given Śrīnivāsa some newly written books and that they were already being copied and distributed.

Turning to the bright-faced devotee who had escorted Narottama to Budhuri, Śrīnivāsa said, "This is my disciple Rāmacandra Kavirāja. He was my companion on my trip to Vṛndāvana. The Gosvāmīs were so pleased with his devotional attitude that they conferred on him the title 'Kavirāja.' This house belongs to his brother, Govinda."

Rāmacandra, who had barely taken his eyes off Narottama since meeting him, smiled lovingly and said, "The Gosvāmīs of Vṛndāvana always remember you with great affection. Śrī Lokanātha Gosvāmī sent his blessings to you."

Narottama's heart filled with love for his spiritual master. Grateful tears rolled down his face as he softly repeated his *guru's* name, but wiping away the tears, he composed himself and began to tell Śrīnivāsa about his own pilgrimage and preaching. He explained how enthusiastically the people of Kheturi had embraced Śrī Caitanya Mahāprabhu's mission, and that even his cousin, the King of Kheturi, Śrī Santosh Rāya, had become his disciple. He also revealed his plans for the Gaura Pūrṇimā festival.

Śrīnivāsa was a little doubtful. "Having personally presided over many *utsavas* I know how difficult it is to organize such an event. Are you sure you can manage? You have no experience with events on such a grand scale. Surely you'll need help."

"With your help . . . " Narottama said, and he folded his hands in *prāṇam*. "I've been waiting for you before setting anything in motion."

"I'm certainly willing to help," Śrīnivāsa said. "But how will you get all of Mahāprabhu's associates to come? Each of them is in such a state of deep separation from the Lord that none of them travel. And they live all over the country. Even if we did manage to bring everyone to Kheturi, how would we accommodate and cook for all of them?"

"I have many men we can send with invitations to the Vaiṣṇavas," Narottama said, his determination as strong as ever. "I'm sure the Vaiṣṇavas will be attracted to come. The temple will soon be completed, and Santosh and his subjects are eager to offer all assistance. If you would help me organize it, and then perform the installation ceremony, we could make a wonderful festival for the Lord's pleasure."

"Your enthusiasm is irresistible," Śrīnivāsa laughed. "Let's begin by drawing up a list of devotees who should be invited."

The two spent glorious hours compiling a long list of exalted souls: Jāhnavā Mātā, Śrī Advaita Ācārya's sons, Śrīvasa Paṇḍita's brothers, Hṛdaya Caitanya, Raghunandana . . . They wrote letters in elaborate Sanskrit poetry to inform each guest about the festival. The invitation made it clear that *all* Mahāprabhu's devotees were invited even if they weren't named in the letter.

As evening approached, Narottama and Śrīnivāsa set aside the festival preparations to relish *kīrtana*. After that, the two sat alone and reminisced about the days they had spent together in Vṛndāvana.

The next morning, Śrīnivāsa Ācārya told Narottama, "I could hardly sleep last night, thinking about all the festival arrangements. I was praying for the understanding how to accomplish this seemingly impossible task when Śrī Caitanya Mahāprabhu suddenly appeared in a vision. He pacified my heart, saying, 'Don't worry. This is My desire – I want this festival.' Then He disappeared. Now I'm fully convinced that we should work on this to fulfill the Lord's desire. We must send out all the invitations immediately. I have already selected fifteen men. I will send them in all directions to invite not only the Vaiṣṇavas but the kings, landowners, poets, scholars, authors, performers, and other illustrious persons."

Narottama beamed.

"There's so much to do and only a few months left," Śrīnivāsa said. "You must return to Kheturi at once. I will come to help you in a few days. Why don't you take Rāmacandra with you? He will make a good assistant. Moreover, I see he is attracted to you."

Accepting Śrīnivāsa's advice, Narottama left for Kheturi and was delighted to have Rāmacandra's company. When they arrived in Kheturi, Narottama felt a fresh burst of enthusiasm and vigor.

Preparations for the festival were now in full swing, and every quarter of Kheturi bustled with excitement.

Walking through the many newly constructed houses built to accommodate his guests, Narottama checked to see that everything had been done properly. Out of deep respect for the Vaiṣṇavas he wanted to offer the visiting devotees the best facilities possible; he didn't want anyone to feel inconvenienced in any way. Narottama noted with appreciation that Santosh had spared no expense. A wave of gratitude washed over Narottama. With the help of Santosh's boundless charity and Śrīnivāsa Ācārya's expert managerial abilities, he felt certain it would be an unforgettable festival.

Walking back down the path, Narottama swept his gaze across the ornately decorated temple gradually rising in the centre of the town. The laborers had been working for months, and they still swarmed the area as they struggled to complete the temple on time. The large storehouse adjoining the temple was already complete, and the elaborate *kīrtana* hall was almost finished too. Gardeners were busily planting flowers and mature shrubs to create gardens around the temple complex, and seeding lotus flowers into the clear water of the freshly dug bathing pond.

As he walked further, Narottama saw lines of newly shaped clay *mṛdaṅga* drums drying in the sun, along with piles of shiny new *karatālas* lying nearby. Each instrument had been specially handcrafted for the *saṅkīrtana* festival. A bit further on he stepped into the large hut where the deities were being sculpted. Narottama studied their forms and faces intently, as he did every day. The five sets of Rādhā Kṛṣṇa Deities were exquisite, but Narottama wasn't satisfied with the Deity of Lord Caitanya. No matter how dedicatedly the sculptors tried to follow his specifications, neither Mahāprabhu's form nor face reflected His true beauty. Disheartened,

Narottama uttered, "Gaurāṅga, Gaurāṅga," again and again. This was the only part of the preparation that wasn't turning out well.

That night Śrī Caitanya Mahāprabhu appeared in Narottama's dream. "My dear Narottama," He said, "listen to Me. You are trying to make a Deity of me, but it will never appear correctly because I do not intend to manifest in that form. I have hidden Myself in the golden Deity in Vipradāsa's storeroom. Because you are My dear devotee I am blessing you with this knowledge." With an enigmatic smile, the Lord disappeared.

At this point in his life, Narottama knew better than to question the Lord's appearance or instruction in his dreams. So, the following morning, after waking and finishing his oblations, he asked the villagers where he could find Vipradāsa, saying nothing about the dream. One of the villagers said he knew of a Vipradāsa who was a wealthy grain seller and offered to take him to his house. Eager to be of service too, or even observers of Narottama's activities, several villagers tagged behind.

Vipradāsa was surprised and delighted to see the famous *sādhu* and his followers at his home, and he welcomed them with great respect, asking, "How can I serve you?"

"Dear sir, kindly allow me to go into your rice storeroom," Narottama replied, struggling to contain his excitement.

Even the villagers were surprised at this unusual request. Surely King Santosh had provided all the grain required for the festival already?

Though a little puzzled, Vipradāsa eagerly tried to anticipate his guest's desire, and said, "Dear Sādhu, please don't trouble yourself – you need not personally go into any of my storerooms. I store nothing but the best quality grain, and in abundance at that. Please sit here comfortably and I'll simply bring whatever you want."

Narottama laughed lightly. "No, it's not grains that I need. I just want to go into your rice storeroom."

Vipradāsa's voice was suddenly filled with alarm – "Mahāśaya, I'm sorry, but that's not possible! That storeroom is infested with snakes! Even if anyone just comes near they hiss loudly! I too would like to go inside, at least to recover the premium quality rice, but not even I dare to enter."

"Don't worry," Narottama said calmly, "the snakes won't bother me."

Vipradāsa begged the other villagers with his eyes to speak up, then fell to his knees. "Please, don't go inside. It's too dangerous. I hired many snake-charmers to try and clear out that storage room, but they were all unsuccessful. I gave up hope of ever getting rid of those snakes long ago. You know it's not a light matter for a merchant like me to surrender his precious stock. But in the name of my family's safety, I have resolved to never try and open it again. I couldn't possibly allow you to go inside! What would I do if any harm came to you? I can think of nothing worse!"

The villagers also looked worried. But Ṭhākura Mahāśaya simply laughed. "Don't be afraid. You'll be relieved and happy when you see what I bring out with me." Before anyone could react, Narottama slipped through the huddle of men and walked through to the back, where he could clearly identify the abandoned storeroom. Without too much endeavor, he opened the large door and disappeared inside.

Vipradāsa and the villagers stood motionless. Their minds raced, anticipating Narottama's shout for help, and what they would do to save him. Seconds passed like hours. Now that Narottama was inside, they could see nothing but the open door, a gaping black rectangle. The wait was almost intolerable. Suddenly snakes began to slither out of the door – at first one by one, then in silent surges. Vipradāsa's mouth hung open. "How did he do that?" The villagers could only sigh with relief.

Now they could see Narottama in the shadows, digging into the rice. He seemed to see something among the grains. Plunging his hands in deeply, he gently pulled out what appeared to be a large golden Deity. Inside, Narottama brushed the rice polish from the exquisite form. He was a perfect image of Śrīman Mahāprabhu, just as the Lord himself had promised. Narottama was overjoyed and clasped Him to his heart.

As he emerged from the doorway, the devotees could now clearly see the enchanting form within his hands, glinting in the sun. A loud cheer went up. "All glories to Ṭhākura Mahāśaya!" someone yelled, as they gathered around to marvel at the exquisite beauty of Lord Gaurāṅga.

Narottama's heart overflowed with ecstasy as he lovingly carried Lord Gaurāṅga through the town towards the hut where all the deities were stored. As he and his entourage passed by, the crowd increased, singing and dancing with joy.

Late that evening, Narottama finished writing the last line of his latest composition: . . . *kahe dina narottama dāsa:* thus speaks the lowly Narottama dāsa . . . Gathering his notes, he hurried to the platform where Gokula Dāsa, Devīdāsa, and the other musicians were practicing. Their exquisite devotional music echoed through the trees, where the birds were settling in for the night. Narottama sat down and presented his new song for them to learn. Once they had grasped the tune and specific beat, Narottama left them to practice it while he composed more verses.

For weeks, Narottama had been making his own preparations for the festival: he was composing songs and then training the best musicians to play them as he sang. All the inspiration Narottama had received as he travelled to Śrī Caitanya's pastime places poured forth into these simple but eloquent Bengali verses in glorification of the Lord. He wrote one superlative song after another, each expertly reflecting the Gauḍīya Vaiṣṇava philosophy and teachings.

Narottama had studied *kīrtana* under the Gosvāmīs of Vṛndāvana, where Rādhā and Kṛṣṇa reign supreme, and had experienced the best *kīrtanas* of Gauḍa-deśa, where Śrī Caitanya Mahāprabhu was adored. Now, guided by the instructions from his vision of Lord Caitanya in Jagannātha Purī, Narottama was harmonizing the two styles in his own unique way. Choosing specific *rāgas* to match each mood, Narottama would first describe Lord Caitanya's pastimes, then Rādhā-Kṛṣṇa *līlā,* expertly blending the Vṛndāvana style of worship with the Bengali style. A new style of divinely inspired *kīrtana* had been born, and it was set to be debuted at the grand festival, just a few days later.

The Guests Arrive

Narottama stood next to Śrīnivāsa on the soft sand of the riverbank. His body thrilled as he studied the scene unfolding on the Padmavatī. The river was teeming with boats of every size, ferrying the festival guests across the water. Devotees from all parts of Bengal and Orissa were streaming into Kheturi. Narottama, Śrīnivāsa, Śyāmānanda, Rāmacandra Kavirāja, and many of their disciples, along with Kheturi's residents, greeted each guest with devotion and respect.

"She must be on that boat over there," Narottama said, pointing to a large boat crowded with devotees. "That's the special boat Santosh built for Śrī Jāhnavā Mātā."

Shading his eyes, Śrīnivāsa too peered across the water. "Yes," he said. "I can see a palanquin. And there are some of her disciples – Minaketana Rāmadāsa, Murāri Caitanya, and that looks like Vṛndāvana Dāsa as well."

"Look at the boat next to them," Rāmacandra said exuberantly. "Isn't that Hṛdaya Caitanya and the devotees from Ambikā Kālnā? And is that Śrīpati and Śrīnidhi from Navadvīpa?"

Narottama's heart pounded. With Śrī Jāhnavā Mātā's arrival, it seemed that everyone who had received an invitation had arrived. The turnout was beyond his grandest expectations. Practically all Mahāprabhu's associates and their disciples: children, and children's children had come. There hadn't been such a gathering of exalted souls since Mahāprabhu's time.

As the boat carrying Ma Jāhṇavā and her entourage neared the shore, everyone rushed to greet them. The air was filled with an unrestrained joy. Some devotees waded into the water to garland the newcomers, while others dabbed cooling sandalwood paste on the guests' foreheads as they stepped off the boat. A few devotees spontaneously scooped up water from the river and playfully bathed their guests' feet. Others helped unload the many valuable gifts the devotees had brought for the Deities. The entire riverbank was alive with excitement. Some devotees were locked in loving embraces while others lay flat in the sand, offering obeisances. Laughter, joyful crying, and loud shouts of "*Hari Bol!*" "*Jaya Nitāi!*" and "*Jaya Gaurāṅga!*" filled the air.

Catching sight of Śrīmatī Jāhnavā Mātā, Narottama, Śrīnivāsa, and the other devotees fell flat, offering *daṇḍavat* obeisances to the revered wife of Śrī Nityānanda Prabhu. Smiling brightly, Śrīmatī Jāhnavā Mātā stepped onto the shore, followed by her son, Vīrabhadra.

Narottama, hands folded, approached her. "Kheturi is now blessed by your association," he said with great humility. "We were worried you wouldn't come, but now that you're here, the festival is certain to be a grand success."

"We could not miss such an opportunity," Jāhnavā Mātā said graciously. "It's Mahāprabhu's desire that we come together to glorify Him."

The devotees stepped aside, making a path for Jāhnavā Mātā, and Śrīnivāsa and Narottama escorted her and her entourage to the town.

As the party entered Kheturi, the guests were amazed and delighted to see the festive decorations. Every lane and path was lined with banana trees, and the buildings were artfully decorated with wreaths of fragrant flowers and garlands of mango leaves. Elaborate rice flour designs adorned the ground at the entranceway of every home.

Narottama and Śrīnivāsa ushered their guests through the busy streets and past the long lines of women and girls who were stringing garlands for the festival, chatting among themselves and singing as they worked. The women stopped to bow respectfully as the party of famous devotees passed by.

A little further down the lane, Śrīnivāsa and Narottama guided their guests past a large group of men grinding sandalwood paste, their muscles bulging as they vigorously rubbed large pieces of sandalwood against heavy slabs of stone. Like the women, the men paused to offer their respects too, then continued with their service of filling the many large vessels with moist, aromatic *candana*.

The guests looked curiously at the gorgeous new temple structure. Many fires had already been lit in the kitchens behind the temple to feed the thousands who would be attending the festival. Already, numerous *brāhmaṇa* cooks could be seen stirring gigantic pots with massive wooden paddles, while scores of helpers busily cut vegetables, cleaned *dal* and rice, or kneaded dough. All of Kheturi was bustling with activity – the children, old people, women, and men – everyone was caught up in the excitement.

Deeply pleased, Śrīmatī Jāhnavā Mātā said, "Narottama, you have created a most extraordinary environment here. It appears that the whole town is in Vaikuṇṭha consciousness."

"I have done nothing," Narottama said. "Actually, all of this has been arranged by the mercy and expert guidance of Śrīnivāsa Ācārya and the kindness and generosity of King Santosh."

Śrīnivāsa then escorted the group to the guest-houses. Many of Kheturi's residents trailed behind, staring unabashedly at the effulgent devotees who had suddenly descended on their village.

Showing Jāhnavā Mātā to her lodging first, Śrīnivāsa then arranged for the accommodations of all the other guests, assigning various devotees to look after their needs. Rāmacandra was to serve Raghunātha Ācārya and his associates, and Govinda, Rāmacandra's brother, was to care for Śrī Raghunandana and his companions. Turning to Śyāmānanda, he said, "You please see to the needs of Śrī Hṛdaya Caitanya and his followers."

As services were being handed out, a fierce competition broke out among the residents of Kheturi, each of them eager for the chance to serve a visiting Vaiṣṇava.

So many devotees came that every possible room in Kheturi and the many surrounding villages was filled. Gradually, the sounds of *kīrtana*, *pūjā*, and discourses seeped into every quarter. All of Kheturi was alive with anticipation.

The night before the festival, massive crowds congregated at the temple for the Ādivasa ceremony to inaugurate the festival and invoke auspiciousness. After worshiping Jāhnavā-devī and showing proper respect to all the assembled Vaiṣṇavas, Raghunandana Ṭhākura sang the invocation prayers signifying an extremely holy event, and the following *kīrtana* roared late into the night.

The Deity Installation

Enthusiastic crowds crammed into the temple courtyard early the next morning, marveling at the beautiful decorations. A massive, brightly colored canopy was draped across the wide courtyard, and the entire area was profusely adorned with banana trees, coconuts, flower garlands, strung mango leaves, and clay pitchers filled with water. In the middle of the courtyard, atop a large, flower-bedecked pedestal, stood the six Deities waiting to be installed, their forms hidden beneath new cloth. In one corner of the courtyard the *yajñas-śāla* stood ready, surrounded by shining copper and brass pots of ghee, sacred water and grains. A pile of neatly chopped wood and a mixture of aromatic herbs and tree barks were ready to offer to the sacred fire.

Narottama, Rāmacandra, and Śrīnivāsa discussed the final arrangements with King Santosh. When Narottama saw that everything was ready, he escorted Jāhnavā Mātā to her seat. Then he and Rāmacandra ushered the other senior guests to their seats.

Standing before the assembly, Śrīnivāsa pressed his palms together in respect and humbly addressed the exalted assembly. "Most dear Vaiṣṇavas, beloved followers and family of Śrīman Gaurāṅga Mahāprabhu, words cannot express our gratitude that you have come to grace this festival with your presence. This is surely a historic gathering, and we have you all to thank for making it possible." He turned toward the senior members of the assembly and, with palms still folded, said "Please give me your permission to begin the auspicious *abhiṣeka*." The senior Vaiṣṇavas nodded their consent, smiling in anticipation.

Śrīnivāsa at once pulled aside the cloth that hid the Deities from view, and the crowd gasped with delight. Amid their loud shouts of approval, and assisted by many *brāhmaṇas*, he proceeded with the bathing ceremony. The courtyard vibrated with a symphony of sounds – conch shells were blown, gongs clanged, bells rang, and women made a shrill ululation of joy. The *kīrtana* began, and *karatālas* chimed in time to the deep pulsating of the drums. The holy names filled the air and mixed with the sonorous chanting of the *brāhmaṇas'* Vedic *mantras*.

Narottama stood transfixed at the sight of golden Lord Gaurāṅga seen through billowing clouds of incense smoke.[14] Śrīnivāsa poured milk over the Deities' bodies, and the devotees chanted, "*Jaya* Gaurāṅga! *Jaya* Nitāi!"

When the bathing was complete, a curtain was raised and Śrīnivāsa Ācārya dressed each Deity in new garments, as the *kīrtana* roared and the fires in the *yajñas-śāla* continued to blaze.

Śrīnivāsa completed the *pūjā* by dabbing sandalwood paste on each Deity's forehead and offering each a fragrant flower garland. Then again, the conches sounded and the curtain was drawn back, revealing the beautiful Deities splendidly dressed in Their new clothing. The crowd, wild with excitement, pushed forward to have *darśana* of their Lordships.

Śrīnivāsa lifted one of the Deities and called out, "*Jaya* Śrī Rādhā-Ballabhi-kāntā, *ki jaya*!" and the crowd roared its approval. He then carried the Deities to the altar. Then lifting the Deity of Lord Gaurāṅga, Śrīnivāsa called out, "*Jaya* Śrī Gaurāṅga Mahāprabhu!" then placed Lord Gaurāṅga on the left side of Śrī Rādhā-Ballabhi-kāntā. One by one the Deities were named and moved to one of the six altars: "*Jaya* Śrī Rādhā-Brāja-mohan!" "*Jaya* Śrī Rādhā-Kṛṣṇa!" "*Jaya* Śrī Rādhā-kāntā!" "*Jaya* Śrī Rādhā-rāmana!" The ecstatic *kīrtana* continued through the offering of a sumptuous feast to their Lordships and the *ārati* that followed.

Mahā-saṅkīrtana

The installation complete, Śrīnivāsa turned to Narottama. "You should begin your *kīrtana* now."

Narottama turned to Devīdāsa and said, "Tell Ballabha, Gokula, and Gaurāṅga to come forward."

The musicians carried their instruments into the courtyard, and Narottama joined them, carrying incense and flowers to worship the *mṛdaṅgas* and *karatālas* before beginning. The crowd pushed forward, straining to get a better view.

After completing the *pūjā*, Narottama garlanded each of the musicians and smeared their foreheads with sandalwood paste. As he turned to face the crowd, his heart flooded with bliss and gratitude. Overwhelmed, he felt to the ground offering his full *daṇḍavats* to all of them. He then offered his obeisances to each senior devotee present, circling the courtyard with great humility, rising and falling again and again as he bowed to each of the devotees.

Finally, he turned toward the Deities. With eyes filled with love, he called out, "Oh Gaurāṅga! Nitāi! Please give us Your blessings."

Silence descended on the courtyard; all eyes were on Narottama's face. Taking the *karatālas* in his hands, Narottama sat down in the center of the musicians and nodded to Devīdāsa to begin. Narottama sat erect and closed his eyes. His face became meditative as he listened to the sound of Devīdāsa's deft hands dancing across the *mṛdaṅga's* heads. With a gentle smile, he began to sing, his voice imbued with devotion. Poignant verse after verse glorified Śrī Caitanya Mahāprabhu, flowing from his mouth like a stream of nectar.

The crowd was captivated. This was a divine sound, a new and extraordinary type of *kīrtana* unlike anything they'd ever heard. Many of the Vaiṣṇavas began to cry as they listened to the poetry praising Śrī Caitanya Mahāprabhu. Narottama gradually increased the tempo, and the devotees in the audience clapped and swayed to the beat.

As Narottama became more and more deeply absorbed in remembrance of the Lord, his brow furrowed and his body trembled. The cymbals in his hands flashed in the morning sunlight, and tears of happiness flowed down his cheeks. One song after another poured forth from the depths of his heart, each a condensed *Veda* conveying volumes of transcendental knowledge. Each *rāga* perfectly matched both the mood of the song and the poetic rendition of Lord Gaurāṅga's activities. As the music flowed forth from Narottama's tongue, the sweet pastimes of the Lord came alive in the listeners' hearts.

Skillfully shifting the mood, style, and tune, Narottama then sang the glories of Rādhā and Kṛṣṇa. The inundation of pure sound flooded the courtyard with spiritual energy, engulfing the audience in *bhakti*. No one remained unmoved – all were swept up in the waves of Narottama's *prema*.

Narottama was now oblivious to his surroundings, and he sang on, his body drenched in perspiration mixed with his own joyful tears. By now, many devotees were dancing, forgetting everything but the bliss of the *kīrtana*.

As Narottama continued, he noticed an extraordinarily sweet scent filling the air. This was clearly not the fragrance of the flowers or incense; it was an unearthly, intoxicating scent, which, as it swept through the crowd, caused row after row of devotees to swoon in ecstasy.

Narottama realized that the fragrance was coming from the Deities.

With this realization, he felt a profound sense of separation from the Lord, and he changed the melody to match this mood. He thus led the crowd into ever deeper states of spiritual emotion. The air became thick with the mood of separation until the devotees were so profoundly affected that it appeared everyone was moving in slow motion – like wading through honey.

Then, like a flash of lightning in a mass of rain-darkened clouds, Śrī Caitanya Mahāprabhu and His associates suddenly appeared beside the musicians. Stunned, Narottama reached out and actually touched Lord Caitanya's hand. It wasn't a dream or even a vision! He was there, and everyone, qualified or unqualified, could see Him! Shivers of ecstasy ran through Narottama's body, his hair stood on end, and tears shot from his eyes like water from a syringe.

Śrī Jāhnavā Mātā burst into wild sobs at the sight of her beloved husband, Śrī Nityānanda Prabhu. Śrīpati and Śrīnidhi stared in stunned shock at their dear brother, Śrīvasa Paṇḍita. Śrī Acyutānanda raced up to his father, Advaita Ācārya, and danced wildly beside Him.

Then the son of Śacī-mātā, Śrī Gauracandra, lifted His long, golden arms and gracefully began to dance. The *kīrtana* exploded. *Karatālas* clashed and the *mṛdaṅgas* thundered like wild elephants stampeding across the desert. Devotees clapped loudly, jubilantly chanting, "Śrī Kṛṣṇa Caitanya! Śrī Kṛṣṇa Caitanya!" again and again. Śrī Caitanya Mahāprabhu showered each devotee with His merciful glance as He whirled and spun with His beloved associates.

Grabbing hold of Narottama's hands, Śrī Nityānanda Prabhu pulled him to his feet and began to dance with him. The earth trembled beneath their feet as Lord Nityānanda's shimmering blue *dhotī* swished from side to side. His reddish lotus eyes rolled with intoxicated joy as He spun around the courtyard. Nearby, Śrī Advaitacandra danced through the crowds of devotees while roaring like a maddened lion, and Gadādhara Paṇḍita danced joyfully beside Śrīnivāsa Ācārya.

Narottama's heart was bursting with ecstasy as he surveyed the assembled devotees. It seemed everyone was there – Rūpa and Sanātana, Raghunātha dāsa and Kāśīśvara, Murāri Gupta and Haridāsa, Svarūpa Dāmodara and Vakreśvara. It was as if the clock had been turned back and once again Mahāprabhu was enjoying His ecstatic pastimes in Navadvīpa.

Utter transcendental madness reigned in the courtyard. Some devotees held hands and danced while others cried or trembled. Some stood motionless, staring in disbelief as Lord Caitanya danced around them, while others fell unconscious. Some lay on the ground drenched with their own tears and others simply called out "Kṛṣṇa! Kṛṣṇa!" again and again. Mad with ecstasy, some devotees, wanting to offer everything they had to the Lord, began to throw coins and valuables, not knowing how much they were giving or even whether anyone was receiving their offerings.

Looking around at this extraordinary scene, Narottama laughed loudly and his body trembled violently in ecstasy. Then his lips began to quiver so rapidly that devotees near him said, "Oh master! Please stop! Your teeth will break!" Narottama could not continue to sing. Unable to suppress his exalted spiritual emotions, he fell to the ground. His body appeared to stretch, then suddenly contract. Witnessing this extraordinary ecstatic state, some of Narottama's disciples tried to hold him down, fearing for his life. Others fell at Narottama's feet, thanking him again and again for granting them this experience of unparalleled devotional love.

The *mahā-saṅkīrtana* thundered on and on, and the devotees dove deeper and deeper into the pure nectar ocean of the holy name. Flooded by waves of ecstasy, the chanters lost all sense of time, place, and bodily identification. They no longer considered themselves higher or lower, larger or smaller, younger or older. All material thoughts were eradicated. Philosophical misconceptions, doubts, and confusions were instantly washed away in the purifying waves of *kīrtana*, and Śrī Caitanya Mahāprabhu's family was united.

Śrī Caitanya Mahāprabhu turned to embrace first Śrīnivāsa and then Narottama. Narottama didn't want the moment to end, but as quickly as they had appeared, the Lord and His associates vanished.

A heartrending wail of dismay rose from the crowd and all was pandemonium. Some devotees fainted while others fell to their knees, shedding tears so profusely that the ground became muddy. Some stood frozen, like statues, staring with unblinking eyes at the spot where only a moment before the Lord had danced. Piteous cries rent the air: "Nitāi! Śrī Kṛṣṇa Caitanya! Śrīvasa! Murāri! Where have you gone? Mukunda! Narahari! Please come back!"

Narottama lay unconscious, barely breathing. When he finally opened his eyes, a circle of anxious devotees stood over him. Śrīnivāsa held his hands and chanted softly. As Narottama came back to consciousness, he spoke lovingly, "Narottama, you have received Lord Gaurāṅga's topmost mercy and you have given the greatest gift of love to everyone here. We are all so grateful to you. Has anyone on this earth ever seen or experienced such pleasure?"

Lost in ecstatic remembrance of the Lord, Narottama barely heard Śrīnivāsa's words. In the distance he saw Śrīmatī Jāhnavā Mātā approaching, and still quivering with emotion, he tried to raise himself in respect.

"Narottama," she said, tears welling in her eyes, "we are all forever indebted to you for arranging this *saṅkīrtana* festival. Because of your intense desire, Śrī Caitanya Mahāprabhu and His entourage personally appeared before us, invoked by your pure chanting.

Narottama simply bowed his head, muttering "Gaurāṅga, Gaurāṅga" over and over.

Gradually, each person in the crowd returned to external consciousness and the loud lamentations slowly subsided. Some of the devotees looked confused, as if they were waking from sleep in a strange place. Some sat quietly, smiling as they replayed the joyous scene in their minds. Some wondered aloud whether it had all been a dream, hardly believing they had actually enjoyed the Lord's association.

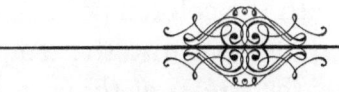

Narottama could appreciate their confusion, for what they had experienced was far beyond the human mind to comprehend. Still, by the Lord's grace, they had each been given divine eyes and spiritual senses by which to see, hear, and dance with the Supreme Lord and His associates. Now the Lord had chosen to hide Himself from their view again, leaving them in a mixed state of intense joy and unbearable separation.

Jāhnavā Mātā suggested to Śrīnivāsa Ācārya that this was the moment to begin the Holi festival. Bowing to Jāhnavā Mātā's request, Śrīnivāsa hurried off to prepare.

Śrīnivāsa gathered the many large containers filled with different colored powders that were waiting to be mixed with perfume. After mixing the substances, he placed the containers before the Deities, and then invited Śrīmatī Jāhnavā Mātā to offer them at the feet of Mahāprabhu.

The *kīrtana* began again, and the devotees came together to watch as teams of *brāhmaṇas* rubbed the Deities with the colorful dyes. Other *brāhmaṇas* showered their Lordships with the colored powders.

The Holi festival spilled out into the temple courtyard and down the nearby streets as thousands of people celebrated the Lord's pastime by playfully throwing colored powders on one another. Clouds of color filled the air, adorning the bodies and clothes of the devotees with rainbow hues as they danced joyfully to songs glorifying Rādhā and Kṛṣṇa's pastimes.

At twilight, thousands of devotees crammed into the temple courtyard to watch the elaborate bathing ceremony of Mahāprabhu's Deity, conducted by Śrīnivāsa Ācārya. The four directions reverberated with the loud chanting of the *abhiṣeka* song commemorating Śrī Caitanya Mahāprabhu's appearance. Hundreds of cooked preparations in clay pots were then carried to the altars to offer to the Lord, and a beautiful *ārati* ceremony followed. With the official rituals over, the altar doors were closed and the Deities put to rest.

But the devotees still surged with devotional energy, and it was too early to end the festivities. As a full moon rose high overhead, Kheturi reverberated with glorification of Śrī Caitanya Mahāprabhu. The *kīrtana* continued to roar as hundreds of devotees stayed on to sing and dance throughout the night. Other devotees wandered around the village, which was lit by hundreds of lamps. Some listened to discourses, joined *bhajan* groups, or watched dramas.

When it was close to sunrise, the devotees returned to the temple for *maṅgala-ārati*. Then they returned to their residences to perform their morning *pūjās* or chant *japa*. Many went to the Padmavatī to bathe, scrubbing off the vivid colors of the Holi powder.

Meanwhile, hundreds of fires were stoked for Śrīmatī Jāhnavā Mātā and a band of expert cooks to prepare a feast in honor of Śrī Caitanya Mahāprabhu's appearance. Teams of cooks and assistants worked for hours under her supervision. Finally, at noon, a fantastic offering was brought before the Deities.

Devotees once again swarmed to the temple, this time to observe the *rāja-bhoga ārati*, and once again Narottama and his band of musicians took up their instruments. As the divine sound of their *saṅkīrtana* filled the air, the audience was again swept up in the joy of chanting the holy names.

Śrīnivāsa was eventually forced to interrupt the *kīrtana* so the devotees could honor *prasāda*. As the chanting came to a close, Śrīnivāsa and his followers swept the temple courtyard clean before ushering the senior

Vaiṣṇavas to their seats. Narottama, Śyāmānanda and their followers helped him by organizing the rest of the devotees. Within minutes, servers were placing banana-leaf plates and clay cups before thousands of people. The lines of devotees stretched from the temple courtyard out into the village.

Pleased to see everyone seated and eager for *prasāda*, Śrīmatī Jāhnavā Mātā encouraged her helpers to serve as quickly as possible. Thus, huge quantities of yogurt, flat rice, bananas, sweets, and hundreds of pots of *pañcāmṛta* were swiftly carried down the lines and distributed to the jubilant devotees. Śrīmatī Jāhnavā Mātā watched carefully to see that everyone was satisfied. Loud shouts of "*Jaya* Gaurāṅga! Hari! Hari!" filled the air as the devotees respected the *prasāda* piled high on their plates. The aroma and flavor of each preparation was so tantalizing that everyone ate far more than their usual capacity. Seemingly endless supplies of fried leafy vegetables, rice, soups, and condensed milk continued to be served until no one could eat another bite.

Śrīnivāsa and Narottama then went to Śrīmatī Jāhnavā Mātā and begged her to be seated and take *prasāda*.

But Jāhnavā Mātā protested. "It's my great desire to feed you first! After you have finished, I shall eat. For my sake, please sit in the courtyard with the others."

Unable to refuse her request, Śrīnivāsa and Narottama sat with some of their associates, and with great affection Jāhnavā Mātā personally served them *prasāda*. She coaxed them to eat to their hearts' content. Narottama, Śrīnivāsa, and the others praised Śrīmatī Jāhnavā Mātā's culinary expertise. The feast was stupendous.

Once all the devotees had been fed, the festivities resumed. For three days Kheturi resounded with the holy name of Lord Kṛṣṇa. There was also a constant flow of *bhāgavata* discourses, *bhajans*, classical dances, and dramatic performances. When the festival finally came to a close, the guests began to leave.[15] The heart-wrenching sadness of their departure was made bearable only by the collective decision to meet again the next year in honor of Śrī Caitanya Mahāprabhu's birth.

As hundreds of devotees boarded bullock carts, palanquins, and boats to begin their journeys home, King Santosh gave each new clothing, plates, and gold coins.

Narottama and Śrīnivāsa humbly bowed before Śrīmatī Jāhnavā Mātā, bidding her and her entourage an emotional farewell. Soon afterward, Śrīpati and Śrīnidhi headed back to Nadia, and Hṛdaya Caitanya gathered his group for Ambikā. The Śāntipura devotees also prepared to depart.

Some of the guests could not bear the thought of leaving Ṭhākura Mahāśaya's association, and so decided to stay on in Kheturi for some time. But eventually everyone was forced to return to their own homes. Only Śrīnivāsa Ācārya and Rāmacandra Kavirāja remained in Kheturi with Narottama and his disciples.

A few weeks later, Śrīnivāsa announced that he would return to Yajigrāma and Vishnupur. Narottama cried in despair at the thought of separation from his dear friend, but Śrīnivāsa consoled him, "Don't worry, by the Lord's grace we'll meet again. In the meantime, Rāmacandra will remain here to keep you company."

Rāmacandra Kavirāja, who had developed a profound love for Narottama, said, "Yes, from now on we will always remain together."

This gave Narottama solace. He had come to love Rāmacandra as they had worked side by side to prepare for the festival. It would be a joy to have his company. And so it was, that after Śrīnivāsa's departure, Narottama and Rāmacandra became inseparable associates. Together, they performed *kīrtana*, attended *ārati* ceremonies, respected *prasādam*, served the devotees and guests, and propagated Kṛṣṇa consciousness in Kheturi and the surrounding areas.

News of the extraordinary Kheturi festival spread far and wide, and Narottama became famous as the former prince of Kheturi who had grown up to become the king of *kīrtana*. People from all over India began to come to Kheturi to take shelter at his lotus feet.

yad-bhakti-niṣṭhopala-rekhikeva
sparśaḥ punaḥ sparśa-maṇīva yasya
prāmāṇyam evaṁ śrutivad yadīyaṁ
tasmai namaḥ śrīla-narottamāya

I repeatedly offer my respectful obeisances to Śrīla Narottama Dāsa Ṭhākura, whose firm faith in devotional service to Kṛṣṇa is like a necklace of precious jewels. His touch transforms like a touchstone, and his words are as authoritative as the four *Vedas*.

Narottama-prabhor-āṣṭaka, Verse 7

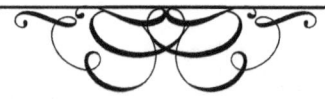

Chapter Seven

Preaching

Harirāma and Rāmakṛṣṇa

One day, as Narottama and Rāmacandra were walking down the shady path to the Padmavatī to bathe, they noticed two young *brāhmaṇa* boys herding goats, sheep, and buffaloes.

"Look at those handsome boys," Rāmacandra whispered to Narottama. "They must be taking those helpless animals to be sacrificed to Goddess Durga. What a shame that such bright-looking boys are wasting their lives worshiping Devī."

Narottama nodded solemnly. Then an idea came to him. Quickening his pace he said, "Come, let's catch up with them."

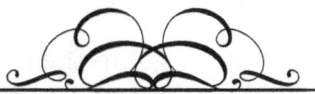

As they approached the boys, Narottama slowed down and began talking to Rāmacandra in a loud voice. "How can people be so foolish as to waste their time worshiping the demigods? The Supreme Lord Kṛṣṇa clearly explains, *yānti deva-vratā devān* – demigod worship is for the less intelligent. People who don't understand the goal of spiritual life worship the demigods in hopes of receiving material gain in exchange. While it's true they may achieve some puny, temporary reward by their worship, they will never stop the cycle of repeated birth and death. Nor will they taste the eternal nectar of pure devotional service to the Supreme Lord."

Rāmacandra played along and speaking even louder, said "Yes, it's unfortunate! And to make matters worse, many demigod worshipers get themselves entangled in animal sacrifice. The deluding power of *māyā* is so strong that such people actually believe they're performing meritorious religious acts by offering the demigods the bloody flesh of innocent animals. But instead of becoming pious they're simply accumulating sinful reactions and have to suffer life after life."

After barely a few moments, it was obvious that their conversation had caught the attention of the two boys. Narottama could see they were listening intently, and gradually edging closer to hear more clearly.

With a faint smile, Narottama continued: "Some people think that animal sacrifice is commendable because it appears to be condoned in some portions of the *Vedas*. But the animal sacrifices performed in Vedic times weren't done to kill animals. They were meant to test the efficacy of the Vedic *mantras*. When the sacrifice was properly conducted, an old animal would emerge from the fire in a new body." Narottama stopped walking and said firmly, "But this is not possible in this age." The two boys stopped walking also, trying in vain to be inconspicuous.

"Why not?" Rāmacandra asked.

"For a start, there are no qualified *brāhmaṇas* to conduct such *yajñas*. Moreover, if there's even a tiny discrepancy in the execution of the sacrifice, the person performing it is held responsible for the animal's death!" He paused dramatically, then added, "It's no different from a murderer being held responsible for killing another man."

The boys looked at each other with alarm.

"I'm sure any intelligent man can understand that animal sacrifice can't be successful in this age," Rāmacandra said as he and Narottama began walking again. "The only sacrifice recommended in Kali-yuga is *saṅkīrtana-yajña*, the congregational chanting of the Lord's holy names – specifically, the chanting of the *mahā-mantra:* Hare Kṛṣṇa, Hare Kṛṣṇa, Kṛṣṇa Kṛṣṇa, Hare Hare/ Hare Rāma, Hare Rāma, Rāma Rāma, Hare Hare. This is the greatest of all *mantras* and is especially intended for this degraded age. By performing the *saṅkīrtana-yajña*, the mirror of the mind will be cleansed, and when that mirror is cleansed, one is automatically liberated. Only then can one go back to Kṛṣṇa, back to Godhead."

Narottama nodded. "That's why Śrī Caitanya Mahāprabhu repeatedly said, *harer nāma harer nāma, harer nāmaiva kevalam/ kalau nāsty eva nāsty eva, nāsty eva gatir anyathā:* In this age of quarrel and hypocrisy there is no other way, no other way, no other way than chanting the holy name."

As they reached the wide bank of the Padmavatī, Narottama and Rāmacandra sat down, continuing their loud discussion. The two boys stood at what they thought was a discreet distance. As the truth of the *sādhus'* words dawned on them, the color drained from their faces. They appeared like two bright blossoms, wilting in the sun. One of the boys whispered to the other, "What they say is true. We have been committing horrible acts by sacrificing animals to Devī. I will never do it again."

"Me neither," the other replied. "Those two Vaiṣṇavas have completely changed my way of thinking. Who are they? They seem to shine like two suns in the sky. My heart is drawn to them."

His brother ventured, "They must be the famous saints everyone has been talking about, Śrī Ṭhākura Mahāśaya and Rāmacandra Kavirāja. They organized a huge festival here in Kheturi not long ago."

"If they are," the other youth answered, "it's our great fortune to meet them. I think we should take shelter of them so we can be forgiven for the sins we've committed."

With guilt-ridden faces, the two boys timidly walked onto the riverbank and fell at the feet of Narottama and Rāmacandra. Sitting up, one boy pleaded with folded hands, "Please save us. Our mission has been sinful, but you have given us new vision."

"Please deliver us," the other begged. "Otherwise, we're doomed."

Touched by their humility, Narottama asked, "Who are you? Where are you from?"

"I am Harirāma, and this is my younger brother, Rāmakṛṣṇa," the first boy said. "We are from Ganeshpura, and our father is Śivānanda Ācārya. He's a devout worshiper of Devī. He sent us here to buy animals for his Durga-pūjā."

"These animals are quite expensive," Rāmacandra noted.

"Yes," the boy confirmed. "My father spends lavishly on worshiping Devī because he wants to get into heaven."

"Ah, yes, I've heard of your father," Narottama said. Then he added, "And do you think he is right?"

"No! Now we know how terribly mistaken he is."

Smiling, Rāmacandra invited, "Why don't you boys come with us. We'll show you Śrī Caitanya Mahāprabhu's temple."

The boys readily agreed. Harirāma unharnessed the animals and set them free. Bleating with glee, they happily trotted off down the riverbank. Narottama, Rāmacandra and the brothers bathed in the Padmavatī River before going to the temple.

After taking *darśana* of the Deities, the boys sat with Narottama and Rāmacandra and were taught about the science of Kṛṣṇa consciousness. The boys sat mesmerized, eagerly drinking in each word. At the end of the day, Harirāma grabbed hold of Narottama's feet and begged, "Please, let us stay here with you. We have no desire to go home."

"It's better that you go home," Narottama said, testing their conviction. "Your father is a wealthy *brāhmaṇa* with great influence in this area. He will not approve of your staying here, and neither will his friends. Have you considered this?"

"If we get your mercy we don't need anything from our father or from society," Rāmakṛṣṇa said. "Please let us stay with you."

Narottama relented with a smile, and the boys moved into his *āśrama*.

Ten days passed swiftly. Harirāma and Rāmakṛṣṇa were deeply inspired by the lively temple environment bustling with melodious *kīrtanas* vibrating twenty-four hours a day, and the frequent discourses on *Śrīmad-Bhāgavatam* and *Caitanya-caritāmṛta.*

With awe and wonder, they closely observed the two *ācāryas* as they interacted lovingly with each other and all the Vaiṣṇavas and visitors. They were amazed to see Narottama Ṭhākura's deep immersion in the worship of his beloved Deities, daily overseeing every aspect of the *pūjā,* especially making sure the cooking was always excellent. The boys were surprised to find out that the Ṭhākura had asked the cook to wear a cloth over his mouth while preparing food to ensure that the offerings were always clean.

They also marveled to see that Narottama and Rāmacandra never wasted any time. They were always busy; attending all the *āratis*—often dancing ecstatically, circumambulating the temple five times every morning, and constantly chanting the holy names. The boys noticed that Narottama never spoke to anyone while he chanted *japa*, and that after respecting Kṛṣṇa *prasādam*, he always instructed his disciples not to touch his contaminated eating plates. The boys were disappointed to not get the remnants of Ṭhākura Mahāśaya, but were delighted to taste the succulent *prasādam* served daily.

In this glorious environment, Harirāma and his brother rapidly transformed. They were now effulgent devotees who fully embraced the Gauḍīya Vaiṣṇava philosophy and practices. Rāmakṛṣṇa took initiation from Narottama, and Harirāma from Rāmacandra Kavirāja. News of their conversion spread quickly, and when their father in Ganeshpura heard it, he sent a messenger to

Kheturi, insisting that the boys come home immediately. Submitting to the command, Narottama instructed Harirāma and Rāmakṛṣṇa to return to their father's house.

The following day Harirāma and Rāmakṛṣṇa entered their father's mansion. They offered respects at his feet, and stood before him with folded palms.

Śivānanda eyed their shaved heads, the *tulasī* beads around their necks, and the Vaiṣṇava *tilaka* on their foreheads with shock, then disdain. "Do you realize how worried we've been? Your mother and I feared the worst. How could you have done this to us?" Then in a harsh tone he demanded, "And what have you done with the money I gave you for Devī's *pūjā*? Have you donated it to your new Vaiṣṇava friends?" Śivānanda practically spit the word *Vaiṣṇava*.

Rāmakṛṣṇa began to protest. "It's not like that at all . . ." but his brother silenced him with a look. Unruffled by his father's demeanor, Harirāma explained, "We were on our way home with the sacrificial animals when we met Ṭhākura Mahāśaya and Rāmacandra Kavirāja. We were so impressed by their knowledge and devotion that not only did we free the animals but we took *dīkṣā* from them."

"You did what?" Śivānanda shouted. His eyes were red with anger. "You fools! How could you be so stupid as to take initiation from a *śūdra*?"

"These Vaiṣṇavas are not *śūdras*," Harirāma said firmly. "They are great saints!"

"Who are you to judge that?" Śivānanda shouted. "I know who Ṭhākura Mahāśaya is – the son of that *kāyastha*, Kṛṣṇānanda Datta! *Kāyasthas* are low-class, paid servants of the Muslim rulers. *Kāyasthas* are nothing compared to our *brāhmaṇa* caste."

Rāmakṛṣṇa interjected, "His father ruled all of Kheturi."

"*Hah*!" Śivānanda scoffed. "Common people may be impressed by such administrators. They may even consider them 'royalty.' But know that a paid servant is a *śūdra* and nothing more. What arrogance it is for a *kāyastha* to pose as a *brāhmaṇa*. How dare he give you boys *dīkṣā*!"

"Please don't speak like this, Pitā," Rāmakṛṣṇa protested. "It's offensive."

"Don't you understand?" Śivānanda asked. "You are *brāhmaṇa* boys. You belong to the highest caste. You are superior to everyone else around you. You cannot take shelter of someone who is inferior to you by birth." Then turning to Harirāma he said, "Not only have you ruined your own caste reputation but you have allowed your younger brother to do the same. How could you live with such people and eat their food?"

Śivānanda stepped back from his sons in disgust. "Stay clear of me or I will be contaminated by your presence. No proper *brāhmaṇa* will allow you to associate with them now. You have become outcastes. You must renounce this false *dīkṣā*, and then perhaps we can consider whether you can be purified by some form of *prāyascitta*."

"Father, you don't understand." Harirāma remained firm as he interrupted his father's rant. Surprisingly,

Śivānanda fell silent as Harirāma went on to explain how Ṭhākura Mahāśaya and Rāmacandra Kavirāja were not ordinary men. "They are exalted manifestations of the Lord's mercy in the world. Everyone loves them for their great and good qualities. You should see them. Their faces are radiant with goodness and spiritual light, and everyone praises their wisdom and humility. No one has ever heard a harsh word from their lips. Why do *you* dislike them?"

Śivānanda 's eyes blazed again with scornful anger. "They may be *sādhus*, but who has given them the right to give initiation. That is the birthright of the *brāhmaṇas* and no one else!"

"But Pitā," Harirāma objected, "if one is in full knowledge of the science of God, then he is a qualified spiritual master, regardless of where he is born. It doesn't matter whether he is a *brāhmaṇa* or a *śūdra*, if he is rich or poor.

Śivānanda shook his head violently. "There are plenty of *brāhmaṇas* who are qualified *gurus*. You had no need to go to low-class persons."

"Don't you see anything but a person's social status?" Rāmakṛṣṇa asked, exasperated. "The qualities a man manifests are far more important than his birth. If someone is born in a *śūdra* family but endowed with *brahminical* qualities, he should be accepted as a *brāhmaṇa*. And one born in a *brāhmaṇa* family but endowed with the qualities of a *śūdra* should be considered a *śūdra*."

"What nonsense! Don't juggle words with me. It's extremely clear: a *brāhmaṇa* is a *brāhmaṇa* and a *śūdra* a *śūdra*."

"Vaiṣṇavas like Ṭhākura Mahāśaya and Rāmacandra are completely above all these bodily designations,"

Harirāma said, irritated by his father's stubborn insistence. "Such great souls are fully engaged in the loving service of the Lord. That makes them superior to everyone. In the eyes of God it is love and devotion that count. It doesn't matter whether one is high-class, middle-class or low-class – the path of *bhakti* is open to everyone. Anyone who uses his actions, mind, and words only to serve the transcendental Lord is a liberated soul even though he may appear to be in material existence."

"More word jugglery," Śivānanda said. "Not only have you become contaminated by low association, they have filled your heads with nonsense. You had no right to accept Vaiṣṇava *dīkṣā*. You belong to a family of Śāktas. We have worshiped Devī for generations. All our wealth and success are due to her mercy." Then, in a quieter tone he said, "Offending her, you have spoiled your lives."

"Actually," Harirāma said, "your Devī is a Vaiṣṇava. She is a maidservant of Viṣṇu. This proves that Vaiṣṇavism is the ultimate religion of every living being."

"That's enough!" Śivānanda roared. "I don't need to be preached to by my own sons. If you refuse to listen to me, I will bring you before a council of *paṇḍitas*. They will convince you to give up this bogus initiation."

"Let the *paṇḍitas* come," Harirāma said boldly. "If they can defeat us through *śāstra* we will give up Vaiṣṇavism and perform whatever purificatory penance they recommend."

Determined to reform his sons, Śivānanda invited many *brāhmaṇas* from across the region to defeat them.

With clean-shaven heads and bold, vertical *tilaka* markings on their bodies, Harirāma and Rāmakṛṣṇa sat like proud lions before the council of learned *paṇḍitas*. Bright faced and alert, they fingered their beads, chanting softly as they waited for the council to begin.

The eldest *paṇḍita* spoke up sternly. "Your Pitā is concerned about you. He tells us you have become confused by bad association, so we've come here to help you sort out your spiritual dilemma." Then, in a softer, friendlier tone, he added, "You have always been good boys and you come from a good family. I'm certain everything will become clear to you once this venerable council of *paṇḍitas* has shown you the error of your ways."

Both boys smiled sincerely at the *paṇḍita*. "We are always eager to increase our understanding of spiritual topics," Harirāma said.

"Good, good." This was an encouraging start, the *paṇḍita* thought. "Then I would like to explain a few things to you from the *śāstras*." The elderly *paṇḍita* launched into a long-winded lecture, quoting this verse and that, determined to set the boys straight. The other *paṇḍitas* on the council nodded their heads as their colleague elaborately explained the foolishness of accepting initiation from lower caste persons. He dwelt particularly on the poisonous effects of bad association, and reminded the boys of their duty as *brāhmaṇas*. He stressed the importance of following family traditions and explained in great detail the importance of the *pañcopāsanā* system, in which Viṣṇu, Śiva, Gaṇeśa, Sūrya, and Devī are worshiped in order to attain oneness with Brahman.

When he finally ended his speech, the other *paṇḍitas* took their turn to express similar views, encouraging the boys to rectify their mistake by rejecting Ṭhākura Mahāśaya and Rāmacandra Kavirāja.

Śivānanda felt smug. Clearly his delinquent boys were now on the road to reform.

When everyone had finished speaking, Harirāma humbly offered his *prāṇams* to the *paṇḍitas,* thanking them for their counsel. "We're grateful that you are so concerned about our wellbeing," he said. "Yet we beg to differ on some points. Although we are just boys and shouldn't disagree with our superiors, please allow us to present some points for your consideration."

"Of course, my son," the eldest *paṇḍita* said. "Speak your mind."

Harirāma spoke slowly and sweetly, and point by point, methodically explained the meaning of Vedanta, the different levels of realization of the Absolute Truth, the qualifications of a *brāhmaṇa,* the qualifications of a spiritual master, the superiority of the devotional path, the ultimate goal of spiritual life, and the process of devotional service. Rāmakṛṣṇa interjected his own comments here and there to further elucidate his brother's points.

The boys spoke at great length, quoting *śāstra* profusely. When they were finished the *paṇḍitas* sat speechless. Śivānanda himself was stunned. His brow furrowed as his feelings vacillated between respect and resentment.

Harirāma added a last point: "Because a Vaiṣṇava has understood the essence of *dharma* and is fully engaged in the loving service of the Supreme Lord, his position is the most exalted. He is a liberated soul, transcendental even to a *brāhmaṇa.* Therefore, we conclude that there is no fault in our taking initiation from a devotee of Lord Kṛṣṇa like Ṭhākura Mahāśaya. On the contrary, by serving such a Vaiṣṇava we will benefit everyone, from the demigods to our family members."

There was silence. No one countered Harirāma's arguments. Rather, the *paṇḍitas* stared at the boys in amazement. Some of them appeared charmed by the boys, while others were bewildered, and some indignant.

One *paṇḍita* said, "The Vaiṣṇavas no doubt have great power."

The eldest *paṇḍita*, flustered and embarrassed, turned to Śivānanda and apologized. "These boys have the blessings of those two great Vaiṣṇavas. No one can defeat them."

Humiliated, the *paṇḍitas* excused themselves and swiftly filed out of the house with downcast eyes. Śivānanda said nothing. He stared at the ground, confused by this turn of events.

News of the *paṇḍitas'* defeat at the hands of Śivānanda's wealthy and cultured sons spread rapidly. As a result, many people were drawn to take shelter of Ṭhākura Mahāśaya. Others became antagonistic toward him. Some members of the *brāhmaṇa* community spread false rumors to discredit him. Some even spied on him, hoping to find fault in his character. Others remained silent, fearing the wrath of the Vaiṣṇavas.

Gaṅgā-nārāyaṇa Cakravartī

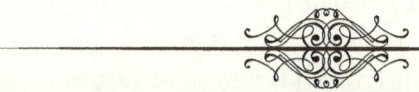

Near the bank of the Ganges in the village of Gambhila, Gaṅgā-nārāyaṇa Cakravartī sat cross-legged on a raised platform, loudly chanting Sanskrit *ślokas*. His attention was distracted by two boys softly singing *kīrtana* as they passed him. Their sweet singing captivated his mind. "There's something extraordinary about those boys," he thought, studying their radiant faces. On closer scrutiny, he recognized them. Intrigued, he called out, "Aren't you the sons of Śivānanada Ācārya from Ganeshpura?"

Surprised, Harirāma and Rāmakṛṣṇa turned to the *paṇḍita*. "Yes, we are," they said, offering *prāṇams*. "And may we ask who you are?"

"I am Gaṅgā-nārāyaṇa Cakravartī," the Paṇḍita said with a smile. "Perhaps you have heard of me."

"Yes, of course," Harirāma said respectfully. "Who has not heard your name? Your reputation as the foremost scholar in this region is widespread."

Gaṅgā-nārāyaṇa smiled at the praise. "You boys have also earned quite a reputation in these parts," he said with a tinge of sarcasm. "Your names are on the tongues of everyone I meet. Is it true that you have left home and taken initiation from Ṭhākura Mahāśaya of Kheturi?"

"Yes, it is true," Rāmakṛṣṇa said, unable to suppress a joyous smile. "After suffering for millions of births I have finally met my divine spiritual master. He has opened my eyes with the torchlight of knowledge and lifted me out of the mire of material existence."

Gaṅgā-nārāyaṇa disapproved. "It's admirable that you aspire to be released from material bondage," he said, his tone patronizing, "but you can only achieve that by strictly following your *brahminical* duties, not by disrespecting your Pitā or seeking shelter of *śūdras*. Your behavior is unacceptable. It goes against all religious convention."

By now accustomed to such challenges, Harirāma and Rāmakṛṣṇa remained unruffled, and at once launched into a defense of their position. Tears of happiness spilled from their eyes as they described their spiritual masters' magnanimous qualities and the glories of devotional service to Kṛṣṇa.

At first, Gaṅgā-nārāyaṇa tried to counter their statements, but it didn't take long to understand that it was useless to argue with these boys. Their philosophy was sound, their faith unshakeable, and their enthusiasm boundless.

Falling silent, Gaṅgā-nārāyaṇa began to listen instead of challenge. "What happened to these boys?" he pondered. "Their faces shine like sacrificial fires, and their lustrous eyes reflect their pure hearts. It's amazing how they convey deep thoughts with such sweet voices, and their use of language is exquisite." Although maintaining a stoic facade, Gaṅgā-nārāyaṇa found himself secretly admiring the boys. "What has Ṭhākura Mahāśaya done to make them glow like this?" he wondered. "They are bursting with love for him."

The exchange was utterly disorienting to Gaṅgā-nārāyaṇa, and he began to wonder if he had perhaps misjudged the famous Narottama Ṭhākura. Desiring to understand more about the boys and the *bhakti* philosophy they were so ably expounding he interrupted Harirāma. "Why don't you two come to my house? We can continue our discussion there."

The boys agreed, and Gaṅgā-nārāyaṇa escorted them home. There, the *paṇḍita* offered them comfortable seats and some *prasāda*. After washing their hands and mouths, the trio resumed their dialogue. Again, Harirāma and Rāmakṛṣṇa described the greatness of

Ṭhākura Mahāśaya and Rāmacandra Kavirāja and what they had learned by studying the *bhakti-śāstras* under their guidance.

The discussion continued late into the night, and Gaṅgā-nārāyaṇa's pride gradually diminished. His heart changed. "I can't argue with anything these young devotees say." This in itself amazed him. "They are certainly far more advanced in spiritual understanding than I am. And they are so happy, so full of love. I simply cannot understand their emotional state. The greatest love I have known in this world is for my daughter, but talking about her doesn't bring me the kind of bliss I see in these boys."

Unable to maintain his air of superiority, Gaṅgā-nārāyaṇa finally expressed his confusion. "My boys," he said, "it's clear you have attained great heights in your spiritual understanding and that the practice of *bhakti* is a path of joy. I don't know whether to rejoice or cry at this. I have always considered myself a learned teacher, but in front of you I feel ignorant. In all the days of my life, I have not tasted even a thousandth of the happiness I see in you. What then is the use of all my learning? After studying hundreds of scriptures and posing as an elevated spiritualist, I have never shed even a single tear of ecstasy."

His voice choked with emotion, Gaṅgā-nārāyaṇa asked, "Why is this? Why is my heart so empty? Why have I failed so miserably? I have always followed my *dharma* explicitly, strictly adhering to all the rules and regulations of brahminical life."

Harirāma gently interrupted him. "You *paṇḍitas* like to talk of *dharma* and rules and regulations, but you seem to lose sight of the real purpose of *dharma*.

The only reason to perform any religious activity is to become connected to Kṛṣṇa, the Supreme Personality of Godhead, through His loving service. Pleasing Him is the goal. And it's not possible to please Him by becoming a perfect *brāhmaṇa*, acquiring knowledge, or observing etiquette perfectly. None of this gives the Lord pleasure. Nor does distributing charity, performing austerities or sacrifice, being clean, or following strict vows. The Lord is pleased only when one has unflinching, unalloyed devotion to Him. Everything else is simply for show. If your activities do not bring you to the point of loving God, they are a useless waste of time. The Lord wants only your love. When you love Him, your life will be filled with bliss. It's as simple as that."

Gaṅgā-nārāyaṇa nodded. "It's truly wonderful how the right way stands out so clearly when you speak. By your kindness my eyes have been opened to the truth." Gaṅgā-nārāyaṇa sighed. "But the truth is sometimes painful. Oh, fie! Fie on my life! Why did I waste my time with dry learning? What's the use of knowing hundreds of *ślokas* when my heart is devoid of love for the Supreme Lord?"

"It's never too late to take to devotional service," Rāmakṛṣṇa said encouragingly. "Kṛṣṇa is always waiting for us to turn to Him."

"You make it sound simple," said Gaṅgā-nārāyaṇa, "but I fear that it's not so easy to develop loving feelings for the Supreme Lord. It's one thing to understand the theory, but how does one do it? How does devotion arise in the heart? By what means can love for Kṛṣṇa be attained?"

"Ah! Now you have asked the right question," Rāmakṛṣṇa said happily. "And the answer is also a simple one: devotion is awakened by the mercy of a pure devotee. Unless you take the dust of the lotus feet of a pure Vaiṣṇava on your head you cannot understand who the Supreme Personality of Godhead is or how to serve Him. This is the secret to success: become the humble servant of the servant a hundred times removed. If you can't understand the importance of serving Vaiṣṇavas, then you will not progress in devotion. To cultivate Kṛṣṇa consciousness you must endeavor to please the Vaiṣṇavas with your body, mind, and soul."

A pain shot through Gaṅgā-nārāyaṇa's heart at these words. Remembering all the horrible things he had said about Ṭhākura Mahāśaya and his followers, he felt the bitterness of remorse.

"If you're serious," Rāmakṛṣṇa continued, "find a real Vaiṣṇava *guru* and take refuge at his feet. Then you will be directed on the path and love will blossom in your heart – *guru-kṛṣṇa-prasāde pāya bhakti-latā-bīja.* The *bhakti-latā,* the seed of devotional service, can be received from a bona fide spiritual master. If we faithfully abide by his orders, then Kṛṣṇa will be pleased. Ṭhākura Mahāśaya always teaches that a genuine disciple must take the *guru's* instructions as his life and soul. Attachment to the lotus feet of the spiritual master is the best way to make spiritual advancement because by the *guru's* mercy, all desires for spiritual perfection are fulfilled."

As the eminent Cakravartī sat quietly digesting these words, hope began to stir in his heart. "These two boys were transformed into brilliant gems by the magical touch of Śrī Ṭhākura Mahāśaya," he thought. "Perhaps, by his mercy, I can also change."

Deeply repentant, the great *paṇḍita* humbly begged Harirāma and Rāmakṛṣṇa to help him. "I have committed so many offenses against your beloved spiritual master and all the Vaiṣṇavas. How can I be forgiven? Is there any hope for a foolish, pompous *brāhmaṇa* like me? If I can't get the mercy of Śrī Narottama Ṭhākura, I will have wasted my life and I will drown in a sea of sorrow."

Greatly pleased by the *paṇḍita's* extraordinary transformation, the two brothers took hold of his hands. They encouraged him, "Don't be afraid, no one is more kind and forgiving than Ṭhākura Mahāśaya. The whole world can find bliss from his loving kindness. Simply by desiring his mercy you have as good as crossed over the ocean of sorrow and reached the other shore."

Their sweet words calmed Gaṅgā-nārāyaṇa and gave him hope. Outside, a thin curve of moon rose in the darkening sky.

"It's late," Harirāma said. "We should rest. Tomorrow, my brother and I will return to Kheturi. If you like, you can come with us and meet Ṭhākura Mahāśaya."

Gaṅgā-nārāyaṇa eagerly accepted their offer and brought *kuśa* mats for the boys to sleep on. The *paṇḍita* also lay down on his bed, but his agitated mind kept him awake late into the night. "What a fool I've been," he thought. "I was so proud of my knowledge that I dared criticize Ṭhākura Mahāśaya. What will happen to me?" Tears filled his eyes. "What will he do when I approach him? Will he condemn me or forgive me?" He is known to be merciful, but will he overlook my offenses?"

Finally, late into the night he drifted off to sleep. In his dream, Narottama Ṭhākura appeared before him, shining with the brilliance of the sun. "You are my servant," he said with a compassionate smile. "Don't lament. All your desires will be fulfilled."

Early the next morning, Harirāma and Rāmakṛṣṇa escorted a contrite but excited Gaṅgā-nārāyaṇa to Kheturi. Arriving at the temple, they first took *darśana* of the Deities, then went to the room where Ṭhākura Mahāśaya sat with his disciples. Gaṅgā-nārāyaṇa was nervous as he entered the room, his face clouded with guilt and shame. But when he saw the golden face of Narottama Ṭhākura smiling so warmly at him – exactly as he had seen him in his dream – tears fell from his eyes and he fell at Narottama's feet. "There is no one as worthless as me," he cried. "I am guilty of performing so many sinful deeds. How can I possibly obtain your mercy? Yet I dare to come here seeking service and sanctuary at your feet."

Ṭhākura Mahāśaya was gracious. "Everyone is welcome in Mahāprabhu's service," he said. "But, what will the other *brāhmaṇas* think of your behavior?"

"Oh Mahāśaya," Gaṅgā-nārāyaṇa exclaimed, "if I can get your favor, nothing else matters. I'm not worried about the opinion of those devoid of devotion. To attain your mercy I'm ready to give up my social position, pride, caste, and family. Whatever is required to get your blessings I am ready to do." Saying this, Gaṅgā-nārāyaṇa bowed low before Narottama.

Ṭhākura Mahāśaya gently placed his hand on Gaṅgā-nārāyaṇa's head and said, "You will certainly receive the mercy of my beloved Guru Mahārāja, Lokanātha Gosvāmī." Then Ṭhākura Mahāśaya lifted Gaṅgā-nārāyaṇa to his feet and embraced him affectionately.

Gaṅgā-nārāyaṇa was speechless with joy. With one simple sentence Ṭhākura Mahāśaya had washed away all his fear and anxiety and flooded his heart with happiness. Turning to Harirāma and Rāmakṛṣṇa he clasped each of them to his chest. "How can I ever thank you enough?" he cried. "It's only due to your kindness that I have had the good fortune to meet Ṭhākura Mahāśaya."

The room overflowed with joy as Ṭhākura Mahāśaya's disciples gathered around Gaṅgā-nārāyaṇa to welcome him.

Gaṅgā-nārāyaṇa told them, "My life has drastically and irrevocably changed. I now know beyond a shadow of doubt that I have found my eternal shelter. I will never leave Ṭhākura Mahāśaya's association.

"Have you heard?" the villager said. "The great *paṇḍita* Gaṅgā-nārāyaṇa Cakravartī, one of the main pillars of the *brāhmaṇa* society, has fallen at the feet of Śrī Narottama Ṭhākura and taken initiation from him."

"You should see him now," someone else said. "He's no longer an arrogant *paṇḍita* but a humble and gentle soul. I never dreamed it possible for such a person to come to the devotional path. I used to see him in Gambhila. He has completely changed. Now he spends all his time studying the *bhakti śāstras* and swimming in a stream of happiness during *saṅkīrtana*."

"Śrī Ṭhākura Mahāśaya is a touchstone," said another. "Whoever comes in contact with him is transformed."

Such talks could be heard in all quarters as news of Gaṅgā-nārāyaṇa's amazing transformation spread from village to village. As Ṭhākura Mahāśaya's fame rapidly increased, more and more people came to Kheturi to seek his shelter.

The Challenge

However, trouble still rumbled amidst the orthodox *brāhmaṇa* community. Already alarmed by Ṭhākura Mahāśaya's growing popularity, they were further shocked to hear of Gaṅgā-nārāyaṇa's unexpected conversion to Vaiṣṇavism. Such a blow to their prestige! The thought of Ṭhākura Mahāśaya infecting even the greatest *brāhmaṇa paṇḍitas* inflamed both their envy and their anger. Opposition to Ṭhākura Mahāśaya's preaching activities was brewing.

One day, a battalion of *brāhmaṇas* strode proudly through the streets of Pakapalli and up the steps of Rāja Narasiṁha's palace. "We must see the king immediately," their leader told the guard.

"Enter," the guard said. "The king's doors are always open to *brāhmaṇas*."

Filing swiftly through the ornate palace gates, the *brāhmaṇas* stepped into the hall where the king was sitting with his court *paṇḍitas*.

"Ah, the sun has risen twice today," Rāja Narasiṁha said in welcome. "Come in. Please sit down. To what do I owe the honor of receiving so many exalted guests?"

As the *paṇḍitas* took their seats the chief *brāhmaṇa* stepped forward. His head held high, he cleared his throat and addressed Rāja Narasiṁha. "My dear King, I and this highly esteemed group of *brāhmaṇas* are here to lodge a complaint against Narottama Ṭhākura Mahāśaya. The *brāhmaṇas* of this region are alarmed by his blatant disregard for brahminical culture and the natural order of *varṇāśrama*. He is acting irreligiously and is influencing others to do the same. Something must be done to stop him."

"*Hmm*," the king said, his eyebrows raised. "I was not aware that Ṭhākura Mahāśaya was causing a disturbance." The king glanced curiously at his court *paṇḍitas*, who remained silent. "It's true that since his famous Kheturi festival he has amassed a large following and wields great power in this region, but I was under the impression that he was truly a great *sādhu*."

"He poses as one," the *paṇḍita* said sarcastically. "But his actions tell us different. This man, though no better than a low-born *śūdra*, is so arrogant that he openly initiates *brāhmaṇas*. Can you imagine," he snorted, "a *śūdra* initiating *brāhmaṇas*? What a farce! Everyone knows that giving spiritual initiation, studying the *Vedas*, worshiping the deity, and performing *yajñas* are duties for *brāhmaṇas*. These activities are never meant to be performed by *śūdras* or *vaiśyas*. What kind of saint is one who gives up his own *dharma* and accepts that of another?" The *brāhmaṇa's* face flushed and his voice rose along with his anger. "By whose authority does this *śūdra* accept the occupational duties of a *brāhmaṇa*? How dare he disregard the ancient system of *varṇāśrama*, which has been respected across this land since time immemorial? Rather than following the path of *dharma* this foolhardy Narottama has concocted his own brand of religion and is now widely propagating it. This is extremely dangerous. If his influence spreads, the *brāhmaṇas* will lose their authority and the entire social structure will fall into chaos."

"This is indeed a serious matter," the king said gravely.

Another *brāhmaṇa* stood and voiced his apprehension in a gentler manner. "Generally, we *brāhmaṇas* are peacefully engaged in *pūjā* and śāstric study. We don't like to speak harshly about anyone or to get involved in politics, but when religious principles are transgressed, we feel it's our responsibility to bring it to your attention. Ṭhākura Mahāśaya now has so much influence that we can no longer sit silently while he makes a mockery of our religious traditions."

"Yes," called out another member of the group. "The *śāstras* warn that as Kali-yuga progresses the *śūdras* will begin to read the *Vedas*. Now it appears that Ṭhākura Mahāśaya is ushering in the Age of Kali by not only studying the *Vedas* but giving instructions to *brāhmaṇas* as well – and even initiating them. Many *brāhmaṇas* have been fooled by his trickery and have come under his influence. Even some of the greatest *paṇḍitas* in this region – Gaṅgā-nārāyaṇa Cakravartī and Jagadīśa Ācārya have just taken initiation from him. It's like he has some kind of mystic power by which he captures people's minds. This Narottama is going to make a laughing stock of the entire brahminical class. It's a disaster."

Inciting one another's fears and insecurities, the crowd of agitated *brāhmaṇas* nodded and continued to defame Narottama. "Ever since Ṭhākura Mahāśaya has been preaching Vaiṣṇavism, the worship of all other gods has been neglected. Many people have taken Vaiṣṇava *mantras* and abandoned all Tantric rituals. Instead, people simply sing and dance like madmen in *saṅkīrtana*."

"It's true," shouted another. "Ṭhākura Mahāśaya must be stopped! The religion of the *brāhmaṇas* is at stake!"

The leader of the *paṇḍitas*, determined to assure the obliteration of Narottama's leadership, appealed to the king with folded hands. "Please," he begged. "You are known as a great patron of the *brāhmaṇas*. Kindly defend our honor and protect *dharma* by severely punishing Narottama Ṭhākura."

"What do you want me to do?" the king asked.

"Your court *paṇḍita*, Rūpanārāyaṇa, is the greatest scholar in this land. If you send him with us to debate this cunning Narottama, you can save our prestige. Once Narottama Ṭhākura has been exposed as a fraud and publicly humiliated, he will lose his influence and be forced to flee in disgrace."

The king turned to the famous old *paṇḍita* Rūpanārāyaṇa, who sat by his side, smiling enigmatically.

Suddenly, another elderly *brāhmaṇa* from Rāja Narasiṁha's court stood up and stepped forward. "My king," he said softly, "if you will allow me, I would like to make a few points, for one should not take action without full consideration."

"Yes, certainly, speak your mind," the king said.

"Don't be deceived by these *brāhmaṇas*. They have misunderstood Narottama Ṭhākura. I have met him, and he is truly the embodiment of virtue. He lives without material possessions and is equipoised, prideless, and free from malice. People are drawn to him because he is pure. His activities may be somewhat unconventional, but I assure you he has no ill intent."

The *paṇḍitas* gasped, stunned by this unexpected challenge. Their leader burst out, "Just see! Even one of your own court *paṇḍitas* has been contaminated by the Ṭhākura."

"Quiet, quiet!" the king called out, raising his hand. "Let him speak."

With folded hands the king's *paṇḍita* calmly addressed the other *brāhmaṇas*. "Please, listen. It's my duty to speak to you a harsh truth. Those who utter good advice even when it's unpalatable are few, and fewer still are those who welcome it. Don't let your pride ruin you. Your sinful plan has not the ghost of a chance of success. Ṭhākura Mahāśaya is a pure devotee. He is protected by the Supreme Lord Himself. Neither guile nor force can bring him down. If you insist on your foolish plan, I see the ruin that awaits you. Offending him will bring your doom."

The other *brāhmaṇas* rose up in outrage, creating pandemonium. The *paṇḍita* tried to continue above the din. "Be careful! Only yesterday I heard that Gurudāsa Bhaṭṭācārya contracted leprosy because of offending Narottama Ṭhākura."

The leading *paṇḍita's* eyes grew wide with indignation. "Do you really expect us to listen to these ridiculous rumors circulated by village women? We are concerned here with the application of religious principles, not sentimentality. Narottama Ṭhākura may make a good show of saintly behavior, but we can't become bewildered by some *śūdra's* melodramatic performances. As *brāhmaṇas* we must understand everything according to *śāstra*, logic, and reason. Tell me, in which scripture does it say that a *śūdra* may initiate a *brāhmaṇa*?" The *paṇḍita's* voice rose in his anger. "How can you have such high regard for a person whose behavior contradicts the statements of the *Vedas*? Shall we listen to your emotional diatribe or accept the verdict of scripture?"

Seeing his words falling on deaf ears the king's *paṇḍita* shrugged and, offering no defense, returned to his seat.

All eyes turned to the king.

"Thank you for your counsel," Rāja Narasiṁha said to his court *paṇḍita*. Then he thought for a few minutes. "It appears there are differing views about the Ṭhākura. How am I to determine who is correct?" Turning to Rūpanārāyaṇa again, the king asked, "Paṇḍitaji, you are said to be the most senior and learned among us. Your good advice has resolved many problems for me in the past. What do you think? What should be done?"

Rūpanārāyaṇa gave his edict without hesitation: "Oh King, taking these *brāhmaṇas* with us, we should leave at once. Let's go to Kheturi and confront Narottama in debate."

"Then it's settled," the king announced. We leave for Kheturi in the morning. I have been curious to meet Ṭhākura Mahāśaya, so I shall accompany you."

A wave of relief swept through the crowd, and the *paṇḍitas* began to talk about the upcoming debate.

The following morning, the king, Rūpanārāyaṇa, and all the *paṇḍitas* began their journey. As the full moon rises brightly before an eclipse, so the throng of *brāhmaṇas* advanced in a proud array.

The news that King Narasiṁha Rāya and his band of scholars was coming to defeat Narottama in debate quickly reached Kheturi. Gaṅgā-nārāyaṇa and

Rāmacandra Kavirāja had seen the look of disapproval on Narottama's face when he heard the *paṇḍitas'* plan. It was clear that Ṭhākura Mahāśaya had absolutely no interest in debating with caste-conscious agitators. Feeling the confrontation would disturb their spiritual master, Gaṅgā-nārāyaṇa and Rāmacandra Kavirāja devised a plan of their own to avert the challenge.

They set off for the nearby town of Kumārapur. There, Gaṅgā-nārāyaṇa disguised himself as a pan-leaf salesman and Rāmacandra Kavirāja dressed as a potter.[16] Wearing turbans to cover their shaved heads, they set up separate but adjacent shops in the marketplace and sat down to sell their wares.

When the king's party arrived at Kumārapur they set up camp, and a few *brāhmaṇas* went to the market to buy vegetables, rice, and cooking pots.

Rāmacandra Kavirāja and Gaṅgā-nārāyaṇa had anticipated this, and they watched as the *brāhmaṇas* walked through the marketplace, finally stopping to examine the clay pots at Rāmacandra Kavirāja's stall.

"How much are these?" one *brāhmaṇa* asked.

Rāmacandra told him the price – in Sanskrit.

Trying to conceal his surprise, the *brāhmaṇa* began to barter for a better price, also in Sanskrit. When Rāmacandra continued to speak in fluent Sanskrit, the *brāhmaṇa* could no longer mask his amazement. "How is it that the shopkeepers of this town are so educated?" he asked.

"We are just humble shopkeepers," Rāmacandra replied meekly. "What little knowledge we have is simply due to the mercy of our Guru Mahārāja."

"And whom may I ask is your spiritual master?"

"Narottama Ṭhākura Mahāśaya. He lives in the nearby town of Kheturi. His knowledge and devotion are beyond compare."

Meanwhile, a few of the *brāhmaṇas* who had moved on to the pan-leaf shop were stunned when Gaṅgā-nārāyaṇa also conversed with them in Sanskrit. Intrigued, the *brāhmaṇas* began whispering among themselves, "This place is amazing. The shopkeepers speak like erudite scholars."

Gaṅgā-nārāyaṇa and Rāmacandra continued to chat nonchalantly with the *brāhmaṇas*, as if Sanskrit were their native language. Skillfully, they turned the conversation toward spiritual topics and gradually drew the proud *brāhmaṇas* into a philosophical debate. As the discussion became heated, crowds of curious villagers pressed in around them, listening with awe as Gaṅgā-nārāyaṇa and Rāmacandra eloquently established their points by quoting many Sanskrit verses. It didn't take long for the two to defeat the *paṇḍitas*.

Mortified, the *brāhmaṇas* stood speechless. "I am not going to stand here in the middle of a marketplace and debate with a *pan-wālā*," one spluttered indignantly to his friends. "Let's go."

The victorious "shopkeepers" chided the *brāhmaṇas* as they strode out of the marketplace. "You had better return to your studies," Gaṅgā-nārāyaṇa teased. "Send your professors to us so we can debate further."

The *brāhmaṇas* swiftly disappeared. But Gaṅgā-nārāyaṇa and Rāmacandra didn't believe the *paṇḍitas* would accept defeat so easily. Suspecting they would return with more of their entourage, Gaṅgā-nārāyaṇa and Rāmacandra remained at their stalls.

The *brāhmaṇas* rushed into their camp and roused their colleagues. "Something terrible happened at the marketplace. We were completely humiliated by two shopkeepers! A *pan-wālā* and a potter started to debate with us, and speaking fluent Sanskrit defeated us in front of everyone."

"What!" one of the *paṇḍitas* chuckled, "A *pan-wālā* and a potter speaking Sanskrit?!"

"Yes. They're students of Narottama Ṭhākura. We were thoroughly disgraced. We can never show our faces here again."

An incredulous *paṇḍita* asked, "What kind of town is this where the shopkeepers speak Sanskrit and discuss *śāstra* in the marketplace?"

"Believe me. Those two shopkeepers are the most erudite scholars I've ever met," said one of the humiliated *paṇḍitas*. "If simple working men like these are so sophisticated, what will the Ṭhākura's scholars be like?"

"And just imagine what Narottama Ṭhākura Mahāśaya must be like if these are his insignificant students," another added. "We had better go home and forget about Kheturi. We've already been defeated by Narottama's pupils."

"Leave now?" the head of the *paṇḍitas* yelled, "Are you mad? Rather, we should go to the marketplace immediately and curb those arrogant shopkeepers' pride.

"Yes! We must defend our honor. Let's go to the marketplace at once."

The group of agitated *brāhmaṇas* entered the marketplace a few moments later. Searching out the *pan-wālā* and clay-pot salesman, the *paṇḍitas* encircled their shops. Their leader confronted Gaṅgā-nārāyaṇa with sarcasm: "Is it a common practice in this town for shopkeepers to offend visiting *brāhmaṇas*?"

"Please forgive me," Gaṅgā-nārāyaṇa said humbly – in Sanskrit. "I didn't mean to offend anyone. We were merely having a philosophical discussion."

Rāmacandra Kavirāja interceded – also in Sanskrit: "I think those *brāhmaṇas* were just too young and inexperienced. You appear to be much more educated. Likely you would fare better in a debate."

Caught by the challenge, the head of the *brāhmaṇas* asserted, "We will discuss whatever you like."

"Perhaps we should make a comparative study between the qualities of the *brāhmaṇas* and the qualities of the Vaiṣṇavas," Rāmacandra said.

"Yes," the head of the *paṇḍitas* replied. "I'm well versed in this topic." And the scholarly *paṇḍita* rattled off numerous verses glorifying the *brāhmaṇas*. He smiled smugly at Gaṅgā-nārāyaṇa. "Would you like to add something?"

"What more can I say?" Gaṅgā-nārāyaṇa said in mock wonder. "You have described the position of the *brāhmaṇa* very nicely. But now, if you will allow me, I would like to say something about the exalted position of the Vaiṣṇavas.

"Of course," the *brāhmaṇa* said with a casual wave of his hand.

Then Gaṅgā-nārāyaṇa began. First, he offered his respects to his spiritual master. Then poetic *ślokas* in glorification of the Vaiṣṇavas flowed from his mouth in an endless stream:

viprād dvi-ṣaḍ-guṇa-yutād aravinda-nābha-
pādāravinda-vimukhāt śvapacaṁ variṣṭham
manye tad-arpita-mano-vacanehitārtha-
prāṇaṁ punāti sa kulaṁ na tu bhūrimānaḥ

"If a *brāhmaṇa* has all twelve of the brahminical qualifications but is not a devotee and is averse to the lotus feet of the Lord, he is certainly lower than a devotee who is a dog-eater but who has dedicated everything – mind, words, activities, wealth, and life – to the Supreme Lord. Such a devotee is better than such a *brāhmaṇa* because the devotee can purify his whole family, whereas the so-called *brāhmaṇa* in a position of false prestige cannot purify even himself."

bhagavad-bhakti-hīnasya
jātiḥ śāstraṁ japas tapaḥ
aprāṇasyeva dehasya
maṇḍanaṁ loka-rañjanam

"For a person devoid of devotional service, birth in a great family or nation, knowledge of the revealed scriptures, performance of austerities and penance, and chanting of Vedic *mantras* are all like ornaments on a dead body. Such ornaments simply serve the concocted pleasures of the general populace."

yasya yal lakṣaṇaṁ proktaṁ
puṁso varṇābhivyaṣjakam
yad anyatrāpi dṛśyeta
tat tenaiva vinirdiśet

"If one shows the symptoms of being a *brāhmaṇa, kṣatriya, vaiśya* or *śūdra*, even if he has appeared in a different class, he should be accepted according to those symptoms of classification.

"If a person is born in a *śūdra* family but has all the qualities of a spiritual master, he should be accepted not only as a *brāhmaṇa* but as a qualified spiritual master.

"A Vaiṣṇava is superior to a *brāhmaṇa* because, whereas a *brāhmaṇa* knows that he is Brahman, not matter, a Vaiṣṇava knows he is not only Brahman but also an eternal servant of the Supreme Brāhman."

On and on, he spoke, his powerful, melodious voice echoing through the marketplace, mesmerizing everyone. The *brāhmaṇas* stood with their mouths agape as Gaṅgā-nārāyaṇa irrevocably established the superior position of the Vaiṣṇava.

When he finally stopped speaking, the entire marketplace was completely silent. With folded hands Gaṅgā-nārāyaṇa turned to the head of the *paṇḍitas.* "So," he said, smiling gently, "the *śāstras* clearly state that the Vaiṣṇava is superior to all. Vaiṣṇavas are beyond caste distinction and should be respected by everyone – even the *brāhmaṇas*."

The chief of the *brāhmaṇas* stood stunned. Wiping sweat from his forehead he sputtered a few weak arguments, which were swiftly refuted by Gaṅgā-nārāyaṇa's razor-sharp intelligence. The color drained from the *paṇḍita's* face. Desperately he turned to the other *brāhmaṇas* for help, but no one spoke. Like a captive elephant hemmed in on all sides, the exasperated *brāhmaṇa* hung his head and admitted defeat. He then slunk away as the crowd cheered.

A few other *paṇḍitas* tried their luck but were swiftly dispatched like moths rushing to a flame. The ecstatic crowd congratulated the two shopkeepers, and the shamed *brāhmaṇas* scurried out of the marketplace.

The *paṇḍitas* returned to their camp, sick with disappointment. After reporting everything to the king, they languished in their sorrow. They had proudly left the camp roaring like the ocean, but now most sulked in silence. A few of them discussed the debate, keeping their voices low.

Their leader was fuming. Turning to the scholar Rūpanārāyaṇa he hissed, "Why didn't you come to my defense? You could have defeated those rascals."

"How can you be so foolish as to call them rascals?" Rūpanārāyaṇa snapped. "Your stubborn pride blinds you. I didn't speak because my heart was filled with awe by their illuminating presentation. It was brilliant, logical, and full of śāstric references. How could you *not* be impressed by those shopkeepers? Their speech, their demeanor, and the knowledge they presented far surpassed those of the greatest *brāhmaṇas*. Both through personal example and śāstric reference they established without a shadow of a doubt that a Vaiṣṇava is situated on the topmost spiritual platform and is worthy of respect even from the *brāhmaṇas*."

Rūpanārāyaṇa's stance was unexpected, and all the *paṇḍitas* stared at him.

Rūpanārāyaṇa glared back. "Are you all too proud to admit that what they said was true? Won't any of you acknowledge that those men know far more about spiritual topics than all of us? Could you not perceive that those saintly shopkeepers were not debating us just to establish their superiority? Nor were they trying to humiliate us. They simply wanted to establish the point that a Vaiṣṇava like their *guru* Śrī Narottama Ṭhākura is beyond mundane caste distinction and is endowed with the power to elevate even the lowest of creatures to the highest spiritual platform. If it weren't so, how could such simple folk become so spiritually advanced? It could only be by the merciful touch of a Vaiṣṇava like Ṭhākura Mahāśaya. Just as bell metal can be turned into gold, a saint of Narottama's caliber can transform anyone into an effulgent, self-realized soul. Such is the power of the Vaiṣṇava."

Exasperated with the *paṇḍitas'* continued silence, Rūpanārāyaṇa stepped into the center of the group. "What's the use of your birth as *brāhmaṇas* if you can't recognize and appreciate transcendental knowledge when it stares you in the face? Isn't the attainment of such knowledge the sole purpose of a *brāhmaṇa's* life? Isn't this what you all yearn for?" He looked around reproachfully at the crowd. "Have you become so caught up in rules and rituals that you've forgotten the goal of your *dharma*?"

No one dared to speak.

Pacing back and forth, Rūpanārāyaṇa continued his impassioned speech. "Do you think you have already attained conclusive knowledge of the Absolute simply by taking birth in a *brāhmaṇa* family? Ha! Don't delude yourself, or others in this way. Spiritual understanding is not so cheap. Simply taking birth in a *brāhmaṇa* family or wearing a sacred thread does not automatically elevate you to the brahminical platform. As a matter of fact, it's said in the *Varāha Purāṇa* that everyone is born a *śūdra* in Kali-yuga. And it is further mentioned that in Kali-yuga even demons may take birth in *brāhmaṇa* families. What have you got to be proud of?"

"No, no, my friends," Rūpanārāyaṇa continued, chuckling lightly, "you most certainly cannot judge a man by his birth. One's nature can only be understood by the qualities he manifests. And to my eyes, those shopkeepers showed themselves to be of the highest character. Just imagine what the characteristics of their *guru* must be."

"Excuse me Paṇḍitaji," one of the reprimanded *brāhmaṇas* objected, "you speak so highly of those shopkeepers, but you seem to have little regard for your own colleagues. Do you not see that there are many great souls in this assembly who possess all the jewel-like qualities of the *brāhmaṇas*? Why are you speaking so harshly to them?"

Rūpanārāyaṇa stopped pacing and turned to address the *brāhmaṇa* respectfully. "Forgive me," he said gently. "I do not wish to offend any of you. My purpose is not to minimize the importance of the *brāhmaṇas* but to point out that coming to the brahminical platform is not an automatic process. Nor is the attainment of Brahman the end of one's spiritual quest. In fact, it is just the beginning. The Absolute Truth is understood in three phases: Brahman, Parāmatma, and Bhagavān. To reach the higher stages you must pass through the brahminical stage and become a Vaiṣṇava situated on the *vasudeva* platform. Only then can you understand the Personality of Godhead, Śrī Kṛṣṇa, and His qualities, name, form, and pastimes."

He fixed his gaze firmly on the questioner and said, "That's why those two shopkeepers could so easily defeat you: they are disciples of a great Vaiṣṇava and have become Vaiṣṇavas themselves, so their knowledge and devotion surpass yours. Consequently, to consider them – or their *guru* – low-class is a grave offense. Regardless of their birth, they are worthy of our worship. Therefore, I humbly ask you to swallow your pride."

Pressing his palms together in *namaskāra*, Rūpanārāyaṇa scanned the faces of his audience, his eyes pleading for understanding, "For your own good, give up your attitude of superiority over the Vaiṣṇavas. This mentality will only lead you down the road to destruction. Take my advice, for I have learned this lesson by experience. I once made the mistake of arrogantly considering myself superior to a great devotee, but by the Vaiṣṇavas' mercy I was humbled."

Mention of Rūpanārāyaṇa's personal mistake caught his listeners' attention. Rūpanārāyaṇa's face softened, and tears welled up in his eyes. Heaving a deep sigh, he sat down. When he next spoke, his voice cracked with emotion.

"Many years ago, when I was a very young scholar, I pompously traveled up and down the countryside defeating *paṇḍitas* in debate. I was so proud of my learning that I demanded a certificate of victory from each of my opponents so I could show everyone that I was Digvijayi, one who had conquered in all directions."

"Eventually I went to Vṛndāvana with the intention of defeating the famous scholars Rūpa Gosvāmī and Sanātana Gosvāmī. But when I rudely challenged them, they humbly declined to argue, saying they were not qualified to debate with such a learned person as me. Hearing this, my head swelled and I thought, 'Ah, now I am the greatest scholar of all time.' When I asked Rūpa and Sanātana to sign the certificate of defeat, they easily did so and sent me on my way."

Intrigued by Rūpanārāyaṇa's intimate disclosure, the *paṇḍitas* moved in closer.

Rūpanārāyaṇa shook his head, shamed by the remembrance of it. "Blinded by vanity, I went straight to the bank of the Yamunā River and bragged to everyone I could find that Rūpa and Sanātana were afraid to debate with me. Śrī Jīva Gosvāmī, their young nephew, happened to come to the Yamunā at that time and heard my prideful boast. Eager to vindicate his uncles' reputation, he said with some anger in his voice, 'I'm a pupil of Rūpa and Sanātana. If you can defeat me, I shall accept you as the winner. You will now learn how clever Rūpa and Sanātana are by debating with me.'

"Well, the debate that followed was heated, and it lasted for days. Śrī Jīva expertly defeated the philosophy of *advaita-vāda* and established the superiority of devotional service above *jñāna* and *karma*. At last I was forced to bow my head in defeat. Yet strangely I didn't feel humiliated; rather, I felt purified. My heart was actually overflowing with transcendental happiness. By the merciful association of the exalted saint Śrī Jīva, my eyes were opened and I understood the truth. Relieved of the heavy burden of my pride I humbly apologized to Śrī Jīva, Rūpa, and Sanātana. At that time Sanātana Gosvāmī told me that in the future I would take initiation from Narottama of Kheturi. Since that time, I have been wandering around eagerly waiting to meet that great soul. When you *brāhmaṇas* arrived at the court of Rāja Narasiṁha to lodge a complaint against Narottama Ṭhākura, although externally I agreed to your plan to defeat him in debate, I was thinking that my good fortune had finally arrived. Now we shall all be delivered by the Ṭhākura's mercy. By his immense spiritual potency, Ṭhākura Mahāśaya is drawing us all to him."

Stunned by this confession, the chief of the *brāhmaṇas* could no longer hold his tongue. "You traitor! You had no intention of helping us." He turned to his colleagues. "We have been harboring an enemy in our own camp." And with that, the *brāhmaṇa* stalked out of the assembly.

Again, mayhem descended. Some of the *paṇḍitas* were amazed by Rūpanārāyaṇa's revelation. Some were bewildered, others dubious, and many more completely won over.

In the meantime, Rāja Narasiṁha had listened silently to all that had transpired. Now he stepped forward and, with a beaming smile, wrapped an arm around Rūpanārāyaṇa's shoulder. "Ah ha! Paṇḍitaji. You are a clever man! Thank you for opening our eyes. Then it is just as I had suspected: Ṭhākura Mahāśaya is an extraordinary saint. So, what are we to do now? What should our course of action be?"

"We should continue on to Kheturi tomorrow," Rūpanārāyaṇa said, "not to debate but to take shelter of Śrī Narottama Ṭhākura Mahāśaya."

"Yes, yes," Rāja Narasiṁha agreed enthusiastically. "We have come so far. Now we must meet this great devotee, seek his shelter, and apologize for our presumption. I have been wanting to meet him for a long time."

Turning again to the *paṇḍitas*, Rūpanārāyaṇa concluded, "So, my friends, your defeat is no cause for shame. You are being offered the greatest opportunity to make spiritual progress. Don't be afraid. Accept your defeat graciously. Let's all go to Kheturi and take shelter of Narottama Ṭhākura. His spiritual power is so great that he can deliver all of us from the ocean of material existence."

Some of the *paṇḍitas* agreed and others still looked dazed by the rapid turn of events.

The king gave his command: "We shall stay here tonight and start for Kheturi in the morning." Saying this, Rāja Narasiṁha and Rūpanārāyaṇa left the assembly, leaving the *paṇḍitas* to ponder.

By morning, most of the *paṇḍitas* had recognized their folly and were eager to meet Ṭhākura Mahāśaya. They discussed their plans for departure.

Suddenly, the chief of the *brāhmaṇas* ran into their camp crying hysterically and fell at Rūpanārāyaṇa's feet. Shocked to see the *paṇḍita* in such a state, everyone gathered around him.

Rūpanārāyaṇa gently pulled the emotional *paṇḍita* to his knees. "What's happened?" he asked.

The *paṇḍita's* face was ashen and his eyes red from crying. "I'm sorry," he sobbed. "Please forgive me. You were right! You were right!"

Amazed by the change in the *paṇḍita's* demeanor, Rūpanārāyaṇa asked, "How have you had such a change of heart?"

Struggling to compose himself, the *paṇḍita* took a deep, trembling breath and wiped his tears. "Last night when I fell asleep," he said, his voice wavering, "the goddess Bhagavatī appeared before me. She was furious. Her blood-red eyes flashed with anger." The *brāhmaṇa* shuddered at the remembrance.

"Holding a sword in her hand she yelled, 'You rogue! You shameless excuse for a *paṇḍita*! I will behead you. All your studies have been in vain because you have criticized the great devotee Narottama Ṭhākura. By this offense you have purchased your ticket to hell. Narottama is the incarnation of the Lord's ecstasy. He is a true *brāhmaṇa* because he not only understands Brahman but he has captured the Supreme Brahman, Kṛṣṇa, in his heart. Thus, a bright sacred thread is permanently imbedded in Narottama's heart. You must become a true *brāhmaṇa* by accepting initiation from him. Only his mercy can save you from the sufferings of hell." The *paṇḍita* clasped his head in his hands. "And then Bhagavatī disappeared. It was horrible! I woke up trembling with fear. Now I realize my grave mistake," he said, fighting back more tears. "Please allow me to come with you to Kheturi."

Ṭhākura Mahāśaya laughed heartily along with his disciples as Gaṅgā-nārāyaṇa Cakravartī and Rāmacandra Kavirāja described their debate with the arrogant *paṇḍitas*. He was relieved to have been spared the confrontation with them. During the discussion, one of

Narottama's disciples entered the garden and interrupted the laughter with an announcement: "The King of Pakapalli and his troupe of *paṇḍitas* just entered the compound. They've gone into the temple room."

Ṭhākura Mahāśaya smiled brightly. "Please bring them here after they have taken *darśana*."

With faltering steps, King Narasiṁha, Rūpanārāyaṇa, and the crowd of *paṇḍitas* approached Ṭhākura Mahāśaya. When they were still at some distance, they fell to the ground in obeisance. Fearful and ashamed, they looked timidly up at Narottama's face.

Narottama smiled as he saw the look of surprise on all the *paṇḍitas'* faces when they saw Gaṅgā-nārāyaṇa and Rāmacandra by his side, dressed in *dhotīs* and with *brāhmaṇa* threads and *śikhās* clearly visible.

"Please sit," Narottama said. "I am fortunate to have the company of such highly learned and noble persons."

Venturing forward, the king fell to his knees in front of Ṭhākura Mahāśaya. "We came on a sinful mission," he said remorsefully. "We wanted to drag you down from your position. But now we have understood our terrible mistake." Tears welled up in the king's eyes. "Please forgive us and give us shelter at your feet."

Ṭhākura Mahāśaya was touched to see the king's tears. Standing he pulled the king to his feet and embraced him. "Don't worry," Narottama said, his own eyes wet with tears. "I am yours and you are mine."

Deeply relieved by Ṭhākura Mahāśaya's warm reception, the king broke out into a huge smile. "These two disciples of yours" – and he motioned to Gaṅgā-nārāyaṇa and Rāmacandra – "saved us from committing a heinous crime at your feet. They have shown us the superiority of *bhakti*. We consider ourselves most fortunate to have been defeated by your glorious disciples."

The chief of the *paṇḍitas* sheepishly stepped forward, his face clouded by anxiety. Falling at Narottama's feet he cried, "Please forgive me. I am the greatest offender." With deep remorse, the humbled *paṇḍita* sorrowfully retold the tale of Durgadevī's anger at him and begged to be forgiven for his offenses.

Ṭhākura Mahāśaya assured the *paṇḍita* that he had not taken any offense. Rāmacandra Kavirāja gently placed his arm around the *paṇḍita's* shoulder, comforting and welcoming him.

"This is Rūpanārāyaṇa," the king said, introducing the famous *paṇḍita*. "He has been waiting for many long years to get your *darśana*."

Rūpanārāyaṇa came forward. After offering his profound respects, he told the story of his meeting with the Vṛndāvana Gosvāmīs and his defeat at Jīva Gosvāmī's hands. Narottama and Rāmacandra heard his tale with amazement and delight.

Rāmacandra Kavirāja then invited everyone to attend the *ārati*. Afterward, Ṭhākura Mahāśaya sat down to begin *kīrtana*. His voice was enchanting, and the king and the *paṇḍitas* gathered around him to listen. Through sweet songs of devotion, Ṭhākura Mahāśaya instructed them all in the science of Kṛṣṇa.

"My dear brothers," he sang, "putting the *yogīs*, *karmīs*, *jñānīs*, and demigod worshipers far away, and rejecting the torments that are fruitive work, ordinary religion, and the other processes of *yoga*, just worship Lord Giridhārī. The innumerable varieties of philosophy and various conceptions of life are all products of the conditioned soul's pride. Trying to understand them brings no real benefit, but only pain within the mind . . . The fruitive work of the *karma-kāṇḍī* and the speculative knowledge of the *jñāna-kāṇḍī* are two pots of poison. If one drinks these two poisons and then proclaims that they are both as sweet as nectar, he will fall from the human realm and spend a long time wandering in many species of life."

The guests swayed to the music, absorbing the profound message in every stanza. Narottama looked up at their joyful faces and knew that the pure, potent teachings of Śrī Caitanya Mahāprabhu were already acting on their hearts.

On and on, Ṭhākura Mahāśaya sang, encouraging his audience to take up the process of Kṛṣṇa consciousness. "Give up the tendency to find fault in others, and simply follow the path of pure devotional service, which is free from any extraneous motive and devoid of fruitive karma, impersonal *jñāna,* and all other selfish desires."

Ṭhākura Mahāśaya's eyes glistened with tears as he lovingly urged his audience to take shelter of his beloved Lord Kṛṣṇa. "Just dive into the shoreless nectar ocean of pure love for Kṛṣṇa. It is larger than the largest salt-water ocean. If you swim in that nectar ocean, Lord Kṛṣṇa will make all your sufferings disappear, and you will attain endless transcendental bliss."

Then, ending the *kīrtana,* Ṭhākura Mahāśaya invited everyone to take *prasāda.* Touched by Ṭhākura Mahāśaya's company, the guests decided to remain in Kheturi for as long as possible.

In that company both the king and his *paṇḍitas* were transformed. Within a short time, all of them fully embraced the Kṛṣṇa conscious philosophy and accepted initiation from Ṭhākura Mahāśaya.

Chand Rāya

One day, noticing two unfamiliar men entering the courtyard, Narottama and Rāmacandra stopped chanting and came forward to receive their guests. After offering them a seat and some *prasāda* Narottama asked, "Where have you come from, and how may I serve you?"

"The ruler of Gaderhat, Śrī Rāghavendra Rāya, sent us here to deliver a message." Pulling a small piece of parchment from his bag, the messenger handed it to Narottama. "Read this letter and you will understand everything."

Narottama opened the letter and silently read:

Respected Ṭhākura Mahāśaya,

I am writing this letter in hopes that you will come to my aid. Recently, my son, Chand Rāya, has fallen into great difficulty, and I believe you are the only one who can save him. Perhaps you have heard of him – he was the powerful Zamindar of the Rajmahāla fort. But some weeks ago, the spirit of a wicked *brāhmaṇa* ghost entered his body and began to torment him. The ghost took complete control of his body and mind, forcing him to speak and behave like a madman. Barely able to eat or sleep, Chand has gradually lost all strength and is now in a terrible state. I fear for his life.

I've tried everything to save him. I brought doctors and Tantrics from all over the country, but no one has been able to help him. A few days ago a psychic astrologer told me that the *brāhmaṇa rākṣasa* who has entered Chand's body is determined to remain there unless and until the son of the Zamindar of Kheturi, Narottama Ṭhākura Mahāśaya, comes here.

So, it appears that the only hope of curing my son lies in your hands. I beg you, please come to my home and help my boy. I will reward you with anything you want – land, gold, cows . . . whatever you desire will be yours if you can cure him.

Please come immediately as he is losing strength rapidly.

Begging for your mercy,

Rāghavendra Rāya

Narottama looked up at the messengers quizzically. "This Chand Rāya – isn't he a notorious dacoit?"

One of the messengers nodded. "Yes, a real debauchee. He was a wealthy and powerful man, extremely brave and skilled in the art of weaponry, but unfortunately, wealth and power went to his head and he became a tyrant. With five thousand horses and infantry under his command he has attacked and looted many villages. Robbing and killing people has been his regular pastime. In carrying out these cruel acts he cares for no one."

The other messenger added, "He even seduced the wives and daughters of the villagers. And his brother, Santosh, joined him in these horrible deeds. Together they would drink, then go into the villages to pick fights. Everyone is terrified of them."

"Sounds like Jagāi and Mādhāi incarnate," Rāmacandra said to Narottama.

"Their father tried again and again to get them to stop their nefarious activities," the messenger continued, "but they just laughed and continued their reign of terror. But now that powerful tyrant, Chanda Rāya, has been reduced to a babbling idiot because a ghost has taken over his body. He's now simply wasting away in his father's house."

Narottama remained grave as he handed the letter to Rāmacandra Kavirāja to read.

"*Hmm,*" Rāmacandra said, noting the contents. "It's a delicate matter."

"What do you think we should do?" Narottama asked. "I'm not sure whether we should get involved."

Kavirāja shrugged. "What can I say? You are the embodiment of love and are free to do as you like."

Closing his eyes, Narottama sat motionless, contemplating the situation. In his meditation he heard the voice of Caitanya Mahāprabhu. "Listen, Narottama. It will be easy for you to deliver this wicked sinner, Chand Rāya. Go to his home and show him your mercy. He is waiting for your blessings. You appeared in this world only to deliver the fallen souls. So, go with Kavirāja and free Chand Rāya from his sins."

Narottama's golden body trembled with ecstasy. Opening his eyes and with a radiant smile he announced, "Tomorrow we will go to the home of Rāghavendra Rāya."

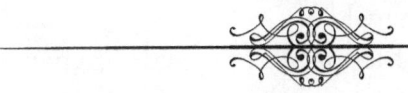

The next morning, after bowing at Lord Gaurāṅga's feet, Ṭhākura Mahāśaya, Rāmacandra Kavirāja, Gaṅgā-nārāyaṇa Cakravartī, and several other Vaiṣṇavas set out for Rāghavendra Rāya's village, guided by Rāya's messengers. Late in the afternoon as they stopped to rest, the two messengers hurried ahead to inform Rāghavendra Rāya of Narottama's arrival.

The next morning, as Narottama and Kavirāja chanted *japa,* their meditation was broken by the sound of musical instruments in the distance. The music grew louder, and finally they saw a band of musicians striding right into their camp followed by a large group of *brāhmaṇas* chanting Vedic *mantras.* A large, burly fellow led the group, and as he entered the camp he looked around until his gaze fell on Narottama. He raised his hand to silence the cacophony. Struck by Narottama's powerful spiritual demeanor, he clasped his hands together in awe.

"You must be Ṭhākura Mahāśaya," he said. Unable to stand in the presence of such obvious spiritual power, the man fell at Narottama's feet. Weeping with joy he cried out, "I am Rāghavendra, Chand Rāya's father. Thank you so much for coming to my rescue. We are blessed to have your association."

Narottama lifted him from the ground and said, "It's our fortune to be of some service. We are simply the humble servants of the servants of the Vaiṣṇavas. We have no other qualification."

"Please, allow me to escort you to my house. Everyone is waiting for your arrival."

Narottama and his party followed Rāghavendra Rāya to his village. Entering the town, Narottama was surprised to see that it had been decorated in his honor. Water-filled jugs and banana trees lined the roads, and beautifully draped garlands of flowers and mango leaves adorned every house. As Narottama and his entourage passed, crowds of people dressed in their best clothes and jewels gathered on the streets to welcome them. Narottama reciprocated warmly, smiling and greeting everyone with sweet words.

As they arrived at Rāghavendra's home, they were received by the family with utmost respect. Rāghavendra offered Ṭhākura Mahāśaya a cushioned seat draped with embroidered cloth, hung a garland around his neck, and smeared sandalwood paste on his forehead. After washing Narottama's feet with great care, he said, "My home has now become blessed by your presence."

"It's very kind of you to invite me," Narottama said. "Now, let me see your son."

Rāghavendra, followed by his wife and family, ushered Ṭhākura Mahāśaya and his associates into the adjoining room. There they saw Chand Rāya asleep on his bed, his skin a ghostly white and his body emaciated. Rāghavendra sat on the bed and gently took his son's head in his lap. "Chand," he said softly, "wake up. Ṭhākura Mahāśaya has come to our home. Offer your respects to him."

Chand Rāya opened his pallid eyes and slowly turned his gaunt face toward Narottama. The moment he set eyes on Ṭhākura Mahāśaya his face twisted and an inhuman voice spoke from within him.

"I have become a ghost due to my past sinful activities. I have behaved just like Chand Rāya. That is why I have taken shelter of his body. I have been living within his body for a long time, but I now desire release from this hell."

Shocked, Rāghavendra's family and friends stepped back in fear, and Narottama could hear the curious villagers peering through the windows gasp in horror.

Again, the ghost called out, "Oh Ṭhākura Mahāśaya, please save me from this cursed life. Your presence here has purified me. I desire to take birth in Kheturi so I can become your humble servant."

"Listen," Narottama said, his voice firm but kind, "Leave this body at once and go elsewhere."

Chand Rāya screamed. His body jerked violently, then went limp as he fainted.

Chand's mother, nearly fainting herself, fanned her son frantically, while his brother, Santosh, sprinkled water on his face.

Within moments, whatever had been distorting Chand's features seemed to leave him and his face regained its normal lines. He opened his dazed eyes and slowly pulled himself to a sitting position.

Shouts of joy and praise for Ṭhākura Mahāśaya filled the room. Santosh knelt at his brother's bedside, "Ṭhākura Mahāśaya has saved your life!" And he explained all that had happened.

Chand was silent at first, then in a small voice, spoke: "I had the most horrible dream . . . " He looked at Narottama and placed his palms together in respect. "Please forgive me. Please forgive . . . " he cried out again, his voice wracked with emotion. "There is no one as cursed as me. I have committed sins not even mentioned in scripture. How can I be relieved of the reactions of my misdeeds?" As he looked into Narottama's eyes he broke down.

Chand's relatives and friends watched with amazement – not only had the ghost left Chand's body but his arrogance had disappeared as well.

Santosh also had a change of heart. He touched the feet of Ṭhākura Mahāśaya. "Although born *brāhmaṇas*, for years Chand and I have performed abominable acts.

Blinded by arrogance, we were lost to the darkness. But your radiant spiritual presence has illuminated our hearts and given us hope of a new life. You know who we are and what we have done," he said, shamed. "We can do nothing but pray for your mercy."

Rāghavendra also fell at Ṭhākura Mahāśaya's feet. "We are all indebted to you life after life. Please consider my entire family your eternal servants."

Villagers pushed at the windows, straining to get a look at what was transpiring inside. What a shock it was to see the two men who had terrorized them, their powerful masters, lying at Narottama's feet begging for mercy.

Narottama spoke compassionately. "Śrī Caitanya Mahāprabhu will certainly bestow His unlimited mercy on all of you. He is *mahā-vadānyāya*, the most merciful. Anyone who surrenders at His lotus feet is most fortunate."

Narottama spent the next few days instructing Rāghavendra and his family about the science of devotional service. Through his association, the whole family became sincere Vaiṣṇavas and renounced their pride and arrogance.

One morning, Narottama instructed Rāghavendra, "Go with your sons to bathe. Dress in new, clean clothing and return."

Rāghavendra and his sons bathed quickly. When they came before Narottama to offer their obeisances, they were visibly excited.

"Come sit by my left side," Narottama said softly. "I shall pour the nectar of the holy name into the ears of each one of you."

One by one, the family members took their place next to Ṭhākura Mahāśaya. Shining like Vaikuṇṭha angels, the two former debauchees and their father humbly came before their spiritual master to receive initiation. After listening to Ṭhākura Mahāśaya chant the *mantra*, Rāya and his sons lay prostrate before their spiritual master.

Cramming into the room to watch the ceremony, Narottama's associates and Rāghavendra's friends, relatives, and servants were moved to tears. The family had truly been transformed by Ṭhākura Mahāśaya's kindness.

After receiving initiation, Rāghavendra and his sons offered many gifts to Ṭhākura Mahāśaya, including clothes, money, horses, cows and calves – even a village! Then a feast of sweets, curries, and scented rice was prepared and offered to the Lord. After Ṭhākura Mahāśaya had eaten, Rāghavendra and his two sons took his remnants and drank the water that had washed his feet.

Ṭhākura Mahāśaya instructed his new disciples for a few more days, then expressed his desire to return to Kheturi. Unable to bear the thought of separation from their spiritual master, Rāghavendra and his sons decided to accompany him to Kheturi.

The following morning, a large party escorted Ṭhākura Mahāśaya and his associates to the river. There, ten boats decorated with gold and jewels awaited them. Rāghavendra ushered Narottama and his associates onto the boat that had been specially prepared for them, and he and his sons boarded another. Rāghavendra had arranged for the other boats to be filled with rice, beans, spices, cloth, blankets, and other gifts for the Deities and devotees of Kheturi.

As the boats pushed off from the shore, hordes of villagers swarmed to get one last glimpse of Ṭhākura Mahāśaya. Narottama realized that during his short visit he had deeply touched their lives and that a great bond of love had grown between them. He knew they would not easily forget the miraculous transformation of the Rāya family. Many of the villagers cried openly, others lay prostrate in the sand, or stood motionless, watching sadly as the boats gradually drifted further downstream.

Onboard the boats, the devotees immersed themselves in talks of Kṛṣṇa. They reached Kheturi at noon the following day, and the party went straight to the temple for *darśana*. Then Ṭhākura Mahāśaya lovingly invited everyone to take *prasāda* in the temple courtyard.

Chand Rāya sat next to his father and brother and the Ṭhākura's exalted associates. Narottama smiled gently as he watched his new disciples devour the *prasāda*.

Chand's eyes met Narottama's. His face flushed and spontaneous praise for his *guru* poured forth. "My good fortune is unfathomable," he said. "Only a few days ago I was lying on my death bed, a horribly cruel man headed for innumerable lives of suffering in hell. By your mercy, I now sit with saints in this pure atmosphere." Tears came to Chand's eyes. "You have saved me from hell and given me real life. But my heart is filled with pain because I know I can never repay my debt to you even in millions of lifetimes."

Narottama smiled. Certainly, Śrī Caitanya Mahāprabhu was the most merciful incarnation. He came to this earth to deliver the most fallen souls and He had done so with Chand Rāya.

That evening the devotees gathered in the temple room as Devīdāsa and other expert musicians began to play their instruments. Narottama then sat among them and took a pair of *karatālas* in his hand. He closed his eyes and began to sing earnestly:

hari hari viphale janama goṅāinu

"Oh Lord Hari, I have spent my life uselessly! Having obtained a human birth and having not worshiped Rādhā and Kṛṣṇa, I have knowingly drunk poison."

golokera prema-dhana, hari-nāma-saṅkīrtana

"The treasure of divine love in Goloka Vṛndāvana has descended as the congregational chanting of Lord Hari's holy names. Why did I never develop my attraction for that chanting? Day and night my heart burns from the fire of the poison of worldliness, and yet I have not taken the means to relieve it."

Narottama's face glowed golden as he sang his compositions, expressing his heartfelt devotion with extreme humility and always presenting himself as the most fallen and unfortunate soul.

hā hā prabhu nanda-suta, vṛṣabhānu-sutā-yuta

"Oh Lord Kṛṣṇa, son of Nanda, accompanied by the daughter of Vrsabhanu, please be merciful to me now. Narottama Dāsa says, 'Oh Lord, please do not push me away from your reddish lotus feet. For who is my beloved except for You?' "

As Ṭhākura Mahāśaya became more and more intensely absorbed, his limbs quivered and his eyes filled with tears. His melodious voice filled the courtyard with the unmistakable mood of true *bhakti.*

"Just meditate on Śrī Śrī Rādhā-Kṛṣṇa," he sang. "Don't desire anything else – even in your dreams! The treasure of love for the youthful Divine Couple is more valuable than gold purified in ten thousand flames. During the life of this body and after its death, Śrī Śrī Rādhā-Kṛṣṇa will always remain my goal and the two masters of my life's breath. I worship the Divine Couple, and I swim and float in the nectarean ocean of love for Them. I pray that the description of their forms, qualities, and pastimes may always remain in my heart."

The crowd in the courtyard swayed to the beat, their eyes also overflowing with tears, as Ṭhākura Mahāśaya expressed his intense yearning for spiritual perfection:

"As a fish without water suffers and dies, so a devotee perishes without love for the Divine Couple. As a *cataka* bird carefully follows the clouds, so a devotee loves the Divine Couple. As a bumblebee yearns for the flower, a chaste wife yearns for her husband, and a pauper yearns for money, so a devotee yearns to attain love for the Divine Couple."

Shivering, he continued, "When will I attain the dark treasure known as Lord Kṛṣṇa? When, agitated with ecstatic love, will I give my heart to Lord Kṛṣṇa?

When will I consider Lord Kṛṣṇa more dear to me than my own life's breath? When will I be able to see Lord Kṛṣṇa's moonlike face?"

Narottama folded his hands in supplication. "I pray that I may now see the two lotus feet of Lord Kṛṣṇa. I will place these lotus feet in my heart and dedicate my entire life and soul to them. If I am not able to see Lord Kṛṣṇa's lotus feet, my heart will burn with suffering. I will end this life by entering a blazing fire, or by jumping into water."

Rāghavendra Rāya and his sons listened intently to the beautiful songs of their *guru*. No one wanted the night to end, but the *kīrtana* was eventually brought to a close very late in the evening.

For many days, Narottama continued to sing his *bhajans* and *kīrtanas* in the evenings, and Rāghavendra and his sons spent their time hearing and chanting with their spiritual master. Narottama knew that simply by hearing songs about the topmost spiritual aspirations, his followers and disciples would be able to imbibe the entire Gauḍīya Vaiṣṇava philosophy, so through his songs, Narottama taught them about the *guru*-disciple relationship, residence in Vṛndāvana-dhāma, the importance of renunciation, the humility of the Vaiṣṇava, the agony the soul feels when separated from God, and the highest spiritual attainments.

One day, Chand Rāya and his father and brother approached the Ṭhākura, their faces gray with sadness. "We have no desire to leave your association," Chand said, "but we must return to our village. We have responsibilities there."

"Of course," Narottama said, nodding consent. "Return to your village, but always remember that the lotus feet of Śrī Kṛṣṇa are the only truth. Everything else is illusion."

With this blessing Rāghavendra Rāya and his sons offered their obeisances and bid their spiritual master farewell. Chand Rāya cried as he turned to Rāmacandra Kavirāja to say good-bye.

"Having met such a wonderful devotee as you," he said, "my life at last has meaning. Please be kind to me and always consider me your servant." Reaching into his shoulder bag, he brought out a package and handed it to the Kavirāja. "Please, take these two garments and one hundred gold coins as a token of my appreciation."

Accepting the gift, Rāmacandra warmly embraced Chand. All the Vaiṣṇavas present gathered around to bid the Rāya family farewell. After offering their respects to Lord Gaurāṅga in the temple, Chand and his father and brother started for home.

Weeks later, Narottama looked up to see one of Rāghavendra Rāya's servants entering the temple compound. The man offered his respects to him, then handed over a letter from Rāghavendra. Happy to finally receive news from his disciple, Narottama quickly opened the letter and read its contents:

My dear Gurudeva,

I am again in terrible anxiety and don't know what to do. A few days ago Chand went to the Gaṅgā with many companions and several horsemen. While they were bathing, one of the Pathan king's spies noticed Chand. It's widely known that the king is angry with Chand for looting many of his villages, so it's not surprising that the spy informed the king of Chand Rāya's whereabouts. The king sent an army and Chand has been captured without protest. Since meeting you he has become so humble that he considers whatever suffering comes his way as due punishment for his past misdeeds. Chand was brought before the Nawab, who ordered him lashed. Even then he remained calm, and he told the Nawab he would willingly pay whatever fine the Nawab considered fit for the crimes he committed. Then the Nawab decided not to whip him but to imprison him. They're holding him in an underground cell and starving him.

My whole family is aggrieved. I've tried everything within my power to get him out, but to no avail.

I am sorry to report this to you, but I'm at my wits' end. How much longer can my son remain alive without food? What should I do, Gurudeva? I await your reply.

Your servant
Rāghavendra Rāya

Deeply concerned for the wellbeing of his disciple, Narottama sent a friend who was influential with the Zamindar to try to get Chand released. But the intermediary returned unsuccessful. As weeks passed and no further news arrived from Rāghavendra, Narottama feared the worst.

One morning, Narottama heard the sound of hooves on the road. He looked up to see Chand Rāya dressed like royalty, frail but radiant, dismounting a horse on the path in front of the temple. Chand then strode into the compound and fell at his *guru's* feet.

Surprised and delighted, Narottama rushed to embrace his disciple. "Come in and sit down," he said lovingly. "I've been so concerned about you."

"By your grace, Gurudeva, I was released from prison a few days ago," Chand Rāya said. "I really deserve to suffer lifetimes in prison for my past sinful activities. It's only your mercy that has delivered me from my sinful reactions. The entire time I was in prison I simply tried to remember your instructions, and this pacified my heart."

Narottama smiled appreciatively. "But how did you get released?"

"Actually, I had a chance to escape some time ago," Chand said, "but I decided to remain in the jail instead."

Narottama was surprised. "Why?"

"Well, a man entered my cell one day. He said my father had sent him to help me escape through a secret tunnel. At first I was excited, thinking that Lord Kṛṣṇa had sent him to save me, but when he said he would first chant *mantras* to Kali in my ear for protection, I knew this was not Lord Kṛṣṇa's plan. I told him, 'Of what use is it to me to hear such *mantras*? Although I have performed many sinful acts, Ṭhākura Mahāśaya has accepted me as his servant. It is impossible for me to hear any *mantra* other than the one he has given me. Tell my father I would rather stay in prison and remain faithful to the feet of my spiritual master. At least here I can chant the Lord's holy name free of all distractions. Tell my father not to worry. My only sorrow is that I am unable to see the lotus feet of my Guru Mahārāja.'"

Narottama smiled broadly. "Your father's servant must have been quite surprised to hear that!"

"Yes," Chand laughed. "He was so shocked that he burst out, 'What do you mean you're not coming with me? You must come right now! Your poor father cannot live without you.'" Chand smiled ruefully and added, "Actually, he was more upset for himself than for me. Apparently, my father had promised to give him horses, cattle, and a village if he rescued me. But I didn't care. I just sat down and began chanting. Exasperated, the man eventually left."

"So how did you get out?" Rāmacandra asked.

"I just kept singing songs about Kṛṣṇa and chanting the holy name," Chand said. "I tried my best to follow your orders to keep my mind filled with thoughts of the Lord's pastimes. One day the Nawab came to the prison and angrily yelled at me, 'You know the end of your life is near. Why haven't you tried to bribe me for your life?' I didn't answer, but just kept chanting in my mind. This seemed to anger the Nawab even more, because he said, 'Never mind then. I'm not interested in your money. I prefer to kill you by throwing you under the feet of an elephant.' "

Narottama and Rāmacandra listened intently to Chand's incredible tale. "He obviously didn't do that," Rāmacandra said.

"Yes, he did," Chand said. He gave orders to have a drunken elephant brought to a nearby stadium. A massive crowd gathered to watch as I was brought from the prison. I could barely walk because I had been fasting for so long, but strangely I wasn't afraid. I thought, 'What's the difficulty? The person who has given me life is now taking it away.' By your grace, Gurudeva, I was ready to die, if that was Kṛṣṇa's desire."

The devotees who had by now gathered to hear Chand's story gasped as he described the peril he had been in.

Narottama bowed his head as he contemplated the firmness of his disciple's faith.

Chand continued, "The Nawab motioned for the elephant to be brought in. Then he gave me one last chance to surrender to him and become a Muslim; otherwise, I would be crushed under the feet of his elephant. I paid no heed to his words and began to chant aloud. Seeing my determination, he signaled to his men that they should release the elephant. I tried my best to fix my mind on your lotus feet. The elephant looked straight at me as it entered the arena, then charged. I expected to die within seconds!"

"*Kṛṣṇa! Kṛṣṇa!*" one of the devotees cried out.

Chand looked at that devotee and said, "Yes, Kṛṣṇa is so surprising. I didn't at first understand what was happening, for when the elephant was within a few feet of me it swerved and spun in the other direction, flinging its head around madly. For a brief moment I thought I was saved, but then the beast pointed its huge white tusks at me and charged again. Again it came so close that I could see its bloodshot eyes – and again I thought I would die. But instead the huge creature let out a deafening bellow and fell to the ground, dead."

"*Sādhu*! *Sādhu*!"

"I was completely amazed and knew it was due to no power of my own," Chand said.

"The Nawab must have been astonished," Rāmacandra said.

"*Everyone* was astonished, including *me*," Chand laughed. The crowd roared and the Nawab rushed to my side and surprisingly, told me to sit on the throne beside him. He asked me how I killed the elephant! I told him my life had been spared by my spiritual master's grace. The Nawab then said he was glad the elephant hadn't harmed me because when he saw me standing without fear before it he himself became frightened. He said he realized I must have some special divine mercy on me because I was willing to die for my Lord. He admitted that he was afraid to punish me anymore because he might invite the anger of God on himself. I could hardly believe what he was saying."

"Then the Nawab announced, 'Chand Rāya shall be set free.' Everyone cheered!

"After we left the arena the Nawab asked me how I had remained so peaceful in prison and why I didn't try to escape. I laughed and told him I wasn't special. Rather, I am nothing but a low-class rogue. But, my spiritual master's power is so great that simply by remembering him I felt no fear. Though they left me without food, I relished the taste of the Lord's holy name and sustained my life. I explained to him that I actually didn't feel unhappy while I was imprisoned. On the contrary, I felt as comfortable as if I were at home.

"He wanted to know how I maintained that peace when he brought me before the elephant. I told him I simply meditated on the feet of my spiritual master."

Chand Rāya touched Narottama's feet. He looked into his eyes, his heart overflowing with gratitude, "By your mercy only, I was saved from the wrath of that elephant."

Narottama stroked his disciple's head. "You are a faithful servant."

"Even the Nawab's heart was softened by hearing about your glories," said Chand Rāya, quietly. "He said, 'Your spiritual master must be an extraordinary person.' Then he embraced me with affection. Calling his guards, he ordered a horse for me and let me go. He also gifted me with a few horses and soldiers and offered to return my property to me. Rather than go home I have come directly to Kheturi. I wrote my father and brother a letter and told them to meet me here. I left the horses and soldiers and traveled here alone."

"What an astonishing story," Kavirāja said.

Narottama hugged his surrendered disciple tightly to his chest, and Rāmacandra Kavirāja patted him affectionately on the back. "It appears that your little creeper of devotion has grown into a tall, strong tree through the fire of ordeal," he said.

As more Vaiṣṇavas gathered around, congratulating and welcoming Chand, Rāghavendra Rāya and Santosh entered the complex and fell flat at Narottama's feet. With great relief they embraced Chand. "We came as quickly as we could," Santosh said.

"No one could believe the Nawab had released you," Rāghavendra said excitedly. "But it is true – you are alive and well. This can only be due to the mercy of Ṭhākura Mahāśaya. We are all tied tightly together, bound to his merciful feet."

Word spread that Ṭhākura Mahāśaya had transformed the notorious rogues Chand and Santosh Rāya into first-class devotees, and that Chand Rāya had defeated a drunken elephant by the power of his devotion to his spiritual master. Thus, people from far and wide came to Kheturi seeking the *darśana* of Narottama Ṭhākura Mahāśaya.

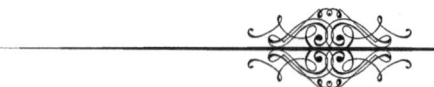

mūrtaiva bhaktiḥ kim ayaṁ kim eṣa
vairāgya-sāras tanumān nṛloke
sambhāvyate yaḥ kṛtibhiḥ sadaiva
tasmai namaḥ śrīla-narottamāya

I repeatedly offer my respectful obeisances to Śrīla Narottama Dāsa Ṭhākura, who is eternally honoured by the saintly devotees, who wonder, "Is he the perfection of renunciation? Is he personified devotional service, descended to this world in a human form?"

Narottama-prabhor-āṣṭaka, Verse 8

Chapter Eight

Final Pastimes

Seclusion

"We've been preaching in Kheturi and the surrounding areas for years," Ṭhākura Mahāśaya said to Rāmacandra, "and by Mahāprabhu's grace we've had some degree of success. Many people have come here from distant places to learn about the science of Kṛṣṇa and to have *darśana* of our beloved Deities. Many copies of the Gosvāmīs' books have been made and distributed. It's most pleasing to see the Lord's *saṅkīrtana* movement flourishing. But Kheturi has begun to feel too crowded to me. The temple courtyard is always dusty due to the hundreds of pilgrims passing through it daily. I feel the crowds are becoming an impediment to my *bhajan*. I'm getting old and have no obligations in this world. My disciples are competent to care for the Deities' service, and continue the preaching mission in Kheturi. I want to go somewhere alone to chant the holy names."

Rāmacandra understood. "Yes, it has become quite hectic here. It's difficult to find a quiet place to chant."

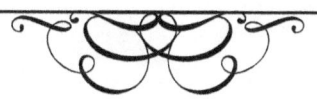

"I know of a beautiful, secluded area not far from Kheturi," Narottama said. "It reminds me of Vṛndāvana. It would be a perfect place for the two of us to perform our *bhajan* in peace. What do you think?"

"Yes!" said Kavirāja, overjoyed to be included. "But who will care for the temple and the Deities?"

"Call my senior disciples here," Narottama said. "I will divide the *sevā* among them. Then we will be free to leave."

Months later, under a lush canopy of leaves, Narottama sat on the bare ground before his hut, a tattered *chādar* draping his thin frame. Absorbed in *kṛṣṇa-kathā* with his dear Rāmacandra Kavirāja, he was deeply content.

Narottama and Rāmacandra heard a rustle and looked up to see Gaṅgā-nārāyaṇa emerging from the bushes. He immediately prostrated himself before the *sādhus*, then triumphantly pulling a large pair of clay pots from his shoulder bag he announced, "My dear masters, I've brought some *mahā-prasāda* from Lord Gaurāṅga for you!" Narottama and Rāmacandra chuckled, charmed by his loving devotion and by the huge amount of *prasāda*.

"Are you expecting guests to arrive to enjoy this enormous feast?" Rāmacandra laughed.

Gaṅgā-nārāyaṇa grinned. "No, no. This small amount of *prasāda* is for the two of you! If you don't accept this meager offering, how can you expect to keep body and soul together?"

"We are quite alive, are we not? Rāmacandra joked.

"Barely," Gaṅgā-nārāyaṇa replied wryly, eyeing the frail frame of his *guru* with concern. "I live in hope that just once you might devour all this *prasāda*. Maybe even ask for more!"

"We have chosen renunciation," Narottama said softly. "We like fasting. It frees us from worries. We're living here in great happiness, fully absorbed in singing, writing, and discussing *kṛṣṇa-kathā*. We're only sorry that this disappoints you."

Gaṅgā-nārāyaṇa sighed, then pulled out a piece of parchment from his bag and handed it to Ṭhākura Mahāśaya. "This letter just arrived from Śrīnivāsa Ācārya."

Narottama took the letter and opened it eagerly. He had not heard from his dear friend for some time, but his heart sank as he read the message. "I am planning to visit Vṛndāvana soon. The journey is long, and I need an assistant. I would like my disciple Rāmacandra to accompany me." Sobered, Ṭhākura Mahāśaya passed the letter to his friend.

As Kavirāja read its contents his expression clouded with concern. This was totally unexpected. He looked quickly up at the gentle face of his beloved friend.

Narottama understood Kavirāja's dilemma. What could be more wonderful than to travel with his Guru Mahārāja to the sacred land of Vṛndāvana, yet how difficult it would be to leave his best friend and their joyful life of *bhajan* behind. "We have become one soul in two bodies," Narottama thought.

Tears filled Rāmacandra's eyes. "How can I possibly leave you here alone?" he cried. "How could I bear to be away from you? You are everything to me – mother, father, master, friend."

A lump formed in Narottama's throat, yet he assured Rāmacandra. "Don't worry, I'll be all right. You should not miss this opportunity to visit Śrī Vṛndāvana-dhāma."

Rāmacandra's head sunk lower and lower. "When I think of how intensely you yearn for the association of Lord Caitanya and His associates in your *bhajan*, I sometimes feel your friendship with me is your only link to this world. Now I will also have to leave you. The thought of bringing you such unhappiness is too upsetting."

"Separation is inevitable in this world," Narottama said gently. "One day we will both return to the Lord's abode and there we will never again be separated. But for now, we must tolerate the pain of separation from one another for some time. When you return, imagine the happiness we will feel."

"No," Kavirāja protested. "There is no need to be apart. You should come with us."

Narottama shook his head gravely. "No, my friend. There is nothing for me in Vṛndāvana now. My Gurudeva has left. Bhūgarbha Gosvāmī is no longer there. Whether Jīva Gosvāmī is there or not we cannot say. All the great gems of Vṛndāvana have disappeared, and without them I would do nothing there but cry." Narottama again shook his head. "No, Kavirāja, I will not go to Vṛndāvana. It seems that it is the Lord's desire that we be separated for some time." Ṭhākura Mahāśaya's lips curved into a slight smile. "Just see our attachment to each other. We are supposed to be renunciants, yet we have become no different from family members tied by the bonds of affection. Perhaps the Lord wants to break our attachment."

"What are you saying?!" exclaimed Rāmacandra. This talk of renunciation is dry. Our Lord, Śrī Caitanya

Mahāprabhu, was always surrounded by His loving devotees, and the Vrājavāsīs also remained close to one another to relish the joy of serving their Lord together. The loving relationships between devotees are not like the mundane attachment between friends or lovers. A devotee cannot bear to live without the association of other devotees, for devotees nourish one another with their sweet talks about the Lord. Without devotee companions how can we taste the mellow of Vrāja? Your *prabhus*, Lokanātha and Bhūgarbha – what did they do but remain attached to each other's association? And the Vṛndāvana Gosvāmīs also had a wonderful family of devotees. We are all part of Kṛṣṇa's family, and naturally we must love each other."

Narottama smiled affectionately. "Yes," he conceded, "but you cannot disobey your *guru's* order. He is old and needs you now. Be happy, and go along to serve him."

Rāmacandra bowed his head. "I know I must go to Vṛndāvana. The prospect is even exciting. But I am concerned about leaving you alone. And I know separation from you will be unbearable."

Sitting alone in the forest, Ṭhākura Mahāśaya picked up his quill and began to write. He had been working on a compilation of songs for many months now. Today he was restless. When would Rāmacandra return? "He should have been back long ago."

Setting his pen down Narottama closed his eyes. "Oh Rāmacandra," he cried out in anguish, "will I ever see you again? Without seeing your face my heart is broken.

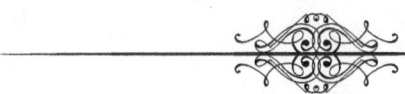

I had a jewel in my possession, but someone cheated me and stole it away. Oh, Śrīnivāsa! Svarūpa! Rūpa! Sanātana! Raghunātha Dāsa! Please be merciful to me."

Narottama sighed deeply and began to sing. *Ei baro karuna koro vaiṣṇava gosai.* His emotionally charged voice echoed through the trees. *Patita toma bine keho nai . . .* Oh Vaiṣṇava Gosvāmī, please be merciful to me now. There is no one except you who can purify the fallen souls. Where does anyone find such a merciful personality by whose mere audience all sins go far away? After bathing in the water of the sacred Ganges many times one becomes purified, but just by the sight of you the fallen souls are purified. This is your great power. The holy name delivers one who has committed an offense to Lord Hari, but if one commits an offense to you, there is no means of deliverance. Your heart is always the resting place of Lord Govinda. And Lord Govinda says, 'The Vaiṣṇavas are in My heart.' I desire the dust of your holy feet in every birth I may take. Please consider Narottama yours and be kind to him."

Trip to Gambhila

Gaṅgā-nārāyaṇa and Harirāma watched their spiritual master from a distance. Their hearts ached to see him motionless, his eyes constantly filled with tears, his body nearly skin and bone. "I dare not tell him the news," Gaṅgā-nārāyaṇa whispered. "Since Rāmacandra Kavirāja left for Vṛndāvana, Ṭhākura Mahāśaya has barely spoken to anyone. He says he has some disease of the throat, but I think he simply wants to be left alone. He is so immersed in *bhāva* that he appears to be burning in a fire of intense yearning for the association of

Mahāprabhu and His devotees. Although physically present in this world, he has little connection with it left."

Anxious tears spilled down Harirāma's cheeks. "You're right. We should not tell him that Rāmacandra has departed from this world. He couldn't bear the news."

Gaṅgā-nārāyaṇa's face was tense with worry. "He has hardly eaten anything for days. I fear he won't be with us much longer." He shuddered. The prospect of his *guru* leaving was unthinkable. "Let's go to him. I have brought some *mahā-prasāda* from Gaurāṅga. Perhaps we can convince him to eat something."

Narottama looked up as Gaṅgā-nārāyaṇa and Harirāma stepped into the clearing and fell prostrate before him. When they had risen, Narottama studied their faces. Their eyes were red and their faces anxious. Both disciples looked at the ground, unable to meet their *guru's* eyes. No words were spoken, but in his heart Narottama understood their news: Rāmacandra Kavirāja had left this mortal world. With trembling hands Narottama accepted the *mahā-prasāda*. Usually he accepted only a few sips of buttermilk, but to quell his disciples' anxiety he took their offering.

When his disciples left, Narottama couldn't restrain his emotions. Tears poured from his eyes, and his lamentation broke out in song: "All the associates of Gaurāṅga Mahāprabhu were qualified candidates for *prema*. Their pastimes were so sweet that even stones would melt to see such beauty. But I am so unfortunate that I was not born in time to witness these events. This pain always remains in my heart." Narottama became choked up as he sang, "Oh Prabhu Sanātana, Rūpa, Raghunātha,

Bhūgarbha, Śrī Jīva, and Lokanātha Gosvāmī! You all performed so many beautiful pastimes in Vṛndāvana. But now you have returned to the spiritual abode, leaving the whole world empty."

Hot tears poured down Narottama's face. "To whom shall I go to express the pain in my heart? I do not want to show my unfortunate face to anyone. I am no better than a dead animal. I had the good fortune to live with Śrī Śrīnivāsa Ācārya, and his words used to cool my heart, but where has he gone now? He and Rāmacandra never came back. Now my heart is quivering with pain. To whom shall I go and tell this story? Now in this burning life I have no hope left. It's as if I have drunk poison, but I am so unfortunate that I do not die. Narottama Dāsa is so ashamed."

The crowd of disciples sat tensely before Ṭhākura Mahāśaya. Staring lovingly at his face they waited anxiously to find out why he had called them to his *bhajan-sthalī*. After a very long silence Narottama finally said, "In this fragile state how can I live?"

No one spoke, and Narottama looked compassionately at his disciples' stunned faces.

Gaṅgā-nārāyaṇa could not accept that his spiritual master was showing signs of concluding his time in the material realm. He knew Ṭhākura Mahāśaya's condition was not caused by any physical problem; rather, he was experiencing intense spiritual emotions. Still, he spoke up boldly, "Gurudeva, we are all deeply concerned for your health. Perhaps it would be good for you to get out of this dark forest and have a change of scenery. I would like to take you to my house in Gambhila. It's a beautiful spot, right on the bank of the Gaṅgā. There you can bathe daily and get some warm sun. And my wife will prepare nourishing *prasāda* for you. I'm certain your health will improve."

Everyone waited. Ṭhākura Mahāśaya appeared to consider the suggestion. "All right," he said smiling slightly. "Let us go for Gaṅgā *snāna*."

Gaṅgā-nārāyaṇa heaved a sigh of relief and the other disciples happily cried out, "*Jaya*! *Jaya*! All glories to Ṭhākura Mahāśaya!"

Arrangements were made, and the following morning Ṭhākura Mahāśaya was carefully ushered out of his *bhajan-sthalī* and brought to the temple in Kheturi. After *darśana* the party continued to Budhuri, Rāmacandra Kavirāja's hometown. There they were greeted by Rāmacandra's brother, Govinda Kavirāja. No one said anything about Rāmacandra, but they sat down at Govinda's home and performed *kīrtana* for the remainder of the day. The next morning, they proceeded to Gambhila.

Arriving at the home of Gaṅgā-nārāyaṇa, the party immediately walked to the bank of the Ganges to take bath. Narottama entered the swiftly flowing water slowly, his smile gentle. His disciples' faces shone with happiness. They had worried about Ṭhākura Mahāśaya's solitary mood and frail health for such a long time; it was a relief to be in his company again and see him step into the sparkling water of the holy river. After a refreshing bath, they sat together on the sandy riverbank, basking in the warm sunlight. They chanted softly, savouring the depth and intimacy of this special experience.

After some time, however, Ṭhākura Mahāśaya's mood unexpectedly changed. His expression grew grave, and he stared intently at the Ganges. Tears flowed from his eyes, forming rivulets down his cheeks. He seemed to have left his associates behind and become inwardly immersed. Without a word, he suddenly lay down on the sand and closed his eyes.

Alarmed, his disciples spoke to him, but he didn't respond. Gaṅgā-nārāyaṇa felt like he had been hit by a thunderbolt. Not knowing what to do, he stared aghast at the peaceful face of his spiritual master. He had thought the change of scenery might be a welcome change, but now it appeared that Narottama had come to Gambhila to leave his body on the bank of the Ganges.

Devastated, they all surrounded their spiritual master and began *kīrtana*. They could do nothing but pray and sing and watch helplessly as their beloved Ṭhākura Mahāśaya's chest faintly rose and fell. The villagers who had followed the party to the Ganges also gathered around, eager to have a last *darśana* of the famous *sādhu*. Sounds of wailing gradually mixed with the *kīrtana*, and one devotee took over the lead, chanting special prayers for the protection of their Ṭhākura Mahāśaya. Another brought garlands and lovingly placed them around his body. Someone else brought water from the Ganges and sprinkled it on him.

Hovering over the precipice between life and death, Narottama remained on the sand for the rest of the day. The tearful disciples continued to huddle around him on the cold damp sand and darkness eventually fell. The sound of the holy name and their sad cries echoed across the water and into the night.

Day broke with a dazzling sunrise and flocks of birds darting overhead. The sounds of the village awakening were faintly heard on the shore, where the men still sat, keeping vigil over their dear master. Narottama's condition had not changed, and as the sun arced through the sky, it remained the same – much to the distress and confusion of his followers.

Gaṅgā-nārāyaṇa sat like a statue, immovable and silent. His spiritual master looked so serene, and yet his own heart was breaking. It was inconceivable that he who had given him life and opened the doors to the sweet mellow taste of devotional service, who had conveyed the superlative teachings of the Vṛndāvana Gosvāmīs in his songs, who had taught him everything he knew about spiritual life, was now about to depart from the world. Gaṅgā-nārāyaṇa's anguish deepened as he recalled the many blessed moments he had spent in his *guru's* association – his countless cherished words of advice and the ecstatic *kīrtanas* they had relished. How could any of them live without him? Who would guide them? Who would protect them and answer their questions? How could that sweet melodious voice of devotion be silenced forever?

When the third day dawned without change, Gaṅgā-nārāyaṇa could no longer tolerate the intensity of his watch. Leaving his spiritual master's side, he wandered down the beach a short distance and sat alone. He rubbed the stubble of his unshaven face and noted with disinterest that his clothes were damp and disheveled. Wracked with anxiety, he watched the hypnotic flow of the Ganges and berated himself for his foolishness in bringing Ṭhākura Mahāśaya to Gambhila. "Instead of helping, I'm responsible for ushering my spiritual master to his deathbed." Tormented by guilt, he sat mournfully on the sand. "I just can't accept his time has come. I can't think of this world without him. But it appears he is determined to depart." Gaṅgā-nārāyaṇa covered his face with his hands. "It's the disciple's duty to assist his spiritual master, but how can I possibly assist him in fulfilling *this* desire? From the depth of his heart, Gaṅgā-nārāyaṇa called out feelingly in prayer, "Oh, Kṛṣṇa! How can you take him away from us? We are weak and unprotected. Please, I beg You, be merciful to us. Let Ṭhākura Mahāśaya stay with us."

As he sat lost in his sea of grief, three *brāhmaṇas* came to bathe near where he was sitting. They placed their water pots on the sand and glanced over at Gaṅgā-nārāyaṇa, who immediately recognized them as die-hard opponents of Narottama's teachings.

The *brāhmaṇas* also recognized Gaṅgā-nārāyaṇa. "Now you see the results of a *śūdra* giving *mantra* initiation to *brāhmaṇas*," one of them sneered, "Due to his offenses your *guru* has been stricken with a disease of the throat and his life is slipping away. How an intelligent man like you could have been taken in by him I can't understand. I would expect that from a gullible villager or a dacoit, but you – who know the *Vedas* – how could you be taken in by a *śūdra* who spends his days wailing, singing songs about his fallen condition and lamenting the loss of his friends?" The *paṇḍita* glanced toward the huddle of disciples down the beach with disdain. "What a pathetic performance for one who is supposed to be spiritually advanced. A true *brāhmaṇa* never laments or hankers for anything. Why doesn't your so-called *ācārya* remember Brahman and be happy?"

Gaṅgā-nārāyaṇa shut his eyes and ears to all this, yet the cruel words had already pierced his heart like poisoned arrows filling him with insufferable pain. He flushed with anger, but controlled himself, even though his eyes continued to blaze. He stood to leave their offensive presence, but as he walked away he couldn't restrain himself from reprimanding them. His anguish broke through and his words were fiery. "Your words are most cruel and unjust," he said, in a voice laden with grief and indignation. "They burn my ears like a red-hot iron. People like you cannot possibly understand the elevated emotions of a pure devotee like Ṭhākura Mahāśaya. You see only the external, so you mistake the highest expressions of the soul's love for God for mundane lamentation. Only one who knows Kṛṣṇa can understand such feelings. Lord Kṛṣṇa is so attractive that one who knows and loves Him finds it impossible to tolerate His separation. To rediscover this inner sense of loss – of being separated from God – is the essence of *bhakti* and the culmination of all Vedic knowledge. Far from taking one away from God, this emotion brings one closer to God through constant remembrance of Him. For a devotee in love with God, even a moment separated from Him feels like ages. Though such devotion appears painful, it's actually most relishable. In fact, there's no higher pleasure than that experienced by a devotee in separation from his Beloved. This is the state of pure love, of union with God, and all great mystics and devotees aspire for it."

Seeing the *paṇḍitas'* indignant looks, Gaṅgā-nārāyaṇa fell silent. He could see that the noose of fate was already around their necks and would drag them to inevitable ruin as a consequence of their blasphemy. But though their abuse was intolerable, Gaṅgā-nārāyaṇa couldn't help but pity the poor souls, for they had not the slightest inkling of spiritual understanding. "There is no use feeding milk to a serpent," he thought sadly. "People of their caliber are attached to dry, speculative knowledge and have no understanding of their relationship with Kṛṣṇa. Their only occupation seems to be criticizing Vaiṣṇavas. They are certainly the most unfortunate, condemned living beings."

Gaṅgā-nārāyaṇa swiftly turned his back on the *paṇḍitas* and headed down the beach. Hot tears burned down his face. In a last attempt to defend his spiritual master's honor he again turned to the *brāhmaṇas* and said in a voice shaking with emotion, "Whether you appreciate Ṭhākura Mahāśaya or not, it is certain that his glory will shine in this world like an undying lamp for as long as the Himalayan mountains stand, the Ganges flows, and the ocean's waves beat against solid earth."

Then Gaṅgā-nārāyaṇa began to run. As he approached Narottama, fear gripped his heart. The devotees were standing now, crowding around Ṭhākura Mahāśaya's body. The *kīrtana* was loud and intense, and he could hear the devotees crying. He could barely breathe. He pushed frantically through the crowd and knelt at Ṭhākura Mahāśaya's side. His worst nightmare had come true; there was no sign of life in Narottama's body. Ṭhākura Mahāśaya had stopped breathing.

Gaṅgā-nārāyaṇa cried aloud and looked at the devastation written on the devotees' faces. He was shocked to see the offensive *brāhmaṇas* standing nearby with some of their associates. They were smiling. Placing his head on his spiritual master's feet, he blurted out, "Ṭhākura Mahāśaya, please come back! We need you. If these foolish *brāhmaṇas* dare to behave so outrageously now, what will happen in your absence? Prabhu, you have delivered many, many fallen souls, yet these *brāhmaṇas* continue to criticize you. If you die now, their claims may be accepted as truth." Gaṅgā-nārāyaṇa's heart raced and his lips quivered. "Please show your mercy to these misguided *brāhmaṇas*. Please don't leave us!"

As he held ever more tightly to his *guru's* feet, Gaṅgā-nārāyaṇa felt a shiver go through Ṭhākura Mahāśaya's body. In disbelief, he looked up and saw that Narottama's chest was moving slightly and his body began to glow a radiant gold. Suddenly, a golden *brāhmaṇa* thread appeared on Narottama's body and his lotus-like eyes softly opened.

The crowd gasped when they heard him utter faintly "Rādhā-Kṛṣṇa, Śrī Kṛṣṇa Caitanya."

Ṭhākura Mahāśaya lifted his hand and motioned for Gaṅgā-nārāyaṇa to come close. Gaṅgā-nārāyaṇa gently placed his hand behind Narottama's neck and slowly lifted him. Narottama smiled and looked at the devotees with great love.

Witnessing this miracle, the crowd was euphoric. Some of them cried, some danced and sang, others laughed with relief, while others shouted, "*Jaya*! *Jaya*! All glories to Narottama Ṭhākura Mahāśaya!" The *smarta-brāhmaṇas* watched the remarkable resurrection with wide-eyed astonishment.

After a few moments, Narottama rose and slowly waded into the Ganges to bathe, his jubilant disciples all around him. He then walked to Gaṅgā-nārāyaṇa's house, the devotees still swarming around him dancing and chanting in boundless ecstasy.

The women of the household were deeply shocked to see Ṭhākura Mahāśaya appear. Narottama smiled brightly at them and said simply, "I'm quite hungry." Thrilled, the women rushed to the kitchen.

Later, while taking *prasāda*, Gaṅgā-nārāyaṇa noticed a crowd gathered before his house. He went outside to investigate and was surprised to see all the caste-conscious opponents of Ṭhākura Mahāśaya.

The *paṇḍitas* fell humbly at Gaṅgā-nārāyaṇa's feet. "You are from our village," one said, "so we are like your family members. Whatever offenses we have committed, please excuse us. We have finally understood that Ṭhākura Mahāśaya is a real *brāhmaṇa*. We have seen how he received the Lord's special mercy. Yet we have done him a great injustice. We have no other recourse than to take shelter at his feet. Please do something so he will show us his mercy."

Gaṅgā-nārāyaṇa was very pleased to bring the *paṇḍitas* before Ṭhākura Mahāśaya. "Prabhu, these people are requesting your mercy," he said, as the *brāhmaṇas* lay prostrate before Narottama.

Ṭhākura Mahāśaya urged them to stand and then embraced each of them affectionately. "In a few days," he said, "I will return to Kheturi. You should come with me. There you can take *darśana* of Gaurāṅga Mahāprabhu and study the *bhakti śāstras* with Gaṅgā-nārāyaṇa."

The leader of the *paṇḍitas* said, "Ṭhākura Mahāśaya, your infectious kindness has melted our hearts and dissolved our animosity. We agree to your plan."

A few days later, Narottama and his disciples returned to Kheturi, accompanied by the humbled Gambhila *paṇḍitas*. The *paṇḍitas* remained in Kheturi for some time, studying the Vaiṣṇava scriptures under the expert tutelage of Gaṅgā-nārāyaṇa.

Disappearance

Narottama returned to his *bhajan-kutir* in the forest. Although frail, he remained there always fully immersed in Kṛṣṇa consciousness. He spent each day and night singing, writing, preaching, and chanting the holy names of the Lord.

With each passing day Narottama's feelings of separation from the Lord and His beloved associates grew. Alone in the forest, he would sometimes call out, "Oh Lord Gaurāṅga Sundara, Oh moon of Navadvīpa! Oh Lord Nityānanda, son of Padmavatī! Oh Lord Advaita, husband of Sītā! Please be merciful to me! I am crying at your feet! Don't neglect me! Please fulfill my desires!" At other times, he rolled on the ground and, with a continuous flow of tears, called out, "Oh Śrīmatī Rādhārāṇī, Kṛṣṇa is Yours. You are always engaged in His service. Please give me the chance to worship You both." Overcome with divine lamentation he would cry, "Where has Śrīnivāsa gone? I had Rāmacandra, but he has also left me. My life has become futile. Svarūpa! Rūpa! Sanātana! Raghunātha! Be kind to me. My heart is pierced with the poisonous arrow of separation from you. If I cannot get your association I will smash my head against the wall and enter into fire."

One morning, Narottama unexpectedly announced to Gaṅgā-nārāyaṇa that he wanted to visit the temple in Kheturi and then travel on to Gambhila.

Alarmed, Gaṅgā-nārāyaṇa protested. "But Gurudeva, how can we let you go back to Gambhila? You nearly left us the last time you were there. Surely you are too old now for such a journey."

Ṭhākura Mahāśaya, however, was unmoved. "We shall leave tomorrow," he said.

Gaṅgā-nārāyaṇa stayed at Ṭhākura Mahāśaya's side as he entered the Kheturi temple with a crowd of his disciples. Narottama lowered his aged body to the ground, bowing respectfully before each Deity, then stood with folded hands before Lord Gaurāṅga. Gaṅgā-nārāyaṇa noticed how his eyes glistened with tears as he stared lovingly at the beautiful golden face of the Lord. He appeared to be locked in a loving exchange with the Lord, oblivious to the crowd of anxious disciples surrounding him.

While Narottama was lost in prayer, the temple swiftly filled up with disciples and other residents of Kheturi. News of Ṭhākura Mahāśaya's unexpected visit had spread quickly. Hundreds of people crammed into the temple, eager to have his *darśana.*

Gaṅgā-nārāyaṇa frowned slightly as he studied his spiritual master's face. Seeing Narottama's lips moving, he couldn't help but wonder what silent prayer he uttered as he communed with the Lord. He had noticed a change in Ṭhākura Mahāśaya. He seemed to have become so deeply immersed in his intense feelings of separation from the Lord, and his longing to be with Mahāprabhu's associates had become so profound, that he appeared to have lost touch with the mundane realm. This intensity sometimes frightened Gaṅgā-nārāyaṇa. He had tried not to think too much of it, but today, seeing Ṭhākura Mahāśaya's state, he couldn't help but wonder how much longer his beloved spiritual master would remain in this world.

Gaṅgā-nārāyaṇa glanced around the packed temple room, noticing the anxiety on many faces. He shuddered to hear someone behind him whisper, "Why is Ṭhākura Mahāśaya going away? Is he leaving forever?"

Stepping a little closer to Narottama, Gaṅgā-nārāyaṇa heard his spiritual master's hushed words: "My dear Mahāprabhu, please give Your mercy to all living beings."

As Narottama turned to leave the temple, Gaṅgā-nārāyaṇa heard him softly say, "I have finished my work in Kheturi." Gaṅgā-nārāyaṇa was stunned by the dreadful import of these words. He dared not ask what his spiritual master meant by them. His heart heavy, he turned and followed his spiritual master out of the temple.

Crowds of people swarmed Ṭhākura Mahāśaya as he left the temple. The people were eager to accompany him to Gambhila. But Narottama turned to the crowd and said. "It's not necessary for everyone to come to Gambhila. You should remain here and serve Their Lordships."

These words broke the hearts of the Kheturi residents, yet they reluctantly conceded to his request. Standing forlorn, they watched in anguish as their beloved Ṭhākura Mahāśaya slowly left Kheturi, accompanied only by a few close associates.

It was a slow journey to Gambhila, as Narottama was now very old, but after a few days, the party arrived. Excited residents rushed to greet him, and Narottama smiled gently, showering his blessings on them all.

Gaṅgā-nārāyaṇa, however, felt uneasy about the look on Ṭhākura Mahāśaya's somber face. His discomfort turned to alarm when Narottama unexpectedly announced that he was going to bathe and then headed toward the river. Gaṅgā-nārāyaṇa kept pace with his *guru*. He didn't need to look at the distraught faces of his godbrothers to know they shared the same foreboding thoughts.

When Narottama reached the riverbank he offered his respects to the sacred water and then stepped into the river without hesitation. Gaṅgā-nārāyaṇa and the others followed him. Slowly submerging his frail frame, Narottama sat, half-submerged in the cool water. He asked his disciples to begin *kīrtana.* As the chanting filled the air, Narottama turned to Gaṅgā-nārāyaṇa and asked, "Kindly massage my body." Eager to render some service, Gaṅgā-nārāyaṇa moved to Ṭhākura Mahāśaya's right side and began to gently rub his spiritual master's body. Rāmakṛṣṇa moved to Narottama's left side to help with the massage. The rest of the devotees continued a melodious *kīrtana.*

All eyes were riveted on Ṭhākura Mahāśaya's face. His eyes were slightly closed and his face lit with an unearthly glow. His mood was unfathomably deep. Gradually, his entire body began to emit a golden effulgence. Stunned, the disciples moved in closer, spontaneously chanting louder and increasing the tempo of their *kīrtana.*

Gaṅgā-nārāyaṇa was astonished to see the water surrounding Narottama's body turning a milky white. He realized that the white substance was flowing directly from his spiritual master's body as he was being massaged. Gaṅgā-nārāyaṇa instantly understood what was happening. He stared in helpless disbelief. Intense anxiety gripped his heart. He wanted to cry out, "No! Please don't go!" He wanted to stop the massage. He wanted to lift his spiritual master out of the water and back to the riverbank! In desperation, he looked at Rāmakṛṣṇa. His eyes were raining tears, yet he did not stop rubbing Narottama's transcendental body. Gaṅgā-nārāyaṇa understood that he too must continue.

Devastation filled the hearts of the devotees, but they continued to chant as they had never chanted before; their hearts bursting with pain as they cried out to the Lord. Louder and louder they chanted as they helplessly watched the milk flow from their spiritual master's body and wash away in the Ganges's current.

Gaṅgā-nārāyaṇa's grief was terrible, but he knew he could do nothing to change what was happening. His beloved spiritual master, that illustrious ambassador of the spiritual world, the guardian of humility, the king of *kīrtana,* had decided to return to the spiritual realm.

As the milky substance poured from the Ṭhākura's body, the Ganges began to swirl furiously and waves lapped high against the shore. The devotees shouted, "*Hari! Hari!*" and sobbed in agony as the cherished form of their spiritual master disappeared from sight, merging fully into the water of the Ganges.

As Narottama's soul ascended on its journey back to Godhead, it appeared as if the entire universe stood still to offer a moment of silent respect to that brilliant luminary, Śrīla Narottama dāsa Ṭhākura Mahāśaya, whose presence on this earth had been more pleasing than a thousand moons, whose words had been more brilliant than a million suns, and whose mercy was worth more than a billion precious gems.

Someone handed Gaṅgā-nārāyaṇa a clay pot and he scooped up some of the milky Ganges water in it and clutched it tightly to his chest. The tears of the devotees now mixed with the Ganges water. Yet even in the agony of separation from their spiritual master, they also rejoiced, knowing that at last, Narottama was reunited with his beloved Lord.

Once again, the *kīrtana* roared: "*Jaya* Narottama dāsa Ṭhākura, *Jaya* Narottama dāsa Ṭhākura!"

rājan-mṛdaṅga-karatāla-kalābhirāmaṁ
gaurāṅga-gāna-madhu-pāna-bharābhirāmam
śrīman-narottama-padāmbuja-maṣju-nṛtyaṁ
bhṛtyaṁ kṛtārthayatu māṁ phaliteṣṭa-kṛtyam

May the graceful dancing of Śrīman Narottama's lotus feet, which delightfully step in time to nectarean songs of Lord Gaurāṅga, and the splendid, melodious sounds of *mṛdangas* and *karatālas*, be ever visible to this humble servant, thus satisfying my fully bloomed desires for devotional service.

Narottama-prabhor-āṣṭaka, Verse 9

Endnotes

1. Primary resources used were *Narottama-vilāsa*, *Bhakti-ratnākara*, *Prema-vilāsa*, and *Karnananda*. Secondary resources used were *Narottama-carita*, an unpublished/untitled manuscript on Narottama dāsa Ṭhākura's life by OBL Kapoor; notes from lectures by Śrīla B.R. Sridhar Mahāraj; and a plethora of seminars and lectures given by senior devotees. And, of course, whatever could be gleaned from Śrīla Prabhupāda's writings.
2. According to *Prema-vilāsa*, this pastime took place in Kānāi Nāṭaśālā, in which case it would not have been the following morning that Lord Caitanya placed the love into the Padmavatī.
3. According to *Prema-vilāsa*, the birth of Narottama was on the fifth day of the bright half of the month of Magha at 6:00 pm.
4. Some accounts state that Narottama was about twelve years old at this time.
5. There are at least three different versions Narottama's escape.
6. There are differing opinions as to which day this occurred and how it transpired. Some say it was a private ceremony.

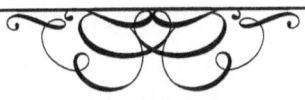

7. There are different versions of how and when these titles were awarded.
8. *Prema-vilāsa* states that they visited only Vṛndāvana.
9. Some commentators say that Lokanātha Goswāmī told Narottama to come back soon so he would be able to see him again.
10. *Prema-vilāsa* says the books were packed at Jiva Goswāmī's *āśrama*, then the devotees walked to Govindajī temple to pray for the success of the mission.
11. This is likely to be the only description within this book that is somewhat contentious. *Bhakti-ratnākara* states that Narottama's parents were not alive when he returned to Kheturi, so that is the version most speakers have adopted.

    However, there are other authoritative descriptions that differ, stating that his parents were indeed alive at the time of Narottama's return. *Prema-vilāsa* (which was written nearly one hundred years prior to *Bhakti-ratnākara*) by Nityānanda dāsa, who was an eye witness to some of these events, mentions the presence of Narottama's parents *several* times after Narottama's return to Kheturi. I chose to utilize the *Prema-vilāsa* version which is supported by other secondary resources.

    In both versions all commentators are in agreement regarding the mood in which Narottama was greeted by former relatives and townspeople and the challenges he faced in returning to his home town.

12. According to *Prema-vilāsa,* Narottama travelled to Jagannātha Purī on another trip at a later date.
13. Some commentators say that Narahari Sarakāra departed the world before Narottama's visit to Śrīkhaṇḍa.
14. According to some commentators, a deity of Viṣṇupriyā was installed along with the Gaurāṅga Deity. However, the Gaurāṅga Deity presently residing in Jiaganj, Murshidabad district, which is supposed to have been installed at the Kheturi festival, is worshipped alone. No deity of Viṣṇupriyā is present.
15. According to *Prema-vilāsa,* Narottama held two festivals. At the first festival two sets of deities were installed, and at the second four more sets were installed.
16. According to *Prema-vilāsa,* Govinda Kavirāja, Harihara, Rāmakrsna and Jagannātha also accompanied Rāmacandra Kavirāja and Gaṅgā-nārāyaṇa Cakravartī, disguising themselves as wine sellers, potters, grain merchants, and oil merchants.

www.ingramcontent.com/pod-product-compliance
Lightning Source LLC
Chambersburg PA
CBHW022059090426
42743CB00008B/658
* 9 7 8 1 8 8 0 4 0 4 2 7 0 *